Executive Agreements and Treaties, 1946-1973

Framework of the Foreign Policy of the Period

AMY M. GILBERT

THOMAS—NEWELL

Thomas—Newell
1201 Monroe Street
Endicott, New York 13760

Copyright © 1973 by Amy M. Gilbert.
All rights reserved. This book may not be reproduced in
whole or in part without the expressed permission of
the author.

First Printing, 1973
Library of Congress catalog card number: 73-82739
ISBN 0-9600-690-1-1

Printed in the United States of America by Vail-Ballou Press, Inc.

To
the memory of
Professor Charles Cheney Hyde
whose wise counsel initiated
my interest in
Executive Agreements

This work was made possible by the cooperation of the staff of the Library of the State University of New York at Binghamton, a depositary of official documents of the United States, and especially by the welcome assistance of Mr. Josiah T. Newcomb, Director Emeritus of Libraries, and of Miss Janet Brown, one of the Librarians of the State University of New York at Binghamton. Gratitude is also extended to Dorothy W. Bowers, Reference Librarian at Dickinson College, Carlisle, Pennsylvania, to Dr. Daniel Gilbert, Head of the History Department of Moravian College, Bethlehem, Pennsylvania, and to Dr. Bernard Mason, Professor of History, State University of New York at Binghamton.

Contents

Introduction		vii
Chapter I—Types of Agreements		1
Chapter II—The Heritage of International Agreements from World War II		10
Chapter III—Post-War International Agreements of the Forties		18
Chapter IV—International Agreements during the Korean War		27
Chapter V—East-West Rivalries and International Agreements of the Fifties		36

        Section A—The Vietnam War
        Section B—Aid as an Instrument of Foreign Policy
        Section C—Deterrents of Communism in the Middle East
        Section D—Weapons or Diplomacy?
        Section E—Summary

Chapter VI—The Assessment of International Agreements, by the Bricker Movement		57
Chapter VII—Uses of International Agreements in the Kennedy Administration		78
Chapter VIII—International Agreements and Their Aftermath in the Johnson Administration		85

        Section A—Defense versus Communism
        Section B—Executive Agreements for Trade

Section C—Changes in Agricultural Aid
Section D—Balance of Payments
Section E—Criticism of the Vietnam War
Section F—Relations with the U. S. S. R.
Section G—World Changes

Chapter IX—International Agreements, 1968–1971   111

Section A—Challenge for Change
Section B—The Vietnam War
Section C—Southeast Asia
Section D—Congressional Criticism
Section E—Developments in Southeast Asia in 1970
Section F—The Pacific
Section G—European Adjustments
Section H—Latin American Problems
Section I—Miscellaneous International Agreements
Section J—The End of an Era

Chapter X—The New Era   155

Section A—Philosophy for the Seventies
Section B—The Nixon Doctrine, 1971–1972
Section C—New Congressional Opposition
Section D—The Pacific
Section E—European Commitments
Section F—The Third World
Section G—The New Challenge

Appendix   193
Bibliography   203
Index   207

Introduction

For over twenty-five years after World War II the United States had commitments, expressed through Executive Agreements and Treaties, that supported her anti-Communist role in the Cold War of the period. The United States was firm and steadfast in her opposition to the spread of the philosophy of the United Soviet Socialist Republics that manifested itself in the immediate post-World War II period in the Far East, in the Middle East, in Europe, in Africa and in Latin America.

The United States acted with strength under the circumstances of the period. She alone, at first, had atomic power; she had a world presence; she had resources; she had technical skills; she sent aid, for relief of war victims, then for recovery of pre-World War II organized powers, then as a means of enhancing her own interests and security through economic and military support to chosen, strategic countries. By 1969 she was a nation still directed by her immediate post-World War II commitments. It is important to review her many commitments since 1946 to understand the relationships of the country and to trace the background of the issues of the United States as she faced the 70's.

By the end of the 60's the world had changed. As the months of 1969 and 1970 went by it was revealed that quiet, preparatory work on the part of the United States had been continuing for the expression of a new philosophy on her own part. After twenty-five years of the United States' efforts to curtail the expansion of Communism, what seemed to be a turning of 180 degrees by the United States came about in 1969. This turnabout was due to experience; to the recognition of reality in the latter part of the 60's; and to the necessity of merging foreign and domestic needs for the 70's. The United States was no longer the sole Great Power

Leader of the world, and the sole power with atomic weapons. The future meant an atomic, nuclear and space age with emphasis on technology and availability of resources. A new mobility of travel throughout the world was bringing new cultural relations, as well, and new needs for international trade on an equalitarian basis. The solution for the 70's was not the old imperialism, not the annihilation of nations through military weapons, not the *imposition* of peace, but a new relationship of *partnership* through negotiations and a quickening of trade throughout the world. The new leadership required a new kind of strength and of imagination, that would be made meaningful by commitments of Executive Agreements and Treaties.

As the 70's dawned the United States still believed in intelligent leadership, for no one state has all of the necessary resources and no one state could be dominant in the 70's. The United States believed, as always, in the role of an organized state or political unit with potentials. There has always been emphasis in the United States upon democracy with its ingredient of equality but there had to be an informed electorate in the 70's as never before. The United States is still "a melting pot" for social groups—but she is not a quantitative formula. She has to have a citizenry who know the heritage of her democratic system, who have historical perspective, who are critically alert to the nature of commitments and who have imagination for the future.

Since the United States has always honored all of her Agreements, it is necessary to be critically aware of their form and content. Because all of the United States' relations with other nations had to be made firm by commitments, it is rewarding to examine them. The country does not have policies because of commitments, but commitments are made because of policies and policies simply express indicated behavior in dealing with world contacts of the time.

In the period since World War II there was a great increase in the number of International Agreements. It is important to see the difference between Executive Agreements and Treaties. A few Treaties have emerged since 1946 but Executive Agreements have increased by the thousands. History has brought a reversal of the utilization of these categories. In 1930 the United States concluded 25 Treaties and 9 Executive Agreements; in 1968 the nation entered into only 16 Treaties but concluded 266 Executive

Agreements, according to the *Congressional Quarterly* of June 24, 1972.

Upon examination it has been realized that some of the Executive Agreements have not been carefully drawn. Where Congress is called upon either before or after a provocation to approve Presidential action, or where there is Presidential action because of the Executive's own power, quite often the result is an elastic interpretation of the authorization. Quite often the time when the Agreement is relevant is not stated; quite often the political state with whom the Agreement has been made has changed; and quite often procedural directions, especially in matters of termination or renewal of the Agreement, are totally lacking. Familiar examples are the wide interpretation of the Tonkin Bay Resolution, the Vietnam War's growing out of an extension of post-World War II aid, and the cost of and the ignorance of the procedure for the removal of NATO Headquarters from French soil.

These inadequacies have led to controversy between Congress and the Executive concerning their respective powers. In the fifties there had been the Bricker Movement, which became a question of amending the Constitution and was of concern, relatively speaking, to professional persons and organizations. More recently there have been resolutions and amendments attached to Congressional legislation to prevent escalation of, and to terminate, the war in Southeast Asia; and these efforts have been of concern to a wider electorate.

Individuals, also, have reacted to the inadequacies. Many have faith in what they hear from newsmen and public officials; identify themselves with the goals of their country as these goals have been indicated; and "couldn't care less" about the background of current issues. Others react emotionally with demonstrations and form groups and movements—when they are personally affected; when personal relationships are disrupted; when they are exposed to the draft; when a loved one has been killed in war; when the costs of international aid projects are high; when there is real inflation at home; when international payments have a deficit; when taxation is high; and when finances are affected. Then the impingement of international affairs on the average citizen becomes real. There are other persons who want to *understand* the role of the United States for there are dilemmas today in this age of technological advancement resulting in conflicts between the Executive and the Congress and it is necessary to consider commitments.

The United States has entered a new era when Executive Agreements and Treaties are going to increase. People need to understand why these Agreements are of different kinds and why they, especially Executive Agreements, will increase. People need to know how these Agreements can be improved in form and in relevance to the times. People need to have historical perspective on the period since World War II and appreciate the chronology in order to live intelligently in the new era of the 70's—hopefully with negotiations and peace. There is need for an informed citizenry!

CHAPTER I

Types of Agreements

Since World War II there has been a great increase in the number of international commitments of the United States, especially in the form of Executive Agreements. These instruments are as old as the United States, and older; yet the term, Executive Agreement, is unfamiliar to the average citizen. Treaties people have heard of and a quick reference to the Constitution of the United States informs one that the President has the power, by and with the advice and consent of the Senate, to make them. But what exactly does one mean by an Executive Agreement?

The Executive Agreement is not mentioned in the Constitution. The only use of "agreement" as a word is in Article I, Section 10, paragraph 3, where it is stated that no State, without the consent of Congress, shall "enter into agreement or compact with another State, or with a foreign power." This refers, however, to limitations upon the powers of the States of the Union and the concept of an agreement is a general one.

In order to understand the meaning of the term, Executive Agreement, and before examining its specific connotation, one must be mindful of a few fundamental concepts concerning our sovereign state and the term, International Agreement. We shall then be able to define Executive Agreement.

In the framework of our federal government, which embraces the Presidency, the Congress, and the Judiciary, the President is the official representative of the United States in foreign affairs and speaks for the nation as a whole. The image of the United States in the eyes of the world is personified by the President and all of the contacts of this sovereign state with other sovereign states are made in his name. Since the routines of life, especially in this affluent era of the twentieth century in the United States, have brought many contacts throughout the world, this intercourse has required International Agreements between our national representative and the national representatives of other states. The philosophy of these agreements is that there is common advantage in accepting a limitation of action or in granting privileges, and that by reciprocal give-and-take there are accomplishments to desired ends, which can be attained by both sides, by means other than violent aggression. These International Agreements are arrived at through conference, conversations, exchange of letters, and telecommunications.

International Agreements made by the United States have the quality of contracts for in international practice over the ages there is a recognized moral obligation to perform the undertaking. While the agreement may not contain a sanction (that is, an enforceable penalty for nonfulfillment), there is a sense of obligation that has a semblance of legal obligation, even though not enforceable by legal process. In International Law and in the fundamental concepts of the United States the honor of the state is involved in respecting commitments. Therefore the making of the commitment assumes importance.

These International Agreements have many forms. They may be expressed in written documents or may not be recorded at all. They may be formal or informal. They may be expressed in detailed phraseology or they may be effected by exchange of notes or joint communiqués. They may be acceptances of *modus vivendi,* expressing the current meeting of minds. They may be negotiated by heads of states or by their agents. They may be multilateral among many states, or bilateral between two parties, even though one party may mean several states.

In diplomatic literature International Agreements go by many names—treaties, agreements, conventions, protocols, procès-verbal, declarations, arrangements, memoranda of understanding, communiqués, aide mémoires, final acts, general acts, etc. In the United States the hundreds of International Agreements that have been made each year since World War II run the full gamut of names for such instruments.

In the United States, however, there are really only two categories of International Agreements, no matter what the name: those that have been submitted to the Senate for advice and approval; and those that have not been so submitted. The first category will also have appended a document signed by the President saying that such consent has been obtained, i.e. the document of ratification, copies of which document will then be sent to the cosignators and deposited with the agreed depositary nation, before the agreement is proclaimed by the President as being effective. These agreements are usually treaties, conventions, final acts, general acts. Agreements of the second category are not characterized by this procedure of being submitted to the Senate and being ratified. They are Executive Agreements, whatever their nomenclature.

The term, Executive Agreement, invites confusion, however, because these Agreements can be subdivided into four classes: (I) those concluded pursuant to a treaty; (II) those concluded to carry out the intention of an act of Congress; (III) those concluded by the President under his Constitutional authority and supported or confirmed by Congressional action such as a declaration of war or a joint resolution passed by majority vote; and (IV) those concluded by the President according to his Constitutional authority and not submitted to or confirmed by the Congress.

Examples of Class I would be implementing agreements arranging for the details concerning the size of military contingents, relative costs of operation, etc. after a Mutual Security Treaty has been entered into. The Security Treaty between the United States and Japan, which entered into force on April 28, 1952, as a case in point, provided in Article III: "The conditions which shall govern the disposition of armed forces of the United States of America in and about Japan shall be determined by administrative agreements between the two Governments."

Agreements of Class II are negotiated by the President upon the authorization of and the directive of the Congress, expressed in a statute. These agreements take place after the authorization and they take care of the specifics indicated by the generalities of the act. The Reciprocal Trade Act of 1934 and its renewals and extensions, for example, gave wide limits between which the Executive could make specific agreements on tariffs with individual states. Also, all of the authorizing statutes for aid to other countries since World War II have been followed by an Executive Agreement with each recipient state.

The President in neither Class I nor Class II acts on his own authority and he does not transcend his authorization.

Examples of Class III are all of the war agreements after a declaration of war; and promises of assistance, usually made in time of emergency, which the Congress by joint resolution approves of, either before or after an act of provocation. Strategy plans of the Allies, armistices, relief and occupation arrangements in World War II; the declaration of policy following the retaliation of the United States against a so-called attack in the Bay of Tonkin in 1964; the promise of protection against overt Communist aggression given to Middle East states after Congressional approval of President Eisenhower's Middle East Doctrine—all were illustrations.

Class IV embraces all other agreements that take care of routine administrative or "housekeeping" matters, such as visa fees for travelers, arrangements for tracking and communication stations in the space age, or arrangements for cultural exchanges between nations. They are instruments whereby the President exercises his Constitutional power of being the Executive and of representing the country in the eyes of the world. They can include unwritten verbal understandings between two heads of state as well as more formal agreements. Their minutiae do not come under Congressional deliberation in order to be effective and they are financed as routine items in the Executive's budget.

Executive Agreements are all different, not only in their Class but in their content. It is impossible to analyze them and have them conform to a rigid pattern. No matter what the Class, however, there are requirements of clarity concerning the duration of the life of the Agreement and of precision in terminology. It is important to know the responsibilities of the parties and to know the procedures for an extension or a termination of the relationship. The life of Executive Agreements should not be left to neglect but should be a fulfillment of standards of international relationships at different eras.

Treaties and especially Executive Agreements of all four classes will be included in this account and will be given attention as conveyors of, or channels expressive of, foreign policy. It is wise to stop at this point, therefore, and assess this term, policy.

Policy expresses indicated-behavior that will be followed to achieve goals. It is a means to an end. The goals of national interest and national security, however, have always been constants and are glibly stated on all occasions by public officials. Surely our *national interest* demands the preservation of our freedoms that have made our open society unique; surely it demands the continuation of the high standard of living that requires the development of our domestic resources, the importation of natural resources not found within our country, and the development of trade in both raw and finished products with potential customers throughout the world; and surely it demands constant attention to the health of citizens. Surely our *national security* indicates that the United States should have the right to develop as her people decide, secure from external attack or interference and from internal subversion.

National interest and national security are expressive of the goals of the United States but the terms are used so tritely that they become the tools of the policymakers, casting an aura over desired behavior and making them seem to be not the goals but the policy itself. Further analysis or questioning is often discouraged as if the goal and the policy were identical and as if a certain policy were not one of many possible means to an end. Unfortunately, until recently, the people of the United States were apt to accept this situation without question. For example, our fundamental policy of animosity to Communism did not change since 1946 and became an end in itself. Understanding of policy as indicated-behavior for desired goals, so necessary in a democracy, was long overdue.

International Agreements are not made by the President alone. He has many assistants, agencies, departments and ministers to assist him and he must bear in mind the will of the Congress. He is also sensitive to public opinion and the press.

The President, however, has tremendous powers in his own right in foreign relations. He not only negotiates all agreements but he nominates and, by and with the consent of the Senate, appoints ambassadors, ministers, and consuls in foreign countries. He is Commander-in-Chief of the Army and Navy in all of their contacts around the world. He also executes the laws of Congress. He is the official who symbolizes the country and his rhetorical speeches may have many implications for commitments.

Congress also has responsibility for the content and policy embodied in International Agreements. Treaties have to have the consent of the Senate; Executive Agreements also involve the Congress—those of Class I being made after Senate approval of treaties; those of Classes II and III being made with direct Congressional approval; those of Class IV receiving implied approval in that they are included in the routine appropriations to carry out the functions of government.

It will be useful to keep in mind the powers of the Congress as they have bearing on foreign relations. Congress has the power to regulate commerce with foreign nations; to lay and collect duties; to establish uniform rules of naturalization; to define and punish piracies and felonies committed on the high seas, and offenses against the law of nations; to declare war, grant letters of marque and reprisal, and make rules concerning captures on land and water; to raise and support armies; to provide and maintain a navy; to make rules for the government and regulation of the land and naval forces; to provide for calling forth of the militia to execute the laws of the Union, suppress insurrections and repel invasions; and to provide for organizing, arming and disciplining the militia and for governing such part of the militia as may be employed in the service of the United States. The states appoint the officers and train the militia according to the discipline prescribed by Congress. Congress also holds the purse strings and has power to appropriate all monies of the United States Government.[1]

The Supreme Court also has responsibility concerning International Agreements for it is the traditional duty of the Court to see that no act of the President or of the Congress violates the Constitutional provisions. In this day of technological advance and of the shrinking of the world, there are many contacts that impinge on the jurisdictions of both the Executive and the Congress and the policy that is reflected in promises of action or is descriptive of present actions and attitudes must be kept consonant with the directives of the Constitution. As in all human organizations, much depends on interpretation by the Supreme Court of the named powers of the President and of the Congress. In the twentieth century the Supreme Court has shown signs of interpreting the Constitution as a whole and has considered its meaning in a twentieth century environment. Knowlegeable and wise decisions are necessary and affect the people whose representatives are speaking. Since Executive Agreements are not mentioned in the Constitution, the Supreme Court, when a suit involving such agreements is before it, has to decide whether Executive Agreements meet or transcend the jurisdictional powers of the President and of the Congress as given in the Constitution.

1. *United States Constitution,* Article I, Sections 7 and 8.

While the President, the Congress and the Supreme Court are all under oath to work toward the goals of national interest and national security, and always have been, it has been very definitely since World War II that these agents, or representatives of the people, have been committed to new tactics. The United States during World War II shed the last shadows of isolationism that had lingered since World War I and adopted openly the policy of internationalism. It was thought after World War II that only by contacts with other people and only by using power to compete with other states, to forestall rivals in ideologies and at times to dominate organizations, could the national interests be served and the country be secure.

The frontier since World War II has become a world frontier. World contacts have been multitudinous and most varied, for it is a technological, nuclear, and space age, and many new sovereign states have come into existence with whom it is desirable to have relations. All kinds of International Agreements have been employed to indicate and guide behavior and are definitely necessary in this complex world. Since World War II their number has soared.

It is impossible to give an accurate number of International Agreements since 1946, for information is hard to come by. A numbered Treaty Series (TS) in pamphlet form was started in 1908 to continue the two volumes of *Treaties, Conventions, International Acts, Protocols and Agreements between the United States and Other Powers, 1776–1909* compiled by William M. Malloy, clerk of the Senate Committee on Foreign Relations. This series included all kinds of International Agreements until in 1929 there was started a separately numbered series called the Executive Agreement Series (EAS) in pamphlet form. These two series were preliminary to their final publication in the *Statutes at Large,* which constituted the authentic evidence in all courts of law and public offices of the United States. In 1946, however, the two pamphlet series were merged, and the first number of the new pamphlet series, Treaties and Other International Acts Series (TIAS), was 1501. In 1950 there was another change. By an act of Congress Treaties and other International Agreements were merged in one compilation and published in a new series of volumes, separate from the *Statutes at Large,* called *United States Treaties and Other International Agreements* (UST). This plan of publication continues to the present time but is usually three years behind the effective date.

TIAS continues in pamphlet form and includes Treaties and Executive Agreements. According to an act of Congress on July 8, 1966 [2] this series is now "competent evidence of the treaties, international agreements other than treaties . . . in all the courts of law . . . and public offices of the United States . . . without any further proof or authentication thereof." TIAS is kept current within the previous few months but pamphlets do not appear in their chronological order.

On February 1, 1971 the number of the last pamphlet containing an agreement was 6985, an increase in 25 years of 5484. Most of these were Executive Agreements rather than Treaties. The increase is indicated by the following list:

Year	Starts with	TIAS No.
1946	" "	1501
1950	" "	2010
1960	" "	4399
1970	" "	6813
1971	" "	6985

This list is not all inclusive, however. It does not include the many oral commitments of the President that are announced as promises. These go beyond the dim line separating them from public announcements of policy that are given out to impress the public both at home and abroad. International Agreements have continued to increase; on January 20, 1973 there were 7470 in the TIAS.

The Executive Agreement, because of its possible immediate implementation and its usually temporary nature (although some have lasted indefinitely), has become a very favored tool or instrument to express the post-war policies. However, the very qualities that make Executive Agreements so easy to use, paradoxically enough, do not always make them instruments for frequent changes of policy. Executive Agreements can, because of their facility of use, escalate policy, as it were; they simply repeat in larger dimensions the behavior necessary to attain the ends—and the retention of the behavior becomes a policy in itself. The reasons for the original behavior are not reviewed and changes of the times are not reflected. It is only when the cost of this continued behavior touches the personal life of the citizen in its toll, both in deaths of loved ones and in high economic costs of living, that

2. 80 Stat. 271; 1 U.S.C. 113.

the problems both of the policy and of the wisdom of using the easy Executive Agreement come into question.

The President, the Congress, and the Supreme Court still have their functions; and the separation of powers, the lack of dictatorship, and free elections are still necessary in the democracy of the United States. But today an educated populace is demanding more and more the shared confidence of the elected representatives and an understanding of foreign policy.

Since International Agreements are essential in international relations, a review of foreign affairs as channeled by them, in the complexities of the post-war era, will contribute to an understanding of the present.

CHAPTER II

The Heritage of International Agreements from World War II

World War II was a turning point for the United States. Her long period of semi-isolation between the two world wars was brought to an end. The United States entered a period of involvement that was to lead to world prominence and this meant the negotiation of many new International Agreements, most of which were Executive Agreements.

It was true that the United States had fought in World War I "to make the world safe for democracy", but she had not ratified the Versailles Treaty, had not joined the League of Nations, had been disillusioned by the war debt controversy, and had only in the thirties joined the International Labor Organization and recognized diplomatically the Union of Soviet Socialist Republics.

The twentieth century had made of the United States a creditor nation; and between 1919 and the stock market crash of 1929, her prosperity continued, private investments and loans went to postwar Germany and other European countries, and private capital helped to develop many parts of the world. The United States had been able to forge ahead, for no battles of World War I had been fought on her soil and her industries were flourishing.

Europe needed dollars, however, both to pay the war debts of World War I to the United States and to pay the interest on private investments in Europe; but imports into the United States declined. There was still resentment in the United States against German-made goods, and Europe's reluctance to pay war debts did not create a cooperative climate of opinion. In 1921 and 1922, and again in 1930 in the Hawley-Smoot Act Congress raised the tariff on imports, with the result that foreign imports diminished and United States exports were promoted.

Wars do not erase fears and suspicions. When Austria after World War I wished to join Germany, France brought financial sanctions to bear against Austria and "called" her short term credits. The lack of money in Europe and the threat of collapse of the economic structure of post-war Europe brought the Hoover Moratorium for one year after July, 1931 and resulted in pressures of governments against private banks' recalling their loans.

1934 was an important year, for that year marked the end of payments of war debts to the United States, except by Finland, and saw the first constructive act to revise the trade policy. The Trade Agreements Act of 1934 authorized the President to negotiate reciprocal trade agreements with foreign countries, within prescribed limits. This was the inception of a new idea of putting the President in a position of decision-making in tariff reduction. There immediately followed Executive Agreements with many countries throughout the world and the fortunate result was an upswing in the United States' foreign trade. This Act and the consequent Executive Agreements of Class II were repeatedly extended to the 1960's. The number of trade Executive Agreements increased from year to year and especially as new states of the world came into existence.

The League of Nations, in the twenties and thirties, was frequently tested in its peace-keeping objective. Where small powers were concerned the League was successful, but when Japan began her expansion throughout northern and central China, when Italy invaded Ethiopia, and when Hitler began to assert himself in Central Europe, the League was severely challenged. Although the United States was not a member, nothing of importance was decided without sounding out of the attitude of the United States through her permanent observer in Geneva in "back-door" diplomacy.

As the thirties progressed the Congress passed four Neutrality Acts but after World War II began in September, 1939, the fourth, in November, 1939, putting arms and ammunition on a cash and carry basis, favored the democracies. Unofficial sentiment in the United States was definitely against any party that was antagonistic to her principles and whose victory as totalitarian would jeopardize her security.

The United States became involved before she declared war because she was a great arsenal for supplies and was a potential granary for Europe and the world. The United Kingdom and her allies turned to the United States for supplies of all kinds. An Anglo-French Purchasing Board came into existence to coordinate supply activities and in late 1939 and throughout 1940 this board and its successor, the British Purchasing Commission, placed orders for supplies and equipment to private companies of the United States. Because of the volume of the needed items, the dollar resources of Great Britain and her allies were quickly reduced.

Another response to the European crisis was the bringing about of closer relations of the United States with Latin America and Canada. Already under the Coolidge and Hoover Administrations the United States had begun to demonstrate its desire to move away from unilateral intervention in Latin America and change the policy of being policeman to a policy of "interposition" when necessary to protect American lives. She wanted above all to have a policy of regional cooperation that would inspire the respect of Latin American nations. The Good Neighbor Policy, enunciated later by President F. D. Roosevelt, had been evolving through this preliminary period and the real Monroe Doctrine was explained as being a protection of freedom and independence of Latin America against Europe and not a policy of the big stick, wielded by the United States. President F. D. Roosevelt redefined Pan-Americanism as having the qualities of the Good Neighbor.

At Montevideo in December, 1933 it was decided unanimously that "no state has a right to intervene in the internal or external affairs of another" [1] ; and at Buenos Aires, December 1, 1936, it had been agreed that the republics would consult together, "in order to find means of peaceful cooperation in the event of war or the threat of war between American countries." [2] The Monroe Doctrine had become a multilateral policy. It was at the Lima Conference in November, 1938 that the principle of cooperation was reiterated and the continental solidarity stood ready to assert itself. "In case the peace, security or territorial integrity of any American Republic is threatened by acts of any nature that may impair them, they proclaim their common concern and their determination to make effective their solidarity, coordinating their respective sovereign wills by means of the procedure of consultation." [3] In 1939 at Panama the foreign ministers of the American

---

[1]. *Documents on American Foreign Relations* (Boston: World Peace Foundation, 1939–), Vol. VII, p. 718.
[2]. *Ibid.*
[3]. *Ibid.*

Republics agreed upon cooperative measures to maintain their neutrality and meet their economic problems and declared that there was a 300-mile neutrality zone around the whole hemisphere except Canada and that each country was authorized to police the waters off its own coast.

In 1940 stronger ties with Latin America and Canada were drawn. On July 30, 1940 the Havana Conference asserted "that any attempt on the part of a non-American State against the integrity or inviolability of the territory, the sovereignty or the political independence of an American State shall be considered as an act of aggression against all the American States."[4] On August 18, 1940 the United States and Canada established a joint defense board. All of these conferences resulted in commitments of the United States expressed through International Agreements.

The Battle of Britain in 1940 soon impressed the United States with the fact that the defense of Britain was a defense of democracy and therefore her own defense. President Roosevelt was able to find rifles, machine guns, bombs and ammunition of World War I days in warehouses and sell them to private firms, that subsequently sold them to Great Britain and France. In May, 1940 Prime Minister Churchill asked the United States for some destroyers of the Government but Acts of Congress prohibited the transfer unless it could be proved that they were not needed for national defense. Getting a new bill through Congress in an election year was not a hopeful prospect and finally, advised by private citizens, President Roosevelt was able through his own executive authority to negotiate the Destroyer-Bases Deal in September, 1940. The United States got naval and air bases on Newfoundland and Bermuda as gifts, and in exchange for 50 destroyers acquired six other bases in the western Atlantic on a 99 year rent-free lease basis.[5] This Executive Agreement of Class IV definitely brought an end to impartial neutrality and the Congress soon passed a peacetime Conscription Act, in September, 1940.

In March, 1941 an "Act further to Promote the Defense of the United States and for Other Purposes" passed the Congress.[6] This was the famous Lend-Lease Act that was the forerunner of all of the Aid Acts of the United States from that time to the present. The President was authorized by Congress "to manufacture in arsenals, factories, and shipyards under their jurisdiction, or other-

---

4. *Ibid.*
5. EAS 235.
6. 55 Stat. 11.

wise procure, . . . any defense article for the government of any country whose defense the President deems vital to the defense of the United States; to sell, transfer title to, exchange, lease, lend, or otherwise dispose of, to any such government any defense article; to test, inspect, prove, repair, outfit, recondition, or otherwise to place in good working order . . . any defense article for any such government, or to procure any or all such services by private contract; to communicate to any such government any defense information pertaining to any defense article. . . ." The Act authorized assistance to the United Kingdom and later, after the United States entered the war in December, 1941, to all other allies. An Executive Agreement of Class II had to follow with each country involved. Requests for defense articles were made to the United States Government through the Office of Lend-Lease Administration (later the Foreign Economic Administration) or the military forces, and at the outset of the program existing stocks met the demand. Reverse lend-lease also took many forms, for "the terms and conditions upon which any such foreign government receives any aid . . . shall be those which the President deems satisfactory, and the benefit to the United States may be payment or repayment in kind or property, or any other direct or indirect benefit which the President deems satisfactory."

Latin American Republics also had lend-lease agreements during the war and were the recipients of grants through the Export-Import Bank that had been established in 1934. On March 31, 1942 there was created the Institute of Inter-American Affairs, a governmental agency responsible for providing United States technical assistance to Latin American countries. The experience with this organization was to prove valuable for European application after the war. The Institute was maintained as a Government Corporation with which the Republics cooperated in the development of health, agriculture and education. Each country made an Executive Agreement with the United States through this Institute.

When the attack on Pearl Harbor occurred on December 7, 1941, the United States, as we have seen, was already geared to cooperate with the Allies against Hitler of Germany. On June 12, 1941 Great Britain and twelve other nations and General de Gaulle of France had signed an Inter-Allied Declaration pledging their intention to work together, and with other free peoples, so that "relieved of the menace of aggression, all may enjoy economic and social security"; and on August 4, 1941 President Roosevelt and Prime Minister Winston Churchill had issued an Atlantic Charter, "somewhere in the Atlantic". This Charter was an informal Executive Agreement of Class IV, stating the common objective of freedom from fear and want, stating their desire to collaborate in the economic field, and stating that they would aid and encourage practicable measures that would lighten the burden of armaments. It was, therefore, only a culminating step for twenty-six nations, that called themselves the United Nations, on January 1, 1942 in Washington, D.C., after the United States had entered the war, to sign the Declaration mentioned above, and later twenty-one other nations adhered to it. It was a war-time measure and all subscribed to the principles of the Atlantic Charter as well and promised not to make a separate armistice or peace with the enemies. These instruments were declarations of principles, and both the Atlantic Charter and the Declaration of the United Nations became Executive Agreements of Class III for the United States, since she had declared war.[7]

When Congress declared war in December, 1941 the President, by his Constitutional right, had unlimited authority to win the war. All of the agreements to that end were Executive Agreements of Class III—agreements with the Allies for strategy, for deployment of troops, for supplies for relief of liberated peoples, for disposition of territory and reparations after the war; and agreements with the enemies for armistices and truces, and control of occupied territory.

During the war there were strategy meetings on a high level. Secretary of State Cordell Hull and the Foreign Ministers of Great Britain and the U.S.S.R. met in Moscow in October, 1943; President Roosevelt and Prime Minister Churchill were in constant touch by cable and by telephone and in eight personal conferences in 1943 at Casablanca, Washington, Hyde Park and Quebec. In November, 1943 Roosevelt, Churchill and Chiang Kai-shek met at Cairo and Roosevelt, Churchill and Stalin met at Teheran. In February, 1945 Roosevelt, Churchill and Stalin met at Yalta, and in July, 1945 President Truman, Churchill and Stalin met at Potsdam. At these meetings the military Executive Agreements that were entered into were naturally kept secret.

At Moscow in 1943 it was agreed that eventually an indepen-

---

7. 55 Stat. 1600; EAS 236.

dent Austria was to be restored; and a European Advisory Commission was to be set up to guide the victors in the occupation period in Europe. Zones of occupation in Germany and temporary ones in Austria were decided upon. Control Councils were subsequently set up for each occupied region. The U.S.S.R. was to profit by the position of her liberating armies and the armistices with the countries of eastern Europe were to show acceptance of boundaries and reparations in her favor. The U.S.S.R. through occupation ensured her future control of these countries as satellites. At Yalta Stalin was promised eastern Poland and it was agreed that Poland should get compensation of territory from eastern Germany. At Cairo the big three decided what would be taken from Japan and at Yalta the U.S.S.R. was promised gains in the Far East. At Potsdam the basic framework of operation after the war was agreed upon and the policies toward the defeated powers of Germany and Japan were made final.

In February, 1945 an Inter-American Conference on Problems of War and Peace was held in Mexico City and resulted in the Act of Chapultepec, which was approved in plenary session on March 6, 1945.[8] It declared: "In case acts of aggression occur or there are reasons to believe that an aggression is being prepared by any other State against the integrity or inviolability of the territory, or against the sovereignty or political independence of an American State, the States signatory to this Act will consult among themselves in order to agree upon the measures it may be advisable to take." It was for the United States an Executive Agreement of Class III until a treaty would be concluded.

While military agreements obtained, Lend-Lease Executive Agreements with all of the Allies continued and in November, 1943 the forty-six nations that were then Allies established the United Nations Relief and Rehabilitation Administration (UNRRA), and the adherence of the United States was by Executive Agreement of Class III. While it was true that the winning armies assumed responsibility for medical supplies, food and the prevention of unrest among civilian populations, this post-combat aid was extended mainly in the occupied areas of Germany and Japan; the relief and rehabilitation work of UNRRA was restricted to countries lacking sufficient foreign exchange to finance essential imports. This help was given to Greece, Yugoslavia, Al-

---

8. *Documents on American Foreign Relations* (Boston: World Peace Foundation, 1939–), Vol. VII, pp. 718 ff.

bania, Poland, Czechoslovakia, Italy, Austria, Byelorussia, the Ukraine, and China.

The conferences of the leaders were also occasions for consummation of plans for post-war keeping of the peace and for interrelations of a permanent nature. Ever since Pearl Harbor special committees had been working in the State Department and post-war planning had been going on in the capitals of the Allies. The summit conferences enabled the plans to be brought together to the state of agreements. At Moscow Secretary Hull achieved a Four-Nation Declaration on October 30, 1943 for an international security organization; in 1943 at Hot Springs the United Nations Food and Agriculture Organization was established; in 1943 at Bretton Woods the International Bank for Reconstruction and Development and the International Monetary Fund were agreed upon; and in 1944 at Chicago the Provisional International Civil Aviation Organization came into being. The conferences dealing with these matters were not secret; the agreements that resulted were in the form of Treaties, not Executive Agreements, and required ratification; and they committed the cooperating countries to post-war long-term policies.

These arrangements then were the heritage of World War II. Some of the commitments as Treaties and others as Executive Agreements were to be projected far into the post-war period. After many years some, still effective, contribute to the dilemmas of the seventies.

CHAPTER III

Post-War International Agreements of the Forties

When World War II was over the United States emerged into a new status of leadership, for battles had not been fought on the soil of continental United States. She had kept her industries going to full capacity by competing for raw materials around the world and she had increased her agriculture to help feed the free and liberated world. The United States had lost in man power and had sacrificed tremendous amounts of equipment, but when the war ended she played her part in the occupation of the Germanies, Berlin and Austria and took the greatest responsibility during the reconstruction of Japan.

Before the war the United States had bases in Cuba, Puerto Rico, the Virgin Islands, Guam, the Philippines, American Samoa, Wake and Midway Islands and Hawaii. Then in 1940 through the Roosevelt-Churchill deal for destroyers she had acquired by Executive Agreement of Class IV additional naval and air bases in Bahamas, Jamaica, St. Lucia, Trinidad, Antigua, and British Guiana on a lease basis and in Newfoundland and Bermuda on a gift basis. On July 1, 1940 the United States and Iceland signed an Executive Agreement of Class IV providing for an American defense garrison to join the British and Canadian troops that were already there. In 1945 the United States still had troops in the occupation zones of Germany, Berlin and Austria, south of the 38th parallel in Korea, in Japan and the neighboring Ryukyus including Okinawa and the Bonin and Volcano Islands. She had asked for no territory but in 1947 she was given a "strategic trusteeship" by the United Nations over Micronesia, 2141 small islands in the Pacific comprising four archipelagoes—the Marshall

Islands, Eastern and Western Carolines, and the Marianas. This meant that she could use these islands for strategic purposes. For four years the United States remained the only nation with atomic bombs, and this possession gave the Americans confidence.

Although potentially powerful, the United States was also internationally minded. One of her goals was the acceptance of the Charter of the United Nations that had been completed at the San Francisco Conference in June, 1945, a conference attended by representatives of the forty-eight nations that had declared war upon the Axis. This Charter was to be accepted by the United States as a treaty and duly ratified by the President with the consent of the Senate. In the United Nations the United States was to play an impressive role. As one of the permanent members of the Security Council, she had the veto power, since no important action would be taken without affirmative action of seven members, including the five permanent ones. The international mindedness of the United States, based on cooperative experience during the war, and prompted by delayed guilt about not having been an active member of the former League of Nations, was to accentuate the normal post-war pacifism that occurs after any war. The United States was eager to bring the G.I.'s home from around the world; to put her faith in international organs to keep the peace; and to get back to normal peace activities that would bring economic, social and cultural relationships. Legislation authorized the United States' membership in the International Bank for Reconstruction and Development (the World Bank) and the International Monetary Fund, which had been established by multilateral treaties during the war, and the United States added to the funds of the Export-Import Bank.

True to her promise the United States gave complete independence to the Philippines in 1946. The concepts of Pan-Americanism and the "Good Neighbor" policy were also reaffirmed in the Inter-American Treaty of Reciprocal Assistance signed at Rio de Janeiro in 1947, and in the Charter of the American States and the American Treaty of Specific Settlement signed at Bogota in 1948. Each of these treaties was followed by an Executive Agreement of Assistance of Class II with each member state after authorizing legislation.

Aside from anticipations in the functioning of structural international organizations, the actual economic conditions in the countries of the world at the close of the war had to receive immediate attention. The large amount of lend-lease for which no terms of payment had been agreed upon was terminated and settlements were negotiated with respect to items in the supply pipeline and to war claims. The United Kingdom, largest recipient of lend-lease, was the first country to negotiate a settlement. On December 6, 1945 in a Joint Statement that country and the United States agreed to settle lend-lease, reciprocal aid, surplus war property, and claims. The result was a Mutual Aid Settlement, incorporating nine specific agreements, which was signed on March 27, 1946 as an Executive Agreement of Class II, and which later was followed by a Joint Congressional Resolution signed by the President making the Agreement one of Class III. In the next year and a half similar settlements were made with France, Belgium, South Africa, India, Australia, the Netherlands and New Zealand. Loans were then extended to Great Britain, France and Italy and were arranged for by Executive Agreements of Class IV.

The close of the war made surplus a vast quantity of United States supplies that were dispersed and stored all over the world. To avoid the expense of their return and their renovation prior to sale in the United States or foreign markets and because few of the nations desirous of acquiring the surplus materials had available dollar resources, the disposal of hundreds of thousands of items had to be coordinated with a wide use of credit financing. This resulted in many Executive Agreements of Class III, of the war category, and were initiated in the Office of the Foreign Liquidation Commissioner starting in October, 1945.

Post-war economic adjustments were very difficult. Prices in the United States were high and few foreign countries had the resources to import necessary articles. The aid furnished by UNRRA during the war was to terminate in April, 1947 and many populations were still in want. By this time international cooperation with the U.S.S.R. was having some problems so the United States decided not to help perpetuate an international agency she could not control and asked Congress to pass the Post-UNRRA Relief Act in May, 1947. This legislation provided that basic essentials—food, medical supplies, seeds, fertilizers, etc.—would be shipped where needed and would be sold for local currencies, with the proceeds to be used by the recipient countries. The act also included provisions for assistance for the International Children's Emergency Fund. And again in December, 1947 the United States passed the Foreign Aid Act to provide emergency aid to Austria, France and Italy, which provided assistance until the end of 1948. All of these acts were in the nature of relief assistance and most amounted to actual gifts in the form of grants. They were effective by Executive Agreements of Class II.

Because the countries of western and northern Europe were seriously affected by the sudden curtailment of lend-lease, it was soon evident that a more comprehensive long-range program of reconstruction, instead of mere relief, was necessary. Loans and grants had not been sufficient to save Europe from monetary and fiscal troubles. War destruction, inadequate maintenance of machinery and utilities, lack of up-to-date plants and processes, and disrupted trade channels—all called for drastic attention. Because of the inconvertibility of international currency there was a general trade paralysis. The loss of European supplies and markets, colonial unrest in Asia and Africa, and the loss of Far Eastern supply sources aggravated the scarcity of goods, and inflation increased prices. Europe had had the fundamental base of institutional devlopment but what she needed after the war was a coordinated program of reconstruction.

It was Secretary of State Marshall, who, in a speech at Harvard University in June, 1947, gave voice to the possibility of a development with assistance from the United States. There followed what was called the Marshall Plan from 1948 to 1952. European nations organized in a collective group to establish a joint plan for economic recovery. The U.S.S.R. and her satellites were invited but refused to join. The Economic Cooperation Act of 1949 launched the program. Sixteen European countries dissolved a temporary economic group and formed the Organization for European Economic Cooperation (OEEC), in which West Germany and Trieste were included.[1] Separate Executive Agreements of Class II were made between the United States and the members of the OEEC. The individual country programs and their requirements were presented to the Economic Cooperation Administration (ECA) for screening and recommendation. After review the process of procurement tried to make a maximum use of private trade channels and to avoid heavy reliance upon United States Government agencies for supplies. The foreign currencies received for the sale of the materials furnished on a grant basis were de-

---

1. The beneficiaries were the United Kingdom, Ireland, France, Italy, Portugal, Austria, Belgium, the Netherlands, Luxembourg, Denmark, Sweden, Jugoslavia, Iceland, Greece, Turkey, Norway, West Germany and Trieste.

posited in an account known as the "counterpart fund," five per cent of which was available to the United States for administrative expenses and for procuring strategic materials. The remaining ninety-five per cent was used by the receiving government with the concurrence of the United States for recovery purposes.

Another means of raising production was by making American management and production techniques available. By arrangements through Executive Agreements of Class IV United States teams explained American manufacturing and agricultural techniques and European business groups came to the United States. This technical assistance was also extended to their overseas territories by the recipient European countries. A number of technical projects were authorized by the United States for overseas territories but the major source of funds for their programs came from United States allotments to the parent countries.

It was not until September, 1950 that the Act for International Development was passed, which provided for the Point 4 Program, so called from the suggestion in the fourth point of President Truman's Inaugural Address in January, 1949. This program of technical assistance and "know how" was limited to economically underdeveloped areas and was implemented by Executive Agreements of Class II.

While these steps were being taken to increase the production of goods it was equally desirable to persuade the countries of the world to modify their import controls and to consider lowering tariffs and other trade barriers. The United States persuaded twenty-three countries to send representatives to Geneva in 1947 to discuss the need of reducing barriers to international trade on a multilateral, or many-party, basis. Their negotiations resulted in a multilateral Executive Agreement called the General Agreement on Tariffs and Trade (GATT).[2] Since 1934 the United States had signed bilateral, or two-party, agreements for trade, and it was this Reciprocal Trade Act of 1934, continued since that date, that permitted the United States to participate in the new arrangement. Pairs of countries, meeting simultaneously to negotiate trade agreements, combined all of their results in a single agreement. Agreements were made on certain articles across the board and the most favored nation principle was incorporated. A code of rules for the conduct of international trade was also

2. *ABC's of Foreign Trade, U.S. Trade Policy in Brief,* Department of State Publication 7713 (Washington: Government Printing Office, 1964), pp. 14–16.

developed and in order to resolve differences of interpretation of these rules, a forum was provided by having the contracting parties meet from time to time and enter into new agreements concerning tariffs.

Meanwhile the United States was being disillusioned by the political action of the U.S.S.R. The close friendship between the United States and the United Kingdom had continued after the war but beginning with the Potsdam Conference in July, 1945 it was quite evident that the U.S.S.R. was going to demonstrate a non-cooperative spirit. She extended Communism to and controlled the countries of Eastern Europe that her armies had overrun; she acquired and transported excess reparations of industries and equipment to her own soil; she raised difficulties in the making of treaties with Italy, Bulgaria, Rumania, Hungary and Finland until the final signing on February 10, 1947; and she raised objections to the application of uniform policies in the occupation zones of Germany, Berlin and Austria. In a speech in Fulton, Missouri on March 5, 1946 Winston Churchill stated: "From Stettin in the Baltic to Trieste in the Adriatic, an iron curtain has descended across the Continent." [3]

The United States developed a policy of resistance to the designs of the U.S.S.R. The war had been an ideological one and it was fought against totalitarianism and the control of states by other totalitarian ones. The United States soon realized that she had not fought the war against one totalitarian power to have the advantage taken by another totalitarian power. The U.S.S.R. had to be deterred.

Early in 1947 both Greece and Turkey requested the United States to assist them in maintaining their territorial integrity. Great Britain had liberated the Greeks from a Communist inspired revolution and Greece had been subject to guerrilla action and territorial demands from contiguous Balkan neighbors. The unsettled conditions and the great flow of refugees had compelled the United Kingdom to provide sizable amounts of civilian supplies. In early 1947, however, the United Kingdom notified the Greek Government that its own resources were becoming so limited that aid could not be continued. It was evident that Communist pressure would soon fill the vacuum. If Greece became a Communist country, Turkey could be surrounded and the safety of the eastern Mediterranean for the West could be endangered.

3. *Current History,* Current Documents, Vol. X (April, 1946), No. 56, pp. 356–361.

Control of the Dardanelles had traditionally been vital from a military standpoint, yet Turkey was also in military and economic difficulties. As early as March, 1945 the U.S.S.R. had announced its intention not to renew the twenty-year old Soviet-Turkish pact of friendship and was demanding that the Dardanelles be controlled and defended jointly by the Soviet Union and Turkey.

In May, 1947 a program of Greek-Turkish economic and military aid was enacted by Congress; it was known as the Truman Plan. To secure the success of military operations, arms were needed so it was arranged that of the $300 million of special aid to Greece half would be earmarked for military and half for civilian use. Turkey was to receive $100 million, entirely for military aid. Executive Agreements of Class II implemented these acts.

It was about this time in July, 1947 that George F. Kennan had presented his analysis of Soviet foreign policy in an article in *Foreign Affairs,* arguing that the policy of the United States toward the Soviet Union "must be that of long-term, patient but firm and vigilant containment of Russian expansive tendencies."

The Greek-Turkish military aid was the forerunner of the many post-war military aid agreements made by the United States. Early in the next year, in April, 1948, additional funds were authorized for the continuance of the military portion of the program. When complete responsibility for economic aid was transferred to the Economic Cooperation Administration (ECA) in July, 1948, with such aid to be provided from the European-recovery funds, the Greek-Turkish program became entirely military. The April, 1948 legislation also authorized military aid to assist the Chinese National Government in its struggle against the Chinese Communists.[4] Executive Agreements of Class II made all of these acts of legislation effective.

The Soviet pattern of aggression had become quite clear by 1948. New evidences were the Communist coup in Czechoslovakia in 1948; and the total blockade imposed on Berlin on June 24, 1948, as a climax to the U.S.S.R.'s lack of cooperation in the Allied Control Council in Berlin and the U.S.S.R.'s reaction to the introduction of a currency reform in the three western zones of occupation. The United States airlift foiled the efforts of the Soviet Union and the blockade was finally lifted on May 12, 1949. Meanwhile from September 1, 1948 to May, 1949 German representatives from the British, French and American occupation zones

4. In 1949 the Nationalists had to flee to Formosa (Taiwan).

were encouraged by the Western powers to meet at Bonn and draw up a constitution for a Federal Republic of Germany. An Executive Agreement of Class III, called an occupation Statute, of April 8, 1949 defined the relations between this new government and the Western powers. It provided for continued occupation of the three Western zones but substituted a civilian Allied High Commission for the earlier military government. The U.S.S.R. refused to cooperate and set up a rival German Democratic Republic in Eastern Germany.

These experiences with the U.S.S.R. led the United States and ten European countries plus Canada to embark on a program of mutual security by the signing of the North Atlantic Treaty on April 4, 1949, in Washington. On August 24, this treaty went into force for the United States. Congress appropriated an initial $814 millions for military assistance to the other NATO countries in the Mutual Defense Assistance Act of October, 1949. On January 27, 1950 an Executive Agreement of Class II, called a Mutual Defense Assistance Agreement, was signed with each of the following: the United Kingdom, Belgium, France, the Netherlands, Italy, Luxembourg, Denmark and Norway. Similar Executive Agreements followed with Iceland, May 5, 1951; and Canada, April 28 and 30, 1952 (in force September 27, 1953). Communist Yugoslavia and totalitarian Spain were not invited to be members of NATO but Yugoslavia, after being denounced by Stalin in 1948, received trade deals and grants for relief from the United States, which were effected by an Executive Agreement of Class II. In 1953 Spain and the United States had an Executive Agreement of Class II whereby Spain was granted economic aid in return for air and naval bases.

Under the Mutual Defense Assistance Act of October, 1949, that had provided for military assistance to the NATO powers, grant aid was also to be made available by Executive Agreements of Class II to nations other than pact signatories, for example, to Greece, Turkey, Iran, Korea, the Philippines, and Nationalist China. Finally Greece and Turkey were admitted to NATO through a protocol to the NATO Treaty, this agreement becoming effective for the United States on February 15, 1952.

The Soviet Union's experimentation with nuclear fission in 1949 made this deterrence policy have more meaning. In 1946 the troops of the U.S.S.R. had been withdrawn from Iran, following the ineffective effort of the United Nations to accomplish this, through a bilateral arrangement with Iran, for the U.S.S.R. was giving priority at this time to conditions in Europe.

The revolution in China, that resulted in the Chinese Communists expelling the Nationalists to the island of Formosa in 1949, was a conflict that the United States refused to be drawn into. From 1945 to 1949 the United States had granted a tremendous amount of aid to Nationalist China by Executive Agreements of Class II but by January, 1950, President Truman announced that the United States would give no further military aid to Chiang Kai-shek and would not defend Formosa in case of attack. The White Paper on China had revealed conditions of corruption in China that it seemed hopeless to correct and the United States did not want to be associated with the traditional concepts of colonialism and imperialism.

The United States' stay in Korea after World War II was regarded by the United States as temporary and it was thought that the United States should concentrate on the defense of Japan, where the United States was still in occupation. The United States should defend only a perimeter that ran from the Aleutian Islands to Japan, the Ryukyus Islands and the Philippines. In 1947 the United Nations had given, as has been noted, a special mandate over the Micronesian Islands to the United States, and she was free to use them for military bases. Excluded, it was thought, from the permanent interest of the United States, therefore, were Korea, Formosa and Southeast Asia.

President Truman put much emphasis upon the newly created United Nations to keep the peace and play an enlarged role in Asia, and looked to the building up of Japan as a democracy. An increase in economic aid to the new countries of Asia, including Indo-China, seemed to be in order, however, for the United States felt her position in the Orient would be stabilized not by military but by economic and political means.

CHAPTER IV

International Agreements during the Korean War

Korea had been almost a forgotten region in the various conferences during World War II. At Cairo in December, 1943, the United States, the United Kingdom and China had declared that "in due course" Korea should become "free and independent." This pledge was reaffirmed in the Potsdam Declaration of July, 1945 and subscribed to by the U.S.S.R. when she entered the war against Japan. When Japan suddenly surrendered in August, 1945 the United States suggested that Korea be temporarily divided along the 38th parallel to prevent the Soviet Union's occupying the country and to obtain the surrender of the Japanese troops. In Moscow in December, 1945 the Foreign Ministers of the U.S.S.R., the United Kingdom, and the United States concluded an agreement of Class III designed to bring about the independence of Korea. This agreement was later adhered to by the Government of China. It provided for a joint United States–U.S.S.R. Commission to meet in Korea and through consultation with Korean democratic parties and social organizations, to decide on methods for establishing a provisional Korean government. The Joint Commission was then to consult with that provisional government on methods of giving aid and assistance to Korea, any agreement reached being submitted for approval to the four powers adhering to the Moscow Agreement.

After two years Korea remained divided at the 38th parallel with Soviet forces in the industrial north and United States forces in the agricultural south with little or no exchange of goods and services between the two zones. The United States and the U.S.S.R. could not agree on the consultative groups and finally the United

States appealed to the General Assembly of the United Nations. The Assembly, on November 14, 1947, resolved that elected Korean representatives be invited to take part in consideration of the question of Korea's freedom and independence and that a United Nations Temporary Commission on Korea be established to travel, observe, and consult throughout Korea to facilitate and expedite participation of Korean representatives.

Elections were first set for March 31, 1948. The elected representatives would consult with the Commission and constitute a National Assembly, which would establish the National Government of Korea. The Government was to constitute its own security forces, take over the functions of government and arrange for the withdrawal from Korea of the armed forces, if possible within ninety days.

The U.S.S.R. was uncooperative concerning the elections, however, and proceeded to set up a Communist regime in North Korea called the Korean Democratic People's Republic. The elections were held by the United Nations' Temporary Commission on May 10, 1948. In July the new Constituent Assembly met, adopted a constitution and set up the Republic of Korea.

On September 20, 1948 the Department of State declared that the U.S.S.R. had not cooperated and on December 12, 1948 the United Nations General Assembly accepted the report of the Temporary Commission on Korea, stating that the Government of the Republic of Korea had been inaugurated on August 15, 1948 and had effective control and jurisdiction over that part of Korea where the Temporary Commission was able to observe and consult, that the Soviet Union had refused to let the Temporary Commission into its zone, that the Government was based on elections on May 10, 1948, and that this was the only such government in Korea. On the same day the General Assembly passed a resolution establishing a New United Nations Commission on Korea, which was to help the Korean people and their lawful government to achieve the goal of a free and united Korea.

The United States terminated her military government in Korea upon the inauguration of the Government of the Republic of Korea and recognized the new government on January 1, 1949. She withdrew most of her forces by the end of June, 1949 but left behind, at the request of the Government of the Republic of Korea and by arrangement of an Executive Agreement of Class III, a few air force personnel and a military advisory group to help

South Korea organize a defense force. The United States made no promise to defend South Korea, if attacked, however.

The U.S.S.R. announced that all of her troops would be gone by January 1, 1949 but by October, 1949 her forces were still there.

On June 7, 1949 President Truman asked Congress for continued economic assistance to the Republic of Korea for the fiscal year ending June, 1950. The United States, he said, was now giving relief and a small amount of assistance in rehabilitation to the Republic of Korea under Public Law 793—80th Congress. "The continuation of that assistance is of great importance to the successful achievement of the foreign policy aims of the United States." [1] "Korea has become a testing ground in which the validity and practical value of the ideals and principles of democracy which the Republic is putting into practice are being matched against the practices of communism which have been imposed upon the people of North Korea. The survival and progress of the Republic toward a self-supporting, stable economy will have an immense and far-reaching influence on the people of Asia. Such progress will encourage the people of south and southeast Asia and the islands of the Pacific. . . . Moreover, the Korean Republic, by demonstrating the success and tenacity of democracy in resisting communism, will stand as a beacon to the people of northern Asia in resisting the control of the communist forces which have overrun them." [2] In 1949 this policy was being enunciated and it was still being reiterated in 1971. The United States was still justifying her Far Eastern policies in this way.

Aid to Korea was administered by the Economic Cooperation Administration since January 1, 1949 and was for recovery; prior to this date it has been for relief and had been administered by the army. Executive Agreements of Class II were entered into for this aid.

On October 21, 1949 the United Nations General Assembly made note of the Commission's report on observing and verifying the withdrawal of the United States troops, but not the Soviet troops, and resolved that the Commission should continue until a new decision of the General Assembly would be made.

On January 26, 1950 the Governments of the United States and of the Republic of Korea signed a Mutual Defense Assistance Ag-

---

1. *A Decade of American Foreign Policy, Basic Documents, 1941–1949*, pt. 2 (Washington: Government Printing Office), p. 680.
2. *Ibid.*, p. 682.

greement.[3] Each government would continue to make available to the other equipment materials, services, or other military assistance; and this Executive Agreement of Class II would be effective until three months after written notice of intention of termination on the part of either government was given. On February 14, 1950, also, the Far Eastern Economic Assistance Act of 1950 was amended to extend the date from February 15, 1950 to June 30, 1950 to enable the President to obligate economic funds already appropriated.

On March 7, 1950 the Secretary of State stated that the United States was providing Korea with political support; was helping Korea develop a sound educational system; and at the request of Korea was maintaining a Military Advisory Group to assist in training Korean security forces. Economic aid was being given under the Economic Cooperation Administration's program. The Secretary of State asked for funds to extend the three-year program to the second year, that of 1951.

While this concern with the development of Korea was manifested by the United States, the China White Paper had been released by the State Department in August, 1949 and revealed corrupt conditions over which the United States had no control.

The U.S.S.R. recognized Communist China after the Nationalists fled to Formosa and in a treaty with that state agreed to renounce some of her Yalta gains in Manchuria. There was uncertainty as to Nationalist China's intention to attack the mainland; and Communist troops were massed along the shores opposite the island.

After a spring buildup, on June 24, 1950 North Korean soldiers invaded the Republic of Korea. President Truman came to the conclusion that the invasion had to be blocked for if the democracies failed to act, the aggressors would keep going.

On June 25, 1950 the Security Council of the United Nations met at the request of the United States. The Soviet delegate was absent because he had walked out in protest against the decision not to seat Communist China in the United Nations. (The U.S.S.R. ended the boycott on August 1, 1950.) A resolution was passed on June 25, 1950 calling for the cessation of hostilities and the withdrawal of the forces of North Korea from South Korea. The resolution called on all members to render every assistance to

---

3. TIAS 2019.

the United Nations in the execution of this resolution and to refrain from giving assistance to North Korea.[4]

In these circumstances the United States President ordered United States air and sea forces to give the Korean Government troop cover and support. On June 25, 1950 it was decided to send arms by airdrop to South Korea and the Seventh Fleet was ordered to protect Formosa, and prevent the Chinese Government on Formosa from having operations against the mainland. It was also decided that military aid would be given the endangered Philippines and military assistance to France and the Associated States in Indochina would be accelerated.

On June 27 the United Nations Security Council recommended that members furnish such assistance to the Republic of Korea as might be necessary to repel the armed attack and to restore international peace and security in the area.

The President of the United States reported on June 30, 1950 that he had authorized the United States Air Force to conduct missions on specific military targets in North Korea and had ordered a naval blockade of the entire Korean coast. The United States sent the first ground forces; General Douglas MacArthur was given full authority by the United Nations on July 8; and the naval blockade of the Korean coast was made effective.

When President Truman decided to oppose the North Korean invasion, his action was interpreted as a reversal of the Administration's policies. The only change, however, was the decision to protect Formosa for Chiang Kai-shek. In regard to Korea all action was to be taken with the consent and support of the United Nations. In connection with Formosa the United States acted alone. The struggle was not only against aggression into South Korea but one of frustrating activities of the two Chinas. The combination of these two goals caused criticism by Europe and created rifts in the conduct of the war in Korea. It was a step which led to Chinese Communist intervention in North Korea for forces were shifted from the provinces opposite Formosa to Manchuria and later were engaged in Korea.

At first, with difficulty the North Koreans were checked and a line was maintained near Pusan. In July, 1950 General MacArthur planned and received approval of his recommendations to strike behind the enemy line by an amphibious manoeuver.

---

4. *American Foreign Policy, Basic Documents, 1950–1955,* Vol. II (Washington: Government Printing Office), pp. 2337–2338.

Chiang Kai-shek had offered 33,000 troops and General MacArthur felt that they could be used as a diversionary force against Communist China but the allies in the United Nations feared that this would precipitate a world war, for the U.S.S.R. now had the atomic bomb. General MacArthur strongly believed that the fight was against Communist world supremacy and the battleground was all of Asia, not just Korea. The Communists had struck in Asia first instead of Europe, and he clung to his own policy of including Formosa in the American security system.

By September 15, 1950 the United Nations troops had regained the 38th parallel in Korea and soon General MacArthur was authorized to try to establish control throughout all of Korea, but not to cross into Manchuria or the U.S.S.R. borders of Korea. Beginning in October, 1950 the United Nations troops advanced toward the Yalu River. President Truman met General MacArthur on Wake Island on October 15, 1950. General MacArthur, at that time, ruled out the Soviet Union's participation and did not feel that there was much danger of Chinese intervention, in spite of Communist China's threat.

By October 30, 1950, however, Chinese troops were encountered south of the Yalu River and the United Nations troops retreated south of the 38th parallel. By the end of November, 1950 war with Communist China seemed imminent. President Truman announced a state of national emergency (which was not formally terminated up to 1973). Meanwhile attempts were made to get negotiations started and a committee was appointed by the United Nations to see if an armistice agreement and a truce could be worked out. Chou En-lai demanded, however, that all foreign troops be withdrawn from Korea before negotiations would be begun. He insisted that Korea's domestic affairs had to be settled by the Koreans themselves. The American forces had to be withdrawn from Taiwan also, he said, and the People's Republic of China had to receive status in the United Nations.

These terms were unacceptable to the United States and to the United Nations. Limited war of attrition rather than a declaration of war on Communist China was decided upon by the Joint Chiefs of Staff. General MacArthur followed the directives and by the end of January, 1951 the war of attrition began; soon United Nations troops reached the 38th parallel once more and were advancing beyond it.

General MacArthur's personal disagreement with the tactics and his inept disregard for proper channels led to his dismissal on

April 11, 1951. On April 19, 1951 he addressed a joint session of Congress and took his point of view to the people. The Senate Armed Service Committee had an investigation and supported President Truman. The Administration made it clear that it would not adopt General MacArthur's program of involving Formosa in an all-out war or pull out of Korea. The morale of the enemy and the fabric of the Chinese armies were to be broken by a war of attrition. Unification of Korea would be sought by diplomatic and political means, not by military conquest.

By the end of May, 1951 the Chinese offensive was repulsed with heavy losses and the war of attrition seemed to be working. By the end of June, 1951 the Soviet Union reported that a cease-fire and armistice might be discussed as a first step. The United States and the United Nations thought that a limited victory might be possible. A quick military armistice could be followed by negotiations to deal with political and territorial issues of the war.

Negotiations began on July 10, 1951 but the Communists used every tactic of delay to wear down the United Nations negotiators.[5] On November 27, 1951 the Communists consented to the United Nations proposal in which the demarcation line would coincide with the actual line of contact when the final truce would be signed. (In July, 1953 it was adjusted to reflect the changes in the battlefield since November, 1951.) Frustrating negotiations, which involved all kinds of propaganda, concerning prisoners of war and charges of use of germ warfare and poison gas, slowed the progress. A deadlock arose in the truce talks from May, 1952 to March, 1953. Meanwhile the war of attrition was stepped up. "Operation Killer" involved tanks, control of Korean waters, aircraft carriers and combat planes. All points of strategic value to the enemy were bombed—hydroelectric plants along the Manchurian border, military targets, the main Communist supply line, and smaller military targets.

By March, 1953 the Communists said that they were ready to exchange seriously sick and wounded prisoners of war and wanted to resume the armistice talks. An Agreement of Class I was signed by the allies with the Communists on April 11, 1953 and two weeks later talks began. On July 27, 1953 the final truce agreement was signed at Panmunjom; and, at Washington,[6] the allies in the United Nations signed an agreement supporting the deci-

5. *American Foreign Policy, Basic Documents, 1950–1955,* Vol. II (Washington: Government Printing Office), p. 2627.
6. TIAS 2781.

sion to conclude an armistice. It was a military truce and not a peace settlement. Syngman Rhee, President of the Korean Republic, was most unhappy and threatened to resume fighting if Chinese troops were permitted to remain in the north. However, the United States pledged to train and equip a South Korean army of twenty divisions, to extend some billion dollars in economic aid, and to conclude a mutual defense treaty to protect South Korea against future Communist aggression. A Joint Statement to this effect, an Executive Agreement of Class IV, was signed at Seoul by the Secretary of State and the President of the Republic of Korea on August 8, 1953. A Mutual Defense Treaty was signed on October 1, 1953 and entered into force on November 17, 1954.[7]

The armistice recommended that a political conference be convened within three months and the General Assembly of the United Nations welcomed this. The conference was delayed, however, until finally on February 18, 1954 the foreign ministers of the United States, the United Kingdom, France, and the U.S.S.R., meeting at the Berlin Foreign Ministers Conference, proposed that a conference of the United States, France, the United Kingdom, the U.S.S.R., the Chinese People's Republic, the Republic of Korea, the People's Democratic Republic of Korea and the other countries, the armed forces of which had participated in the hostilities in Korea, should meet in Geneva on April 26, 1954 for the purpose of reaching a peaceful settlement of the Korean question. It was agreed that the question of restoring peace in Indochina, also at war at this time, would be discussed as well; and the United States, France, the United Kingdom, the U.S.S.R., the Chinese People's Republic, and other interested states were to be invited for this purpose.[8]

On June 15, 1954 at the final session of the Geneva Conference, sixteen nations that had contributed military forces to the United Nations Command in Korea issued a declaration that as long as the Communist delegations rejected 1) the idea that the United Nations was fully and rightfully empowered to take collective action to repel aggression and 2) the idea that free elections should be held under United Nations supervision, further consideration and examination of the Korean question would serve no useful

---

7. *American Foreign Policy, Basic Documents, 1950–1955*, Vol. II (Washington: Government Printing Office), pp. 2675–2676.
8. *Ibid.*, p. 2685.

purpose.[9] The General Assembly approved the report of this phase of the Geneva Conference on Korea on December 11, 1954 and even in 1973 was still seeking a solution of the Korean problem in accordance with its objectives.[10] The Armistice Agreement still stood in 1973 and administrative control over the territory between the 38th parallel and the armistice demarcation line, which was handed over to the Republic of Korea, still obtained.[11]

During this difficult period of the Korean War, President Truman had enunciated the Far Eastern policy of the United States, a policy that was the same in 1971. All of the commitments were expressed in Executive Agreements and one treaty. Aid had advanced from relief to recovery and then both economic and military aid had become a tool of foreign policy. Korea had indeed become a "testing ground" in which the principles of democracy were matched against Communism. Moreover, the Chinese Communist interference had accentuated the fear of the United States concerning an international conspiracy; and when the French departed from Indochina in 1954 it was easy for the United States to see this region as another avenue of expansion of Communism.

9. *Ibid.*, pp. 2692–2693.
10. *Ibid.*, p. 2701.
11. *Ibid.*, p. 2694.

CHAPTER V

East-West Rivalries and International Agreements in the Fifties

Section A—The Vietnam War

For two decades prior to World War II the Vietnamese, under the leadership of Ho Chi Minh, an exiled Communist from Annam, French Indochina, had carried on an underground struggle for independence from France; and this movement had continued during the occupation of the Japanese troops. When Japan was defeated in 1945, according to the Potsdam Agreement in 1945, the Chinese Nationalist troops were to disarm and intern Japanese forces north of the 16th parallel and the British and Indians were to perform the same task in the south. The whole country would be placed under trusteeship without participation of France in the administration. On August 19 Ho Chi Minh seized control of Hanoi, however, before the Allies would land and on September 2, 1945 he proclaimed from Hanoi the independence of *all* of Vietnam, under the name of the Democratic Republic of Vietnam.

In reply the British rearmed and used the defeated Japanese troops to throw representatives of the new government out of Saigon; and they rearmed approximately 5000 French troops that had been interned in Saigon. The result was that the British allowed a French *coup d'etat,* which returned Southern Vietnam to its colonial position under Paris rule. The old colonial war against France led by Ho Chi Minh was renewed; but gradually the French control was restricted to forts and a few large cities.

On June 5, 1948 Bao-Dai, the "Supreme Advisor," who had fled to Hong Kong, and who then was off the coast of North Vietnam, signed a document with the French that recognized the independence of Vietnam but proclaimed its adherence to the French

Union as a state associated with France; but actually only part of Vietnam was under the control of France. On March 8, 1949 French-Vietnamese agreements provided the basis for the evolution of Vietnamese independence within the French Union. On March 14, 1949 elections were held in Cochinchina and on April 23, 1949 Cochinchina became the Republic of Vietnam.

The United States Ambassador-at-Large, on January 27, 1950, congratulated the Chief of State of Vietnam upon the assumption of these new powers and on February 7, 1950 the United States accorded diplomatic recognition to the Governments of the State of Vietnam, the Kingdom of Laos and the Kingdom of Cambodia as independent states within the French Union. "This recognition is consistent," it was said, "with our fundamental policy of giving support to the peaceful and democratic evolution of dependent peoples toward self-government and independence." [1] The consulate-general of the United States was raised to a legation and a Minister appointed by the President was accredited to all three states.

On May 8, 1950 the Secretary of State announced this policy of the United States and said that he and the French Foreign Minister were in general agreement as to the urgency of the situation in Indochina but the problem was recognized as primarily the responsibility of France and the governments of the people of Indochina. The United States, he said, recognized "that the solution of the Indochina problem depends both upon the restoration of security and upon the development of genuine nationalism and that United States assistance can and should contribute to these major objectives. . . . The United States Government, convinced that neither national independence nor democratic evolution exist in any area dominated by Soviet imperialism, considers the situation to be such as to warrant its according economic aid and military equipment to the Associated States of Indochina and to France in order to assist them in restoring stability and permitting these states to pursue their peaceful and democratic development." [2]

By May 24, 1950 the American Chargé d'Affaires at Saigon announced that the United States had decided to initiate a program of economic aid to Cambodia, Laos and Vietnam to assist them to restore stability and pursue their peaceful and

1. *American Foreign Policy, Basic Documents, 1950–1955*, Vol. II (Washington: Government Printing Office), pp. 2364–2365.
2. *Ibid.*, pp. 2365–2366.

democratic development and was establishing a special economic mission in Saigon, associated with the United States legation. Before this the aid to this region had gone through NATO. A separate bilateral Executive Agreement of Class II with each of the Associated States on the part of the United States was to follow, but the Secretary said that initial economic operations "may begin prior to the conclusion of these agreements." [3] This was the situation when the Korean War began in June of 1950.

In August, 1950 a Military Assistance Advisory Group of thirty-five men was sent to Indochina to advise on the use of American equipment. On October 17, 1950 a statement of the Secretary of State revealed that a review of the United States contribution to the implementation of the French rearmament program within the framework of NATO by officials of the United States and of France had been made and this review included the question of additional United States military aid to Indochina. Military equipment, including light bombers, for the armed forces of France and the Associated States of Indochina, had to be given high priorities.

In the Assistance Acts of October 6, 1949 and July 26, 1950 for the fiscal years of 1950 and 1951 France was assigned the largest single part of the amounts earmarked for military equipment to the members of NATO. In addition to a sum appropriated by Congress for military assistance to the Far East a major part was used to provide military equipment, including light bombers, for the armed forces both of France and of the Associated States of Indochina. The United States signed on December 23, 1950 a Mutual Defense Assistance Agreement of Class II with France and the Associated States for indirect military aid in combating Communist forces under Ho Chi Minh; and on September 7, 1951 the United States signed another agreement with Vietnam of Class II for direct economic assistance.

On September 23, 1951 in discussions between French officials and officials of the Departments of State and Defense the participants agreed "that the successful defense of Indochina is of great importance to the defense of all Southeast Asia." [4] Additional aid from the United States was to be studied, and at any rate improve-

---

[3] *American Foreign Policy, Basic Documents, 1950–1955*, Vol. II (Washington: Government Printing Office), p. 2365 and *Department of State Bulletin*, June 12, 1950, pp. 977–978.

[4] *American Foreign Policy, Basic Documents, 1950–1955*, Vol. II (Washington: Government Printing Office), pp. 2366–2367.

ment was to be made in rate of deliveries of many items of equipment already pledged.

On June 18, 1952 in a communiqué regarding discussions between representatives of the United States, France, Vietnam, and Cambodia it was stated that the "principle which governed this frank and detailed exchange of views and information was the common recognition that the struggle in which the forces of the French Union and the Associated States are engaged against the forces of Communist aggression in Indochina is an integral part of the worldwide resistance by the Free Nations to Communist attempts at conquest and subversion." [5] It was recognized that the United States had primary responsibility in Korea and the French in Indochina. "The partners, however, recognize the obligation to help each other in their areas of primary responsibility to the extent of their capabilities and within the limitations imposed by their global obligations as well as by the requirements in their own areas of special responsibility." [6] Our increased aid, then approximating one-third of the total cost of Indochina operations, would be especially devoted to assisting France in the building of the national armies of the Associated States. This communiqué for increased aid was virtually an Executive Agreement of Class II, for the United States.

On December 17, 1952 the NATO Council said the campaign of the French Union forces in Indochina deserved continuing support from the NATO governments.

This was the Vietnam situation when the Truman Administration came to an end. The policy of aid as a diplomatic tool was the same as in Korea, but the war continued. By May 8, 1954 French forces in Vietnam had to surrender at Dienbienphu. The United States had contributed more than two billion dollars in American aid to the French military efforts, and these sums were made effective through Executive Agreements of Class II.

From May 8, 1954 to July 21, 1954 at Geneva, Switzerland the U.S.S.R., the United Kingdom, France, the United States, the People's Republic of China, Laos, the State of Vietnam, Cambodia, and the Vietminh regime (the Democratic Republic of Vietnam) met in a Conference under the chairmanship of the U.S.S.R. and Great Britain. Agreements were reached whereby the

5. *Ibid.*, p. 2367.
6. *Ibid.*

military partitioning line at the 17th parallel in Vietnam was recognized as provisional, and elections leading to reunification were to be held by July 20, 1956.[7] The International Supervisory Commission, made up of representatives of India, as chairman, Canada, and Poland, was to supervise the implementation of these agreements. The United States and South Vietnam did not sign the Geneva Agreements for the United States was not active as a participant in the war and South Vietnam did not recognize the partition. The United States in a unilateral declaration said that she would refrain from the "threat or use of force to disturb" the agreements and that she "would view any renewal of the aggression in violation of the aforesaid agreements with grave concern and as seriously threatening international peace and security."[8]

Soon after this Geneva Conference the United States sponsored a meeting in Manila, where she and seven other states (Thailand, Australia, New Zealand, Pakistan, the United Kingdom, France and the Philippines) signed the Southeast Asia Collective Defense Treaty on September 8, 1954.[9] This treaty was to declare publicly the unity of these states and to coordinate their efforts for collective defense and for the preservation of peace and security. The parties separately and jointly by means of self-help and mutual aid would resist armed attack and would prevent and counter subversive activities against their territorial integrity and political stability. Economic measures and technical assistance would also be strengthened.

By a special Protocol the states of Cambodia, Laos and the free territory under the jurisdiction of the State of Vietnam were designated as having the provisions of the treaty applicable to them. The signatories established a Council, constituting an organization, which could meet at any time; but each party could act against aggression by armed attack in the treaty area, since each party recognized that such armed attack would endanger its own peace and safety. Each state would meet the common danger in accordance with its own constitutional processes. In case of aggression by means other than armed attack the parties would

---

7. *American Foreign Policy, Basic Documents, 1950–1955*, Vol. I (Washington: Government Printing Office), pp. 785–786; and *Current History*, Current Documents, February 1966, pp. 113–114.
8. *American Foreign Policy, Basic Documents, 1950–1955*, Vol. I (Washington: Government Printing Office), p. 788.
9. *Ibid.*, pp. 912–916.

consult. Any action had to be at the invitation of the government concerned.

The United States made it clear in an attached Understanding that her obligations in case of armed aggression were meant to be applicable against Communist aggression. In case of other aggression or armed attack she would consult with the other parties.

On the same day, September 8, 1954, all eight states proclaimed The Pacific Charter, an Executive Agreement of Class IV for the United States, upholding the principles of equal rights and self-determination and promising to strive to promote self-government and to secure the independence of all peoples that desire it and are able to undertake its responsibilities. They would take practical measures in accordance with their constitutional processes and would cooperate in the economic, social and cultural fields. They would prevent or counter any attempt to subvert freedom and destroy sovereignty or territorial integrity.[10] The Charter was to prevent the impression that the signatory states of the SEATO Treaty were trying to impose a new kind of imperialism in their efforts against Communism.

On October 24, 1954 President Eisenhower wrote to President Ngo Dinh Diem of South Vietnam that the United States would give aid directly to South Vietnam but expected the aid would be met by performance on the part of the government in undertaking needed reforms. This aid was begun on January 1, 1955 by an Executive Agreement of Class II and the United States by February 12, 1955 began to train the South Vietnamese army.

The elections that were mentioned in the Geneva Agreement and were to take place by July, 1956 were never held. President Diem knew that there were more votes in the north than in the south, that Ho Chi Minh was better known as a leader than he was, and that the International Control Commission could not supervise the election in the north, where Ho Chi Minh could manipulate the election. He did not permit the election and defended his position by saying that he had not signed the Geneva Agreement.

This decision was followed by a renewal of guerrilla warfare. In 1957, when South Vietnam had not collapsed before the onslaught of the Communists of Hanoi, the government of North Vietnam reactivated the subversive network of their followers

10. *Ibid.*, pp. 916–917.

whom they had left south of the 17th parallel after the Geneva Conference and introduced terrorism and sabotage. Even this effort was changed and stepped up when in 1959 the "National Liberation" movement was instigated and proclaimed and guerrillas were imported in an aggressive movement from the north. During 1960 and 1961 3000 civilians were killed and 2500 were kidnapped; and people in many areas came under the new organization in South Vietnam called the Vietcong and were forced to supply food and recruits to the insurgents.

The International Control Commission had no real means to implement the decisions of the Geneva Conference and proved to be merely a forum for registering reports. South Vietnam in desperation called on the United States to increase its military and economic aid. In reply in May, 1960 the military advisory group from the United States was increased from 327 to 625.

Section B—Aid as an Instrument of Foreign Policy

Aid had not been hard to get from Congress during the turbulent years from 1950 to 1954. After the Korean War broke out the character of aid began to change, and emphasis was put on the support of rearmament. In 1951 the Mutual Security Act provided for military and economic programs of friendly nations. The Economic Cooperation Administration became the Mutual Security Administration and there was a Director of Mutual Security. Defense was under the Defense Department and economic and technical assistance was under the Technical Cooperation Administration of the State Department.

After the Korean War was over, the entire foreign aid program was revised and all of the various phases of aid were consolidated by the passage of the Mutual Security Act of 1954. All earlier legislation was repealed.[11] In 1955 President Eisenhower in keeping with this Act of 1954 established the International Cooperation Administration (ICA) as an agency within the State Department. The non-military programs were transferred to the ICA and the Defense Department was placed in charge of the military programs. An Executive Agreement with each recipient country implemented the aid grants and loans that were decided upon

---

11. This act has been extended each year by amendments, mainly to authorize the funds to be appropriated. Authorization acts require a vote of both the House and the Senate but the appropriation act is passed by the House alone.

by the ICA and the Defense Department. By this act Congress brought greater efficiency to the aid program.[12]

Aid had been tending to emphasize military assistance or military support, whereby a country could spend its own resources on military matters when it was relieved of economic burdens. The Battle Act of 1951 had assured that no aid found its way to Soviet satellites. Now in 1954 there was a real recognition that aid could be used, either directly or indirectly, as a foreign affairs tool through the military implication. Aid was not only to recognize the presence of a great power, or to secure compensatory favors such as bases, but it was definitely used as a diplomatic instrument, and, as such, it had delicate implications. Continuing from the Eisenhower Administration, aid was an indispensable part of foreign policy and the number of Executive Agreements had increased as the number of the states of the world had grown larger. The recipients were the esconced rulers and it was easy to seem to be involved in internal dissension, and even in revolution.

The year 1954 saw the passage of Public Law 480, whereby surplus grain was sold to underdeveloped countries for local currency; and this currency was then loaned to the government for use on other projects. Aid grants were still used but loans, even soft loans at very low interest over long periods of time, were being favored to outright grants. The loan might never be repaid and was perhaps a cloaked grant but this device seemed to meet the approval of Congress. Many Executive Agreements of Class II followed these 1954 laws.

In 1956 the aid figure for 1957 was reduced and a study was initiated to see whether the programs were in the best interests of the United States. The next year the Development Loan Fund was established as a semi-independent agency under the policy supervision of the Department of State. It provided capital for long term development to less developed countries when capital was not available from other sources. The capital was provided on favorable terms, often including the option to repay in the borrower's own currency. Many Executive Agreements of Class II were entered into.

In 1957 Sputnik I had been launched by the U.S.S.R. as the first man-made satellite to circle the earth; and pressure with political motivation for aid to free countries was increased. There

12. *U.S. Foreign Aid in Review,* 1945–1960 (Washington: Government Printing Office).

was a trend toward loans rather than grants. The Mutual Security Act of 1958 had Section 503 (c), which was added as an amendment. This required the Administration to formulate a specific plan for each country receiving grant assistance whereby, whenever practicable, such grants should be progressively reduced and terminated. The establishment of the Inter-American Development Bank was in keeping with this emphasis, also, and the United States' participation in this bank was authorized by the Inter-American Development Bank Act, in 1959.

By 1960 there was a general organization of aid that reflected the policy of the United States at that time. More than forty countries were receiving Grant Aid through Executive Agreements of Class II under the Military Assistance Program of the Department of Defense. Many of these countries were members of the defense pacts of NATO, CENTO and SEATO. In Europe emphasis was on newer weapons, which were not within the production or financial capability of the allies of the United States, while in less developed areas modernization of conventional equipment was emphasized. These countries through Executive Agreements of Class II received military aid: in Europe—Belgium, Denmark, the Netherlands, Norway, France, Germany, Italy, Luxembourg, Portugal, Spain, the United Kingdom, Yugoslavia; in Africa—Ethiopia, Tunisia, Liberia, Libya, Morocco, Sudan; in the Middle East and South Asia—Turkey, Greece, Iran, Iraq, Israel, Jordan, Lebanon, Pakistan, Saudi Arabia; in the Far East—Taiwan, Korea, Australia, Cambodia, Japan, Laos, the Philippines, Thailand, Vietnam; in Latin America—all countries except French and British Guiana, Surinam, Bolivia, Panama, and British Honduras, most of the aid going to Brazil and Venezuela.

Defense Support was administered by the Interational Cooperation Administration, an agency of the State Department. It was economic aid through Executive Agreements to assist countries to make a specific contribution to the common defense effort without incurring political and economic instability. The recipients were Cambodia, China (Taiwan), Greece, Iran, Korea, Laos, Pakistan, the Philippines, Spain, Thailand, Turkey, Vietnam. Most of the Defense Support went to Korea, Taiwan and Vietnam.

Technical Cooperation was administered by the International Cooperation Administration. There were bilateral technical cooperation programs in sixty countries and territories arranged for by Executive Agreements of Class II. Only two were in Europe—

in Spain and in Yugoslavia. These programs and those in Africa, the Middle East, the Far East and Latin America meant an exchange of technical knowledge and skills to improve standards of living.

There was also Special Assistance administered by ICA for twenty-two countries and territories. These projects that were arranged for by Executive Agreements of Class II were functional ones such as malaria eradication, community water supply development, international medical research, aid to American schools abroad, investment incentive programs, the United Nations Emergency Force, and education and vocational training in tropical Africa.

From the P.L. 480 program of 1954, sales of surplus United States agricultural commodities for foreign currencies were also occurring and the uses to be made of the proceeds of the sales were set forth in sales agreements in the form of Executive Agreements of Class II.

On October 20, 1959 the Development Loan Fund announced that in the future its lending policy would place primary emphasis on the financing of goods and services of United States origin.

There were also changes in the aid policies of the agencies set up on a multilateral treaty basis. In July, 1956 the International Finance Corporation was created as an affiliate of the International Bank for Reconstruction and Development to enable financing of riskier enterprises through loans.

From September 28 to October 2, 1959 at the annual meeting in Washington of the boards of governors of the International Bank for Reconstruction and Development, the International Monetary Fund, and the International Finance Corporation, the United States emphasized that many countries had now "recovered" industrially and could help the underdeveloped. As a result, the International Development Association (IDA) was formed as an affiliate of the International Bank for Reconstruction and Development. It was to finance economic development in the less-developed countries and to finance specific projects; interest could be at any level or none; loans could be repaid in local currencies.

Another group that came into existence was the Development Assistance Group that was formed to encourage bilateral agreements for programs. This group had its first meeting March 9–12, 1960 in Washington to discuss means of expanding and facilitating the flow of long-term capital funds to less developed areas. In the group were Belgium, Canada, France, Germany, Italy, Japan, Portugal, the United Kingdom and the United States.

Through all of these means the United States had channeled its aid for definite ends. She had the cooperation of many allies and by 1960 aid was a definite, political tool in foreign policy, and was arranged for through the instrumentality of the Executive Agreement.

Section C—Deterrents of Communism in the Middle East, Latin America and the Pacific

The activity of the United States in the forties and early fifties was countered by the revival of the U.S.S.R. The Soviet Union also was in a position to use aid as an intrument of foreign affairs and her aspirations manifested themselves. Her satellites in Europe had been drawn into the Warsaw Pact in 1955 but other borders than Europe's were open for influence. The U.S.S.R. was in a position to offer arms and loans and the Middle Eastern countries were especially inviting, to insure her presence in the Eastern Mediterranean.

Conditions had changed since 1947. The Truman Policy in 1947 in giving military and economic aid to Greece and Turkey and the extension of technical assistance through the Point 4 Policy in 1949 had bolstered the political security of the region. In 1951 Greece and Turkey became members of NATO by treaty.

The Shah of Iran, also, had visited the United States on December 30, 1949 and was assured of aid and "certain military assistance" through Executive Agreements of Class II. The countries of Turkey, Iran, Iraq, Pakistan and Great Britain formed the Baghdad Pact in 1955, which brought into existence the Middle East Treaty Organization. Each country promised to aid the others if attacked by an outside power. The United States was not a member but she immediately through Executive Agreements of Class II extended military aid to each member of the Pact and to the organization. This regional pact for the Middle East was the counterpart of NATO for Europe.

Cyprus was also the scene of turbulence until a plan was worked out in 1959 under United Nations sponsorship recognizing the claims of Turkey and Greece to their own sections of the island.

The State of Israel had asserted its existence in the war of 1948–1949, against the Arab nations that had emerged after World

War II and had brought an end to their mandated status. The three big powers, Great Britain, France and the United States, issued simultaneously the Tripartite Declaration on May 25, 1950, which for the United States amounted to an Executive Agreement of Class IV. It insured a ban on an arms race and warned both Israel and the Arab states against resorting to force. The three powers "pledged themselves to ration the supply of arms to the Arab countries and to Israel so as to prevent the development of an arms race and the creation of an 'imbalance' between the antagonists; and they also made themselves the guarantors of the armistice borders against any attempt to alter them by force." [13]

The animosity of the Arab states against Israel's claim to existence continued after 1949 with the Arab boycott of Israel's trade and a partial blockade of Israel in the Suez Canal and the Gulf of Aqaba. Egypt even barred goods to and from Israel carried on third-party ships. Israel was cut off from Asian and African markets and suppliers and from Persian oil sources. In 1955 Israel decided in principle to go to war to remove the Aqaba blockade and seized the circumstances of October, 1956 to attain that end.

Great Britain had completely withdrawn her forces from the Suez Canal zone in 1954 and thereafter the U.S.S.R. had found ways of extending her influence into the Middle East. In September, 1955 Egypt, who had opposed the Baghdad Pact and especially Iraq's entering it, made an arms deal with the U.S.S.R. by contracting to receive cotton from Czechoslovakia. This development precipitated an arms race between the Arab states and Israel. The latter asked the three western powers to be allowed to purchase modern equipment to counteract Egypt's equipment and the United States promised "sympathetic consideration". By the end of February, 1956, however, Israel was advised by Secretary Dulles to rely on the United Nations. The United States procrastinated on the arms request and by implication diluted her diplomatic commitment of the Tripartite Declaration concerning security and the balance of power guarantee. This response was considered unfavorable.

In 1956 the United States tried to woo Egypt by offering to help to build the Aswan Dam. France feared the implications for Algeria of the Soviet Union's arms deal and began to sell arms to Israel. The United States, irked by Egypt's promotion of the

13. Harry N. Howard, "The United States in the 1967 Middle East Crisis", *Current History*, December, 1967, p. 361.

overthrow of the government of Jordan in March, openly associated itself with the French action. Nasser retaliated by recognizing Communist China and Secretary Dulles replied by canceling the Aswan deal.

On July 26, 1956 the nationalization of the Suez Canal by Egypt precipitated the military attack by Great Britain and France, in collusion with Israel. The ineffective plans of the United States for international operation of the Canal and the ineptitude of the United Nations' interposition, in which the United States and the U.S.S.R. found themselves on the same side, brought an end to the influence of Great Britain and France in the region. The United States had had the Sixth Fleet in the Mediterranean since World War II, although she had no home port in the Mediterranean. The result of the 1956 turbulence did not add to Israel's lands but brought free passage through the Gulf of Aqaba, although it was not recognized juridically. The United Nations troops were stationed at the entrance to the Gulf and the Egyptians had the right at their discretion to dismiss them from this location and along their border with Israel.

After the crisis of 1956 the Eisenhower Administration was challenged to assume more responsibility in the Middle East, for British and French influence was destroyed. The Soviet Union was likely to win easy control of all economic and strategic prizes of the Eastern Mediterranean. On January 5, 1957 President Eisenhower asked Congress for authority to extend economic and military aid to any Middle Eastern country that desired it, and to employ armed services "to secure and protect the territorial independence of such nations . . . against overt armed aggression from any nation controlled by international communism." [14] This became known as the Eisenhower Doctrine. On March 9, 1957 a joint resolution of Congress sanctioned this power of the President and an appropriation of 200 million dollars was made for economic and military aid to the Middle Eastern countries.

As a result, King Saud of Saudi Arabia made a goodwill trip to the United States and recieved aid through an Executive Agreement of Class III; [15] and former Congressman Richards visited fifteen Middle Eastern nations to explain the Eisenhower Doctrine and by Executive Agreements of Class III to line up a solid

---

14. *American Foreign Policy, Current Documents, 1957* (Washington: Government Printing Office), pp. 829–831.
15. *Ibid.*, pp. 1031–1032.

anti-Communist front.[16] Oil of the Middle East at that time made that region a great prize.

Most of the troubles of this period were internal and domestic in the Arab States and the Eisenhower Doctrine as such could not secure territorial integrity, for there was not overt aggression from the U.S.S.R. Communism at this time worked through internal subversion. In Jordan for a time the British presence was dismissed but in April, 1957 the King restored a pro-Western government. The United States moved the Sixth Fleet to the eastern Mediterranean as a warning and granted ten million dollars in special aid to King Hussein through an Executive Agreement of Class III.

Syria accepted economic and military aid from the U.S.S.R. and in February, 1958 joined Egypt in establishing the United Arab Republic. The next month Yeman joined this new republic.

On July 14, 1958 in Iraq a rebellion by pro-Nasser and pro-Soviet elements raised fears that all the pro-Western governments would be overthrown. The result was that President Eisenhower sent marines into Lebanon, in keeping with the Eisenhower Doctrine and in compliance with an Executive Agreement of Class III, and Great Britain sent troops into Jordan, at the request of these states. The Soviet Union remonstrated to Washington but neither side wanted serious trouble. The matter was brought to the United Nations. The Security Council was deadlocked because of the veto of the U.S.S.R.; but finally the General Assembly passed a resolution presented by nine of the Arab states, providing for the withdrawal of foreign troops from Lebanon and Jordan, calling on the Arab League to observe their pledge of non-interference in one another's internal affairs and requesting the United Nations Secretary General to uphold the purposes of the United Nations Charter in relation to Lebanon and Jordan. A middle-of-the-road candidate was elected President in Lebanon on July 31, 1958 and American forces were withdrawn by October 25, 1958. There followed the evacuation of the British from Jordan.

The situation in Iraq deprived the Baghdad Pact of an important member. To prevent the alliance's collapse the United States was committed to its full support by an Executive Agreement of Class III in July, 1958 and in October, 1959 the name of the organization without Iraq was changed to Central Treaty

16. *Ibid.*, pp. 831–860.

Organization (CENTO). This was followed by Executive Agreements of Class II for aid for defense from the United States with Iran, Turkey, and Pakistan and the United States served on some of the committees of CENTO.

The contest between the United States and the U.S.S.R. for influence in the Middle East continued. Nasser's alliance with the Soviet Union was an unnatural one. His government received arms and loans from that country but suppressed Communists in Egypt.

In Europe the United States was blamed for propaganda encouraging rebellion in East Germany in 1953 and in Poland and Hungary in 1956. The U.S.S.R. was blamed for brutality in Hungary but the conflict was dulled by the coinciding of the Suez incident in 1956 and the requisite cooperation of the United States and the Soviet Union in that affair. The U.S.S.R.'s relation to the United States was, therefore, unpredictable at that time.

The East-West struggle for influence extended into Latin America. In 1958 Vice-President Nixon on a goodwill tour of Latin America encountered anti-American demonstrations in Argentina, Paraguay, Peru and Venezuela. The United States was accused of aiding the rest of the world but neglecting Latin America. Also the United States was accused of manipulating the aid she did give to strengthen the position of the Latin American dictators—a charge hard to change since the dictators represented the governments.

The people of Latin America soon rose against their dictators in Argentina in 1955, in Colombia in 1957, in Venezuela in 1958 and in Cuba in 1959. The Cuban revolution threatened to spark other revolutions in the Caribbean region. In April, 1959 the Organization of American States nipped an attempt of Cuban adventurers to seize control of Panama. In 1960 the United States patrolled the Caribbean Sea to protect Guatemala and Nicaragua and in 1963 she gave her blessing to the overthrow of the President of Guatemala, who was accused of complicity with the Communists.

As a result of this confusion the State Department initiated a review of its trade and aid policies to see what more could be done to alleviate Latin American problems.

Meanwhile in the Pacific the United States was guarding her security. By the fifties her bases stretched from South Korea, Japan, Okinawa and the Ryukyus to Formosa, the Philippines,

Vietnam and Thailand. There were three islands, Tachens, Quemoy and Matsu, near the mainland of Communist China that still belonged to Nationalist China but were desired by the Communists, as well. They could have been used as a base for attacking the Communist mainland by the Nationalists from Formosa but the spectre of a third world war was always present. The United States did sign a Mutual Defense Treaty with Nationalist China on December 1, 1954, whereby the United States promised to come to her aid if Formosa or the Pescadores were attacked and whereby she stated that additional territories might be brought under guarantees, by mutual agreement. In an Executive Agreement of Class IV Chiang Kai-shek promised not to attack the mainland without prior consultation with the United States.

The Communists invaded Tachens and there was no attempt by the United States to retain the territory but to make the United States policy clear Congress passed a joint resolution on January 28, 1955 authorizing the use of the Armed Forces by the President "as he deems necessary for the specific purpose of securing and protecting Formosa and the Pescadores against armed attack, this authority to include the securing and protection of such related positions and territories of that area now in friendly hands and the taking of such other measures as he judges to be required or appropriate in assuring the defense of Formosa and the Pescadores." [17] It was not until 1958 that the Communists bombarded Quemoy and the question of United States protection came to the front. President Eisenhower made clear that Quemoy and Matsu had become related to the defense of Formosa and the United States convoyed supplies to three miles off Quemoy but full scale war was avoided and Chiang Kai-shek made a statement renouncing the use of force to regain the mainland. Thus through diplomacy, backed by a Joint Resolution, and Executive Agreements with Chiang Kai-shek, the United States steered clear of war with Communist Russia.

Section D—Weapons or Diplomacy?

The Eisenhower Administration was also the great period of challenge concerning weapons and bases. The United States, who had her first atomic bomb in 1945, was soon followed by the

---

17. 69 Stat., Pub. Law 4, chap. 4 (Jan. 29, 1955), (H. J. Res. 159).

U.S.S.R. with her first atomic bomb in August, 1949. Great Britain had her first atomic test on October 3, 1952. The United States then had her first hydrogen test in November, 1952 and by March, 1954 had fully developed her hydrogen bomb. Meanwhile the U.S.S.R. had her first hydrogen bomb in August, 1953.

Up to the fifties the United States had maintained her superiority over the U.S.S.R. in nuclear weapons. The defense of Western Europe was no longer dependent on ground troops with tactical air support, but on the United States Strategic Command that carried nuclear warheads. In October, 1957, however, the U.S.S.R. launched the first Sputnik into outer space and seemed to be attaining superiority in both IRBM's (intermediate range ballistic missiles) and ICBM's (intercontinental ballistic missiles).

In December, 1957 the NATO heads of state, meeting in Paris, decided to establish a NATO nuclear missiles force with IRBM sites through Western Europe. This was to strengthen the capabilities of the ground forces. Both the United States and Great Britain knew how to manufacture nuclear weapons but the other members of NATO did not. American law forbade the sharing of this knowledge. To meet this situation the national contingents were supplied with weapons capable of firing nuclear warheads but the warheads were stockpiled under the control of the NATO Supreme Commander, an American. This gave the United States and the United Kingdom the responsibility of deciding whether or not nuclear weapons would be used in any given situation. This was galling to France, a country that redoubled its efforts to develop nuclear weapons.[18] Everyone anticipated the future use of ICBM's and this brought doubt concerning the decisions of the United States about small aggressions in Europe, when retaliation could reach the continental United States.

This rivalry about weapons had emphasized the importance of bases around the world. Bombs had to be carried by planes and the role of the Strategic Air Command for security was realized by the Defense Department. The United States had major bases in at least twenty countries in the 1950's and more than 3000 minor bases were scattered around the world. The United States had advisory teams in thirty-eight countries and had more than a million G.I.'s abroad. All of these contacts were arranged for by Executive Agreements of Classes II and IV.

18. This effort culminated in February, 1960 with the explosion of the first French atomic bomb and in August, 1968 with the first French hydrogen bomb.

This was the period of global strategy. Secretary John Foster Dulles kept flying from one focal point to another, meanwhile keeping his authority over details of the State Department, promising massive retaliation against provocation, and boasting that he had kept the peace by bringing the world to brinkmanship.

It was because of this uncertainty that a long drawn out attempt at disarmament was made through negotiations of the United Nations Atomic Energy Committee, that had first been set up in January, 1946 to plan for reserving atomic energy for peaceful purposes. A United Nations Commission on Conventional Armaments had also been set up in 1946, but nothing was accomplished. The United States had lessened its attention to conventional arms as it stressed nuclear weapons. President Eisenhower was persuaded to attend a summit conference with the heads of government of Great Britain, the U.S.S.R. and France at Geneva from July 18 to 23, 1955 and suggested the "open skies plan" whereby each side would provide the other with complete information about all the military establishments and permit aerial reconnaissance against surprise attacks. No international commitments resulted, however. Stalin had died in 1953 and his heir, Nikita Khrushchev, worked hard to support policies for the Soviet Union's best interests.

International cooperation for beneficial uses of the atom did not have to wait for control of nuclear weapons, however. In December, 1953 President Eisenhower had appeared before the United Nations General Assembly to suggest that the governments possessing atomic industries should make joint contributions from their stockpiles of uranium and other fissionable materials to an International Atomic Energy Agency. This body was to devise methods whereby these supplies would be allocated to serve the peaceful pursuits of mankind. In 1955 an International Conference on the Peaceful Uses of the Atom was held in Geneva with sixty nations, both Communist and non-Communist, represented. In 1957 six West European countries organized the European Community of Atomic Energy (EURATOM) for the purpose of pooling resources for atomic power development. Finally in October, 1957, East and West both participated in the establishment of an International Atomic Energy Agency with headquarters at Vienna "to accelerate and enlarge the contribution of atomic energy to peace, health and prosperity throughout the world." [19]

19. 8 UST, Part I (1957), pp. 1093–1224.

Meanwhile, authorized by the Atomic Energy Act of 1954, the United States by a series of bilateral Executive Agreements of Class II had supplied over seven tons of U235 to Italy and smaller quantities to France, West Germany, the Netherlands, and some other twenty countries. In 1957 the United States made available for peaceful uses, through Executive Agreements of Class II, "a research reactor and other equipment, a complete library on the peaceful uses of atomic energy and generous quantities of U235 and natural uranium" to the International Atomic Energy Agency.[20]

Meanwhile a treaty with Austria had finally been consummated in 1955. West and East, however, were still having a period of sparring for disengagement in Central Europe, for separation of the powers by a neutral area, etc., but nothing came of the many suggestions. In this climate of opinion Khrushchev served notice in 1959 that he was abolishing the occupational regime in Berlin and was making of West Berlin a demilitarized free city. If negotiations to this end did not succeed in six months, he said that he would put the plan into effect by a separate peace treaty with East Germany.

Secretary Dulles retired in April, 1959 and died in May but his policies lived on. A summit meeting was urged but the United States insisted that a Four Power Foreign Ministers Conference should precede it. Nothing was accomplished until there was injected an ingredient of personal diplomacy. Executive Agreements of Class IV arranged for American symphony orchestras to go to the U.S.S.R. and for Soviet ballet companies to come to the United States. Vice-President Nixon opened an American Exhibit in the U.S.S.R. and the Soviets sent an Exhibit to New York City. President Eisenhower invited Khrushchev to come to the United States and Khrushchev reciprocated with an invitation to Eisenhower to visit the U.S.S.R. (The trip to the U.S.S.R. was never realized.)

President Eisenhower started a round of globe trotting to Bonn, London and Paris. Khrushchev came to the United States in September, 1959 and at Camp David cleared the diplomatic air. By saying that he had not meant to put a time limit on the Berlin negotiations he dissolved the ultimatum to the West.

Soon President Eisenhower went, in December, 1959, to eleven countries of Europe, Asia and the Middle East and in February,

---

20. 8 UST, Part I (1957), pp. 1093-1224.

1960 he visited four Latin American countries. He was greeted with friendliness (although he had to cancel a trip to Japan). Khrushchev countered by making many trips to various countries of Asia and Europe.

Meeting at Paris in December, 1959, the Western Four invited Khrushchev to meet with them in the spring. Questions of Berlin, disarmament, and nuclear test bans were the issues of the time. The Soviet Union, however, shot down an American plane 1300 miles from the Soviet border in the Urals. At the first meeting of the Summit in Paris on May 16, 1960 Khrushchev demanded an apology and punishment of those responsible. President Eisenhower said that the incident would not be repeated but Khrushchev walked out of the conference. There was, therefore, little hope to have easy solutions to the issues between East and West.

Section E—Summary

We have seen that the Eisenhower Administration had experienced a climax of many issues. The cold war had been evolving since 1946 and 1947 and the anti-Communist policy was the dominant catalyst. The United States' role was activated in the Far East, the Middle East and Latin America. The aid program was reorganized and made more efficient and more effective; loans rather than grants were favored; consideration of the underdeveloped countries was promoted; mutual security assistance around the world was emphasized; new weapons were developed and efforts were made to obtain their peaceful use. The President's executive power was used to the utmost. In two instances, during the Quemoy and Matsu incident and during the Middle East uncertainties, the President asked for Congressional approval of his policies through joint resolutions.

During the Eisenhower Administration there was a great increase in International Agreements, especially Executive Agreements. In the decade from 1950 to 1960 International Agreements in TIAS rose from No. 2010 to No. 4399. Many new sovereign states had come into existence since the war and most of these qualified for aid or military assistance. In addition, there were the many relationships that reflected the social, economic and cultural needs of the United States itself and were arranged for through Executive Agreements of Class IV. This kind of Executive Agreement is always in existence in any period, for it is the activating of administrative housekeeping, but by the fifties post-war desires had become normalized and new interests of the time demanded Executive Agreements. Telecommunications were improved. Radio was commonplace and TV was no longer a novelty. Commercial air travel had increased. The space age had dawned. Travel all over the world had increased for business, education and recreation. Cultural exchanges had begun with the U.S.S.R. and other countries. Science was bringing new sources of food; synthetic processes were giving new resources for clothing, for industry and for strategic security; etc. Each of these areas of interest for improved and changed standards of living brought Executive Agreements of Class IV with other countries that enhanced the national interest of the United States.

CHAPTER VI

The Assessment of International Agreements, by the Bricker Movement

As life had become reorganized toward normalcy and progress after World War II there arose questioning of some of the executive arrangements with the enemy and of some of the decisions of conferences concerning the disposition of territory. The very secrecy of the work of conferences, such as Yalta, raised speculation concerning the positions taken and how the national interest was served.[1]

What the U.S.S.R. got in Eastern Europe and in Asia, it was gradually realized, was something to be accepted, and the containment policy was being built up; but the Soviet Union's subversive policy became more known and emphasized. Internally, as well as externally, the strategy of the Communists was suspect and in the fifties the Alger Hiss trial and the Joseph R. McCarthy accusations of Communism in high places and the Army made frontpage headlines and lent drama to a post-war era.

There was also a change in international relationships. The United States was not only one of the victors but during the war she had already taken steps of leadership as an international power. She had by the treaty process become a member of the United Nations and of the Bretton Woods agencies of internationalism. During World War II, as in World War I, the United States had played the role of being the arsenal of the war and of doing a tremendous job of feeding the world; after the war she was a power on the international scene. There were many "new

---

1. The complete texts of the agreements at Yalta were published in 1947 and it was revealed that most of the terms were already known and nothing startling had been kept secret.

internationalists" who were enthusiastic about the United States' being a positive participant in international affairs but many citizens were hesitant about this role. Now the traditional attitudes of the people of the United States began to assert themselves again, in that the functioning of international organizations brought all kinds of concern to the people.

The issue that arose in people's minds became a Constitutional one, whether people recognized it as such at first or not. Was the great increase in the use of International Agreements significant? Were the many Agreements, through their commitments of the United States, affecting the freedoms of the people that they were long used to? Were the citizens still protected by Constitutional provisions or could Treaties and Executive Agreements bring revisions of the Constitution and create internal laws of the country without the electorate playing a part? Citizens with good memories were mindful of the fight against the acceptance of the Covenant of the League of Nations after World War I and of the dedication of persons like Senator Henry Cabot Lodge to the principle that the sovereignty of the United States should not be sacrificed. Now, however, some of the after-effects of the United States' being a member of the United Nations were being experienced and some concepts had to be tested. For example, does a Treaty, such as the Charter of the United Nations, which is made under the authority of the United States, and which expresses the contractual relation of the United States with sovereign states, transcend the eighteen categories of delegated powers in its effectiveness as domestic law of the United States; does a Treaty, by dealing with subjects unlimited, bring about domestic law in a way that a Congressional Act does not do? These were big questions that had been bothering lawyers and other scholars for many years and they now came home to citizens because of developments since World War II. Such questions were to precipitate a controversy over the power of the Executive and the power of Congress that has lasted for decades.

It will be recalled that the Constitution states: "This Constitution and the laws of the United States which shall be made in pursuance thereof and all treaties made, or which shall be made, under the authority of the United States, shall be the supreme law of the land. . . ."—Article VI, Section 2; "The powers not delegated to the United States by the Constitution, nor prohibited by it to the States, are reserved to the States respectively, or to the people."—Amendment X.

This meant that Congressional acts made "in pursuance of" the Constitution and made in the eighteen categories of the enumerated powers of Congress are the Supreme Law of the land. It also meant that treaties, already made before the Constitution was ratified, or made thereafter, under the authority of the United States, were the Supreme Law of the land.

A second problem related to Executive Agreements. These were not mentioned in the Constitution. The President, by and with the advice and consent of Congress, provided two-thirds of the Senators present concur, has the power to make Treaties; he nominates, and, by and with the consent of the Senate, appoints ambassadors and other public ministers and consuls; but he also has executive power in his own right. The Executive Agreement with other sovereign states is, therefore, an exercise of executive power; and Congress in the eighteenth enumerated power has the power to make all laws which shall be "necessary and proper for carrying into execution the foregoing powers and all other powers vested by the Constitution in the Government of the United States. . . ."—Article I, Section 8, Par. 18. Can the Executive Agreement, therefore, like the Treaty, go beyond the limitations of the delegated powers of the United States?

These problems post the further question whether Treaties and Executive Agreements are self-executing as far as domestic legal effect is concerned, or create a situation where a consequent, implementing act of Congress is obligatory, even though the subject may not be among the other seventeen enumerated categories mentioned in the Constitution and may be "reserved to the States or to the people."

It was as early as 1948 that the spectre of the invasion of the internal law of the United States by Treaties framed by international organizations or agencies of the United Nations began to be raised and the question of internal, domestic law became very important. The International Commission on Human Rights of the United Nations issued a Declaration of Human Rights, which was approved by the General Assembly of the United Nations in December, 1948. It stated that everyone "has the right to just and favorable conditions of work, to protection against unemployment and to just and favorable remuneration; to rest and leisure and periodic holidays with pay; to food, clothing, housing and medical care and social services; and to security in the event of unemployment, sickness, disability, widowhood, old age, without any provision that he shall work for it or help establish a fund to pay for it."[2] This Declaration was only a blueprint or a "declaration of aspirations" and not a legal document but many members of the United Nations and staff considered it merely an interpretation of the economic and social provisions of the Charter, which was a Treaty. A matter's mere consideration, they said, made it no longer a domestic matter. This was a new concept and amounted to a challenge. An article in the January, 1948 issue of the *Annals of the American Academy of Political and Social Sciences* had warned that this was a preemption of the relationship between a state and its individuals.

The Genocide Treaty for the prevention and punishment of genocide was approved by the General Assembly of the United Nations on December 9, 1948 and was signed and submitted to the United States Senate on June 16, 1949. In 1950 hearings were held by a subcommittee of the Senate Foreign Relations Committee, changes were suggested, and reservations were drafted by the full committee. (The discussion was not revived after that session of the 81st Congress; the Treaty was not considered again until the Second Session of the 91st Congress,[3] and to 1973 was not made effective.)

In 1950 the House of Delegates of the American Bar Association authorized a study of the subject of an amendment to the treaty-making power of the United States, to be undertaken by the Committee on Peace and Law through the United Nations.[4]

In 1951 the United Nations Draft Covenant on Human Rights as revised by the seventh session of the International Commission on Human Rights was published. This was the Treaty that had been awaited. On July 17, 1951, Senator John W. Bricker, Ohio, Republican, introduced S. R. Res. 177 (82nd Cong.) that declared it to be the sense of the Senate that the Covenant "would, if ratified as a treaty, prejudice those rights of the American people

2. *Documents on American Foreign Relations* (Boston: World Peace Foundation, 1939–), Vol. X, pp. 430–435 (1948).

3. By 1955 there were fifteen treaties drafted in organizations, committees or subcommittees of the United Nations that were open for signature and acceptance. Of these the United States had accepted four and ratified them according to constitutional processes: two protocols dealing with narcotics; one dealing with the White Slave Traffic; and one with the suppression of the circulation of obscene publications.

4. U.S. Senate, 84th Congress, 2d Sess., Committee on the Judiciary, Constitutional Amendment Relative to Treaties and Executive Agreements, Report No. 1716 by Mr. Dirksen on S. J. Res. 1, p. 2; and U.S. Senate, 85th Congress, 1st Sess., Hearing before a Subcommittee of the Committee on the Judiciary on S. J. Res. 3, Proposing an Amendment to the Constitution of the United States Relating to the Legal Effect of Certain Treaties and Other International Agreements, Statement of Views by Frank E. Holman, p. 411 (Washington: Government Printing Office).

which are now protected by the Bill of Rights of the Constitution of the United States." This defined the issue already stated, although the resolution was not voted on.

Meanwhile the efficacy of the United Nations Charter in the internal law of the United States was being tested in the courts. In 1952 Sei Fujii, a Japanese, bought land in California, violating the California Land Law which prohibited aliens from holding real property. Fujii brought a suit contesting the constitutionality of the Land Law and claiming it to be a violation of the Fourteenth Amendment of the Constitution and of the Charter of the United Nations, a Treaty. The Court of Appeals upheld Fujii on both counts but the Supreme Court reversed the decision.[5]

The Charter of the United Nations was mentioned in the dissenting opinion of the Youngstown Sheet and Tube Company against Secretary Sawyer in 1952 concerning the President's directive for the Secretary to take temporary possession of the nation's steel mills.[6] The United States Supreme Court held that the President's directive was unconstitutional but the dissenting opinion claimed that the United Nations Charter was the supreme law and was violated.

In 1955 Mrs. Rice buried her husband, killed in the Korean War, in the cemetery of Sioux City, Iowa. After the services she was notified that her husband, an Indian, could not be buried in a cemetery reserved for Caucasians. Mrs. Rice brought action claiming a violation of the Constitutions of Iowa and the United States and of the United Nations Charter. The Iowa Supreme Court overruled Mrs. Rice on both counts. The case was taken to the Supreme Court of the United States and resulted in a 4-4 vote (The death of one member had occurred and a new member had not yet been appointed.). This decision had the effect of upholding the Iowa Court but it was remembered that four judges were on Mrs. Rice's side.[7]

These cases since World War II and the establishment of the United Nations by Treaty had accentuated the questions before the public and Congress that had been growing in importance. Several previous Supreme Court decisions of the twentieth century also had bearing on International Agreements and were well remembered. In the case of Missouri v. Holland in 1920 the Su-

---

5. Sei Fujii v. the State of California (1952, 38 Calif. (2d) 718, 242 P. (2d) 617).
6. 343 U.S. 579,667 (1952).
7. Rice v. Sioux City Memorial Park Cemetery, Inc., et al., and 1954, 348 U.S. 880.

preme Court decided that the United States had the right to pass the Federal law of 1918 prohibiting the capture or shooting of wild fowl in migration consequent upon a Treaty with Great Britain in 1916, even though all sources of food supply within State lines were subject to State regulation only, according to the Constitution. The Supreme Court held that the United States statute was not illegal and stated: "If the treaty is valid, there can be no question of the validity of the statute." [8] The essence of the matter was that a Treaty enabled the Federal Government to pass a statute that it had tried to pass previously but could not pass because it was not among the enumerated powers of the Federal Government in the Constitution.

In 1934, during the Chaco disputes between Bolivia and Paraguay, Congress passed an arms-embargo act and President Roosevelt invoked the embargo by proclamation. Curtiss-Wright in 1936 was indicted with conspiracy to sell fifteen machine guns to Bolivia. The Supreme Court decided the United States had the power to pass the legislation even though it was not among the enumerated powers bestowed by the Constitution because this power was derived from the fact of sovereignty, and not from the power bestowed by the Constitution.[9] A distinction was, therefore, drawn between external sovereignty and internal law.

The most recent challenge to Constitutional tradition was in the decision in 1942 that the United States in recognizing the U.S.S.R., a right given in the Constitution, had the power to remove obstacles to full recognition such as settlement of claims. The President had, as an Executive Agreement of Class IV, accepted the Litvinov Assignment, which in effect gave the United States title to the New York assets of the Moscow Fire Insurance Company, in payment of old debts of Russia to the United States. These funds had been frozen since World War I and the U.S.S.R. could not seize the funds in New York. The company had been nationalized by the U.S.S.R. but Russian aliens in the United States and certain United States citizens claimed that the U.S.S.R. Government was not the owner and could not assign them. Mr. Pink, the Superintendent of Insurance in the State of New York, needed a court decision to tell him what to do with the money; the United States creditors had all been paid in full; and a balance remained in the hands of the Superintendent of Insurance. He wanted to

8. 252 U.S. 416 (1920).
9. 299 U.S. 304, 316–319 (1936).

know whether these funds should be distributed to creditors of the company in other countries or to emigré Russians in other countries who had been members of the board of directors of the Russian insurance companies. The Litvinov Assignment allowed this excess to revert to the United States to be used to pay persons in the United States who had old claims against the Russian Government. "It took nothing away from a United States citizen." The Superindendent, to play safe, had merely asked for a court ruling.

The Supreme Court eventually ruled: "If the President had the power to determine the policy which was to govern the question of recognition, then the fifth amendment does not stand in the way of giving full force and effect to the Litvinov Assignment." [10] It decided that there was nothing in that fifth amendment that interfered with the effectiveness of the Executive Agreement, for no citizen was being deprived of property, and that, just as United States creditors of the insurance companies had priority over creditors in other countries, the United States creditors of the Russian Government had priority over creditors from abroad. Here was a case of an Executive Agreement's bringing about a change in domestic law, for property control was regulated by the states according to the Constitution.

In 1951, after the decision of the California Appellate Court in the Fujii case, which upheld Fujii before the final decision of the Supreme Court, the California Legislature recommended adoption of a constitutional amendment "to protect the basic structure of the American government" for it was seen that the Constitution was being amended by means other than those expressed in Article V. Subsequently Representative Usher Burdick, N. D., Rep., introduced in the House a proposed constitutional amendment relative to the treaty power. On September 14, 1951, Senator Bricker introduced S. J. Res. 102; and on the House side of the Capitol various proposals were offered. In 1951 Senator McCarran, Nevada, D., chairman of the Senate Committee on the Judiciary, presented S. J. Res. 122 to impose limitations with regard to Executive Agreements.

On February 9, 1952 Senator Bricker, in behalf of himself and fifty-eight cosponsors, introduced the important S. J. Res. 130, proposing an amendment to the Constitution of the United States. The House of Delegates of the American Bar Association, after a

---

10. 315 U.S. 203, 230 (1942); and U.S. Senate, 84th Congress, 2d Sess., Report No. 1716 by Mr. Dirksen on S. J. Res. 1, p. 9 (Washington: Government Printing Office).

debate of the question, in February, 1952 adopted a resolution differing in text but similar in purpose to S. J. Res. 130. It stated: "A provision of a treaty which conflicts with any provision of this Constitution shall not be of any force and effect. A treaty shall become effective as internal law in the United States only through legislation by Congress which it could enact under its delegated powers in the absence of such a treaty." [11] At that time the peace and law committee of the American Bar Association had not completed its research with respect to Executive Agreements but in September, 1952, at the annual meeting in San Francisco the House of Delegates adopted the following recommendation to the Congress: "Executive agreements shall not be made in lieu of treaties. Congress shall have power to enforce this provision by appropriate legislation. Nothing herein contained shall be construed to restrict the existing power of Congress to regulate executive agreements under the provisions of this Constitution." [12]

It was on April 12, 1952 that John Foster Dulles, before he was Secretary of State, in a formal address before the regional meeting of the American Bar Association at Louisville, Kentucky, issued this warning:

"The treatymaking power is an extraordinary power liable to abuse. Treaties make international law and also they make domestic law. Under our Constitution treaties become the supreme law of the land. They are indeed more supreme than ordinary laws, for congressional laws are invalid if they do not conform to the Constitution, whereas treaty laws can override the Constitution. Treaties, for example, can take powers away from the State and give them to the Federal Government or to some international body and they can cut across the rights given the people by the constitutional Bill of Rights." [13]

This statement was one of the most forthright declarations of the dangers of treaty law and the need to preserve American rights, the American form of government and American independence.

11. U.S. Senate, 84th Congress, 2d Sess., Committee on the Judiciary, Report No. 1716 by Mr. Dirksen on S. J. Res. 1, p. 8; and U.S. Senate, 85th Congress, 1st Sess., Hearing before a Subcommittee of the Committee on the Judiciary on S. J. Res. 3, Statement of Views by Frank E. Holman, p. 412 (Washington: Government Printing Office).
12. *Ibid.*
13. U.S. Senate, 83rd Congress, Hearings on S. J. Res. 1 and 43, p. 862; and U.S. Senate, 84th Congress, 2d Sess., Report No. 1716 by Mr. Dirksen on S. J. Res. 1, pp. 4–5; and U.S. Senate, 85th Congress, 1st Sess., Hearing before a Subcommittee of the Committee on the Judiciary on S. J. Res. 3, p. 412 (Washington: Government Printing Office).

There were six Joint Resolutions offered in the Senate by Senator Bricker and several amendments and substitutes by others in the 82nd, 83rd, 84th and 85th Congresses from 1952 to 1957 for the amendment of the Constitution of the United States to insure Treaties' and Executive Agreements' being in compliance with the Constitution and to prevent their making domestic law without legislation under Constitutional limitations, and thus to prevent their being themselves another method of amending the Constitution.

There were hearings on these resolutions by a Senate subcommittee or the full Senate Judiciary Committee from May 21 to June 9, in 1952; from February 18 to April 11, in 1953; from April 27 to May 12, in 1955; and on June 25, 1957—28 days in all and yielding approximately 3303 pages in print.

There were presentations in person or by letter from dozens of individual witnesses and organizations; the best legal talent of the country expressed arguments pro and con; public opinion was directed by publicity and editorials to this matter, although the real issues were not always made clear; the amendment was said to be most important; there were changes in the original wording of the Joint Resolution, and Senators Ferguson, Dirksen, and George presented substitutes that were considered; and at least five votes of the full Senate were taken on various sections and amendments, the George substitute failing by only one vote on February 26, 1954.[14]

Senator Bricker's early resolutions had many co-sponsors, 58 for the first in 1952, 63 for the second in 1953; and the votes reflected the widespread interest of the Congress. President Eisenhower, although criticized by the proponents, expressed his will and desires, for making Treaties and Executive Agreements are administrative matters, even though the President has no Constitutional role in amending the Constitution. He opposed the amendment as being "unnecessary and dangerous." [15]

14. See sequence of amendments in APPENDIX A.
15. The following is a partial list of organizations and individuals who filed with the Committee on the Judiciary resolutions or statements *in favor of* the Bricker Amendment:
Vigilant Women for the Bricker Amendment
National Small Businessmen's Association
American Medical Association
American Bar Association—Standing Committee on Peace and Law through the United Nations
American Legion
Association of American Physicians and Surgeons

Senator Dirksen had said that the issue had to be dealt with; so more than five years of attention were given to it in the Senate and its committees; but the hearings on the one day in 1957 were closed "on call of the chairman of the sub-committee" and no more was heard of the subject. The real issues that brought the matter up were not resolved. They faded out but at the time they seemed imperative.

The arguments pro and con referred to both Treaties and Executive Agreements. All International Agreements were being discussed and some versions of the amendment gave a special section to "executive or other agreements" or to "executive agreements."

The first point of argument for the proponents, usually expressed in the first section of the "Bricker Amendments," was to

Long Island General Assembly, Fourth Degree (Patriotic), Knights of Columbus, Brooklyn, N.Y.
National Association of Pro America
Daughters of the American Revolution
National Sojourners, Inc.
Veterans of Foreign Wars
Marine Corps League
Military Orders of World Wars
United Spanish War Veterans
The Catholic War Veterans
Kiwanis International
The Chamber of Commerce of the United States
National Association of Life Underwriters
National Grange
American Farm Bureau Federation
National Defense League of America
National Society, Sons of American Revolution
Colonial Dames of America
Patriotic Women of America, Inc.
United States Flag Committee
Minute Women of U.S.A., Inc.
Women's National Patriotic Conference on National Defense, representing more than 30 prominent women's organizations throughout the United States
American Council of Christian Churches
National Association of Evangelists
American Federation of Women's Clubs
National Society for Constitutional Security
National Economic Council, Inc.
Committee for Constitutional Government
American Flag Committee
Constitutional Foundation, Inc.
Steuben Society of America
American Medical Association, Women's Auxiliary
Conference of State Manufacturers' Association
Southern States Industrial Council
National Cotton Compress and Warehouse Association
National Labor-Management Council on Foreign Trade Policy
Junior Order United American Mechanics
Conference of American Small Business Organizations

ensure that Treaties and other International Agreements, including Executive Agreements, were consonant with the Constitution of the United States. The wording of this section changed repeatedly. An example will illustrate the many attempts to get the better of semantics to accomplish the end. The wording went from the statement that "no treaty or executive agreement should be made respecting the rights of citizens of the United States (protected by the Constitution), or abridging or prohibiting the free exercise thereof"; to the statement that "a provision of a treaty which denies or abridges any right enumerated in the Constitution should not be of any force or effect"; to "a provision of a treaty which conflicts with any provision of the Constitution shall not be

National Association of Real Estate Boards
Freedom Clubs, Inc.
The American Progress Foundation
Clarence Manion, Former Dean, Notre Dame Law School
Judge Leander H. Perez, District Attorney, Plaquemines District, La.
Joseph L. Call, Judge of Superior Court, County of Los Angeles, State of California
Frank E. Holman, Former President, American Bar Association
Margaret Rambaut, Wyckoff, New Jersey
Wm. L. McGrath, President, Williamson Heater Co., Cincinnati, Ohio
George A. Finch, Member of the Bar of the District of Columbia, Vice-Chairman of Committee on Peace and Law through the United Nations of the American Bar Association
Eberhard P. Deutsch, Member of New Orleans Bar and Member of American Bar Association's Standing Committee on Peace and Law through the United Nations
Hon. John W. Bricker, United States Senator from Ohio

The following is a partial list of organizations and individuals who filed with the Committee on the Judiciary resolutions or statements *against* the Bricker Amendment:

AFL–CIO
American Veterans' Committee
Committee for Defense of the Constitution by Preserving the Treaty Power
League of Women Voters
Minnesota Committee Opposing the Bricker Amendment
Committee on Federal Governmental Processes of the Bar Association of St. Louis
Friends Committee on National Legislation
Association of the Bar of the City of New York
Committee on Federal Legislation and International Law of the Association of the Bar of the City of New York
Hon. Thomas C. Henning, Jr., Senator from the State of Missouri
Philip B. Perlman, Former Solicitor General of the United States
Bethuel M. Webster, Former President, Association of the Bar of the City of New York
Quincy Wright, Professor of International Law, University of Chicago
Hon. Herbert Brownell, Attorney General of the United States
Dana C. Bachus, Attorney, New York City
Hon. John Foster Dulles, Secretary of State of the United States
Erwin N. Griswold, Dean, Harvard Law School
Hon. Jacob K. Javits, Attorney General, State of New York

of any force or effect"; to "a provision of a treaty or other international agreement which conflicts with this Constitution shall not be of any force or effect"; to "a provision of a treaty or other international agreement which conflicts with this Constitution, or which is not made in pursuance thereof, shall not be the supreme law of the land nor be of any force or effect"; to "a provision of a treaty or other international agreement not made in pursuance of this Constitution shall have no force or effect. This section shall not apply to treaties made prior to the effective date of the Constitution." [16]

In the course of the debates it had been brought out that the difference in wording in Article VI of the Constitution about the supreme law of the land, concerning statutes that were made *in pursuance* of the Constitution, and Treaties that were made *upon the authority of* the United States, was because of the existence of some Treaties made before the Constitution was formed and effective at the time, such as the "Treaty of Amity and Commerce" with France during the Revolutionary War, the "Treaty of Peace" with Great Britain at the end of the Revolutionary War containing provisions in favor of certain British creditors, etc. These Treaties could not have been made "in pursuance of the Constitution." This accounts for the added statement in 1954: "Notwithstanding the foregoing provisions of this clause, no treaty made after the establishment of this Constitution shall be the supreme law of the land unless made in pursuance of the Constitution." This idea was finally condensed into Section 1 of the last "Bricker Amendment" of 1957 that read: "A provision of a treaty or other international agreement not made in pursuance of this Constitution shall have no force or effect. This section shall not apply to treaties made prior to the effective date of this Constitution."

Many Supreme Court decisions since the beginning of the United States had been accompanied by statements of judges to the effect that a Treaty or Executive Agreement could not violate the Constitution. The Bricker forces, however, pointed out that the decisions that upheld the Constitution were nineteenth century decisions and reflected the legal traditions of the time. Moreover, they said that the statements concerning the Constitution

---

16. U.S. Senate, 84th Congress, 2d Sess., Report No. 1716 by Mr. Dirksen on S. J. Res. 1, p. 24; and U.S. Senate, 85th Congress, 1st Sess., Hearing before a Subcommittee of the Committee on the Judiciary on S. J. Res. 3, pp. 10, 22, and 415 (Washington: Government Printing Office).

were mere dicta of the judges, with no legal effect in a future court; that dicta changed; and that decisions were often 5 to 4 and even contradicted previous decisions at times. The proponents also stated that in the twentieth century the Pink Case, the Holland v. Missouri Case, the Curtiss-Wright Case, and other cases had brought other interpretations. The Court was moving "in the direction of submitting the American people to superior treaty law regardless of constitutional rights and was suggesting authority in the President superior to or separate from the Constitution." [17] For these reasons the Bricker advocates wanted a declaratory statement in the Constitution to remove any doubt that a provision of a Treaty or other International Agreement that violates the Constitution or that deals with matters of purely domestic concern would be invalid.

The cases in the twentieth century made the issue acute and seemed to indicate that the Federal Government was not violating the Constitution when it took action and Congress passed consequent laws that were not in accord with its enumerated powers and infringed upon the reserved rights of states and of the people. In other words, the Bricker followers said that, since by Treaty or Executive Agreement the President was making applicable in domestic law his implied rights as the executive and could expect Congress to pass legislation that was "necessary and proper" for the execution of those rights, it seemed wise to spell out how a Treaty or Executive Agreement could be made effective as internal law. This gave birth to the famous "which clause" in the following form in 1953: "A treaty shall become effective as internal law in the United States only through legislation which would be valid in the absence of treaty." Also other agreements "shall be subject to the limitations imposed on treaties, or the making of treaties. . . ." This meant that Federal legislation had to comply with the enumerated areas of Federal jurisdiction.

By February 26, 1954 the George Substitute had only two sections, as follows:
"Section 1. A provision of a treaty or other international agreement which conflicts with this Constitution shall not be of any force or effect.
"Section 2. An international agreement other than a treaty shall

---

17. U.S. Senate, 85th Congress, 1st Sess., Hearings before a Subcommittee of the Committee on the Judiciary on S. J. Res. 3, p. 37 (Washington: Government Printing Office).

become effective as internal law in the United States only by an act of the Congress."

It was this substitute for the Senate Judiciary Committee's text that eliminated the "which clause" for all purposes and thereafter failed, by a vote of 60 to 31, to obtain the necessary two-thirds vote for an amendment to the Constitution.

New Joint Resolutions were proposed by Senator Bricker in August, 1954 and on January 6, 1955; by the Committee on the Judiciary on March 27, 1956; and by Senator Bricker on January 7, 1957. The Joint Resolutions proposed by Senator Bricker continued to include the concept of implementing legislation for Treaties and Executive Agreements "valid in the absence of international agreement," that is, valid according to enumerated powers.

The Bricker people saw that it was essential to have an explicit statement concerning Executive Agreements. There is no express constitutional sanction for the conclusion of Executive Agreements but Treaties and Executive Agreements are closely related. Both obligate the United States to some course of action. The exact line of demarcation between a Treaty and an Executive Agreement has always been undefined. The existence of such a line was not seriously questioned before 1940, but some authors recently had asserted that Treaties and Executive Agreements were wholly interchangeable; and some had asserted that controversial matters should be handled as Executive Agreements and routine matters, as Treaties. Also there was the point of view expressed by Assistant Secretary of State Francis B. Sayre in 1939: "International agreements involving political issues or changes of national policy and those involving international arrangements of a permanent character usually take the form of treaties. But international agreements embodying adjustments involving arrangements of a more or less temporary nature usually take the form of executive Agreements." [18]

However tenuous the line between Treaties and Executive Agreements was, the recent court cases of U.S. v. Pink, U.S. v. Curtiss Wright, and U.S. v. Belmont had recognized the power of the President to make Executive Agreements. The Supreme Court in the Pink case, for example, had stated: "A treaty is a 'law of the land' under the supremacy clause (Art. VI, clause 2) of the Consti-

18. Francis B. Sayre, "The Constitutionality of the Trade Agreement Act," 39 *Col. Law Review*, 751, 755.

tution. Such international compacts and agreements as the Litvinov asignment have a similar dignity. . . ."[19]

Other cases raised the question of the priority of an Executive Agreement over an act of Congress. In 1955 in Seery v. U.S. a citizen of the United States brought suit against the United States in the Court of Claims.[20] This citizen had owned property in Austria, which was used by the military forces of the United States during the occupation of Austria, and, therefore, sought payment for such use. The United States Government through the Department of Justice opposed payment for several reasons, one of which was that the plaintiff's claim was negated by the terms of an Executive Agreement between the United States and Austria. By this Executive Agreement the United States had agreed to pay Austria a specified sum for all obligations incurred between April 9, 1945 and June 30, 1947. The Executive Agreement covered such claims as this citizen's. The Justice Department expressed its opinion in its brief: "The agreement between the United States of America and the Federal Government of Austria is, therefore, a part of the supreme law of the land and must be regarded as equivalent to an act of Congress."[21] The Court of Claims, however, rejected this proposition that the Executive Agreement withdrew jurisdiction conferred by statute, for the jurisdiction of the Court of Claims is statutory.[22] Thus a statute was considered superior to an Executive Agreement.

This decision, however, was at variance with the opinion of the U.S. Court of Appeals, Second Circuit, in Ozanic v. U.S.[23] A Yugoslav vessel was in collision with a vessel belonging to the United States in 1942. In 1948 the United States had an Executive Agreement with Yugoslavia settling claims for lend-lease benefits of World War II. The Yugoslav Government released its claims "arising out of maritime collisions occurring on or after April 6, 1941 and prior to July 1, 1946," and the Court denied the Yugoslav citizen the right to sue the United States. The Court observed:

"Although the agreement of 1948 was not a treaty, and did not in terms profess to repeal the consent of the United States to be sued which the Public Vessels Act had granted, we regard it as

19. 315 U.S. 203, 230.
20. 127 F. Supp. 601 (1955).
21. U.S. Senate, 84th Congress, 2d Sess., Report No. 1716 by Mr. Dirksen on S. J. Res. 1, p. 16 (Washington: Government Printing Office).
22. 28 U.S.C. 1491 et seq.
23. 188 F. 2d 228 (1951).

overriding that consent, and asserting the immunity of the United States from suit upon any claim whose release was part of the consideration of the United States for the release of its lend-lease claims against the Yugoslav Government. . . . These considerations alone would go far to persuade us that, even though the agreement of 1948 stood only upon the constitutional power of the President to come to an accommodation with a foreign government upon mutual claims between two nations, it would suffice to withdraw the consent to be sued." [24]

This extension of the doctrine of "similar dignity," enunciated in the Pink case, to enable an Executive Agreement to allow the Executive to modify or repeal enactments of elected representatives of the people in Congress gave rise to the need for specific statements concerning Executive Agreements in the Amendment to the Constitution. It was thought absurd, therefore, not to have a statement limiting the Executive Agreement, as well as the Treaty, method of concluding International Agreements; and since there was no settled meaning of an Executive Agreement, the Amendment used the term International Agreements as including all agreements other than Treaties.

Some people felt that one-man control of foreign policy might well lead to complete executive control of domestic policy and that this might be the price of survival in an atomic age but the Bricker group felt that world leadership and national security were objectives not incompatible with the preservation of liberty as protected in the Constitution.

The opponents of the "Bricker Amendment" put faith in a long line of Supreme Court decisions from 1870 to 1953 that had stated that a Treaty cannot violate the Constitution or do what the Constitution forbids.[25] There were also cases that were current to the

---

24. U.S. Senate, 84th Congress, 2d Sess., Report No. 1716 by Mr. Dirksen on S. J. Res. 1, p. 17 (Washington: Government Printing Office).

25. The following cases were quoted by the opponents to prove the point:

Doe et al. v. Braden (16 How. 635 (1953)):

"The treaty is therefore a law made by the proper authority, and the courts of justice have no right to annul or disregard any of its provisions, unless they violate the Constitution of the United States."

The Cherokee Tobacco (11 Wall. 616 (1870)):

"It need hardly be said that a treaty cannot change the Constitution or be held valid if it be in violation of that instrument."

Hauenstein v. Lynham (10 Otto 483 (1880)):

"We have no doubt that this treaty is within the treatymaking power conferred by the Constitution * * * * *. There are doubtless limitations of this power as there are of all others arising under such instruments; * * * * *."

last period of the Senate hearings that seemed to clinch the arguments for the opponents to the Amendment. For example, an important decision was handed down by the Supreme Court on June 10, 1957, concerning two cases that were combined for final consideration. Dorothy Krueger Smith had killed her husband in Japan on October 4, 1952 and Clarice Covert had killed hers in England on March 10, 1953. Both women were convicted of murder of their servicemen husbands in courts-martial.

There had been Security Treaties with Japan and Great Britain, followed by Executive Agreements of Class I, which determined the conditions governing the disposition of the armed forces of the United States in those countries and which included a section authorizing the military trial of dependents accompanying the armed forces. The Uniform Code of Military Justice (UCMJ) was considered to carry out the obligations of the Executive Agreements.[26]

The cases involved the constitutionality of the courts-marital proceedings against civilian wives of overseas servicemen. The cases were appealed and finally the Supreme Court overruled, on June 10, 1957, its own decision of June 11, 1956 and held that Congress could not constitutionally subject these American civilian wives overseas to courts-martial jurisdiction in capital cases in time of peace. The Government's efforts to sustain courts-martial jurisdiction under an Executive Agreement was rejected by Mr. Justice Black, joined by three other Justices, and later two other

Geofroy v. Riggs (133 U.S. 258 (1890)):
"That the treaty power of the United States extends to all proper subjects of negotiation between our Government and the governments of other nations, is clear * * * * *. The treaty power, as expressed in the Constitution, is in terms unlimited except by those restraints which are found in that instrument against the action of the Government or of its departments, and those arising from the nature of the Government itself and of that of the States. It would not be contended that it extends so far as to authorize what the Constitution forbids, or a change in the character of the Government or in that of one of the States, or a cession of any portion of the territory of the latter, without its consent * * * * *."

Missouri v. Holland (252 U.S. 416 (1920)):
"We do not mean to imply that there are no qualifications to the treatymaking power; * * * * *. The treaty in question does not contravene any prohibitory words to be found in the Constitution."

Asakura v. City of Seattle (265 U.S. 332 (1924)):
"The treatymaking power of the United States is not limited by any express provision of the Constitution, and, though it does not extend 'so far as to authorize what the Constitution forbids' it does extend to all proper subjects of negotiation between our Government and other nations."

26. U.S. Senate, 85th Congress, 1st Sess., Hearing before a Subcommittee of the Committee on the Judiciary on S. J. Res. 3, p. 34 (Washington: Government Printing Office); and 50 U.S.C.A. 242.

Justices wrote concurring opinions. The statement of the four Justices read:

"Even though a court-martial does not give an accused trial by jury and other Bill of Rights' protections, the Government contends that section 2 (11) of the UCMJ, insofar as it authorizes the military trial of dependents accompanying the Armed Forces in Great Britain and Japan, can be sustained as legislation which is necessary and proper to carry out the United States obligations under the international agreements made with those countries. The obvious and decisive answer to this, of course, is that no agreement with a foreign nation can confer power on the Congress, or on any other branch of Government which is free from the restraints of the Constitution." [27]

This decision was heartwarming to the opponents of the "Bricker Amendment" and proved, they said, that it was unnecessary.

These critics were also against implementing legislation's being required for all Treaties and Executive Agreements. They said that this procedure would have disastrous effects for it could preclude treaties of friendship and commerce, extradition treaties, consular conventions, narcotic drug control treaties, road traffic conventions, and wildlife preservation treaties. All of these protect American citizens abroad and are essential to continued friendly relations with other nations.

The procedure would also cause delay. In some cases all of the states would have to legislate before Treaties or Executive Agreements became effective. A survey of all treaties since 1789 showed that approximately 30% could not have been concluded in the absence of legislative action of *all* of the states, as well as by the Congress, under the amendments proposed.[28]

There was also the retroactive possibility of the Supreme Court's declaring invalid past Treaties that conflicted with "any provision of the Constitution." This would result in chaos for it would result in years of litigation.

Implementing legislation would deprive the President of his constitutional authority to give effect within the United States to agreements made with other nations in carrying out his respon-

---

27. 77 S. Ct. 1222, 1230 (1957); and U.S. Senate, 85th Congress, 1st Sess., Hearing before a Subcommittee of the Committee on the Judiciary on S. J. Res. 3, pp. 6, 13, 21, 23, 24, 429, 430–432 (Washington: Government Printing Office).

28. U.S. Senate, 84th Congress, 2d Sess., Report No. 1716 by Mr. Dirksen on S. J. Res. 1, p. 28 (Washington: Government Printing Office).

sibilities under the Constitution and tranfer powers of the President in foreign relations to the Congress. The traditional separation of powers and the Constitutional balance among the branches of Government would be impaired.

There were also the "new internationalists" who claimed that the Amendment would put crippling restrictions on the conduct of foreign relations. They said that it was a camouflaged manoeuver designed to undermine American leadership in international affairs, for the necessity of implementing Executive Agreements would mean that there could no longer be self-executing ones.

"The 'Bricker Amendment' became a symbol or a line of demarcation dividing those who believed that the American concept of government and individual rights should not be sacrificed to international plans and purposes, and those who believed that such a sacrifice should be made in the interest of so-called international cooperation." [29]

All forms of the Amendment from 1954 on contained the section providing for the yeas and nays of the ratification vote to be taken and recorded on the Journal of the Senate. This had been the recent practice and it was argued by the opposition that a Rule of Procedure, even though possibily changeable later, could be put into the Senate Rules, and a Constitutional Amendment was not necessary.

It was also stated that there were ambiguities in the Amendment, that there were pitfalls in changing the Constitution, that it was dangerous, and that no useful purpose would be served. The opposition felt that the real intent was to limit the power of the United States to make Treaties and other International Agreements.

Senator Bricker, on the last day of the hearings, admitted that the President had and should have power to make Treaties and Executive Agreements under the general terms of the Constiution, for the states had ceded such power to the Federal Government and it was supreme. He admitted that there were certain categories of acts that had to be dealt with by Treaties and Executive Agreements but that these categories involved the relationship of this country to other nations. He still believed that the President alone should not be able to make law and that implementing legislation

---

29. U.S. Senate, 85th Congress, 1st Sess., Hearing before a Subcommittee of the Committee on the Judiciairy on S. J. Res. 3, p. 413 (Washington: Government Printing Office).

by Congress was necessary when domestic law was to be created. He agreed with one of the proponents who said: "Because of the changes in the judicial concept as to treaties, and the changed international point of view, treaty law has become omnipotent, a kind of 'Frankenstein' instrumentality, which can change and even destroy the liberties of the American people and their form of government." [30]

When the "Bricker Amendment" was let die by the Committee on the Judiciary, it seemed that the whole movement had been an exercise in futility and that it had been a semantics farce. It seemed that the remedy was considered worse than the disease. The number of proponents and sponsors had dwindled and no issues were resolved. People could still ask: Is the United Nations Charter self-executing? Can a Treaty or an Executive Agreement go beyond the enumerated powers of the Constitution? What is the Constitutional status of an Executive Agreement? Can an Executive Agreement negate a previous statute or vice versa? Is the real issue one between Congress and the Executive?

Perhaps the greatest result of the Bricker Movement was an educational one. People realized that they have a Constitution and that there are questions arising under it upon which patriotic men and women, respectable lawyers and legal scholars may differ.[31]

---

30. U.S. Senate, 85th Congress, 1st Sess., Hearing before a Subcommittee of the Committee on the Judiciairy on S. J. Res. 3, p. 423 (Washington: Government Printing Office).

31. A long awaited decision of the Supreme Court was announced after the hearings were over and would have had effect upon the Bricker Movement, had it come earlier. It had to do with the suit of Charles E. Wilson, Secretary of Defense, et al., Petitioners, v. William S. Girard, United States Army Specialist 3/C (no. 1103) and the suit of William S. Girard, Petitioner, v. Charles E. Wilson, Secretary of Defense, et al. (No. 1108) (354 US 524, 1 L ed 2d 1544, 77 S Ct 1409). The cases were argued July 8, 1957 and decided July 11, 1957.

"(William S. Girard), an American soldier, while guarding a machine gun and clothing left in an Army exercise area in Japan, fatally wounded a Japanese woman who was gathering expended cartridge cases in the area. The Secretary of Defense and the Secretary of State determined that the respondent should, as requested by Japanese authorities, be delivered for trial on criminal charges in the Japanese courts. These American authorities acted pursuant to an Administrative Agreement (Executive Agreement), authorized by the Security Treaty between Japan and the United States, which, although providing that the United States should have primary jurisdiction over members of the Armed Forces in relation to offenses arising out of any act or omission done in the performance of official duty, also provides that a state having primary jurisdiction in any particular case may decide not to exercise jurisdiction and that the authorities of the state having the primary right shall give sympathetic consideration to a request from the authorities of the other state for a waiver of its right where such other state considers the waiver to be of particular importance. Seeking to avoid trial in the Japanese courts, respondent sought a writ of habeas corpus in the United States District Court for the

The long struggle in the 1950's involved the American public but it was a public of special scholars and of organizations—not of the average, individual citizens. The issues were between the Executive and Congress as two institutions. They were only the first manifestation of the resultant problems when the Executive power was increasing as a mark of leadership in a complicated world; the consequences of keeping the status quo were academic and did not seem crucial at the time. The general public did not see the relation of this question that involved lawyers and statutes and International Agreements to the life of the individual in its everyday routine. It was to take war, inflation, and domestic upheaval to bring home the question of whether the individual is protected by the separation of powers in the Constitution and this climax would come after another decade.

District of Columbia. The writ was denied, but the respondent was granted declaratory relief and an injunction against his delivery to the Japanese authorities (___F Supp___). The United States appealed to the United States Court of Appeals for the District of Columbia Circuit, and, without awaiting action by that court on the appeal, invoked the certiorari jurisdiction of the United States Supreme Court. The respondent cross petitioned to review the denial of the writ of habeas corpus.

"Having granted certiorari, the Supreme Court reversed the District Court's judgment granting declaratory and injunctive relief, and affirmed its judgment denying habeas corpus."

The decision of the Court took into account the fact that "a sovereign nation has exclusive jurisdiction to punish offenses against the laws committed within its borders, unless it expressly or impliedly consents to surrender its jurisdiction." It was also brought out that, although the Senate had ratified the Security Treaty with Japan after the Executive Agreement had been signed, the NATO Agreement had been signed later with full knowledge of the Executive Agreement with Japan, so that Article III of the Security Treaty really authorized the making of the Executive Agreement and the subsequent Protocol embodying the NATO Agreement provisions governing jurisdiction to try criminal offenses.

Here was clearly an Executive Agreement of Class I authorized by a Treaty, and a Treaty is the supreme law of the land. The Executive Agreement was merely carrying out the provisions indicated. Also the important point was that "neither the Constitution nor any statute enacted subsequently to the effective date of the Security Treaty between Japan and the United States bars the carrying out of an Administrative Agreement." The wisdom of the provisions of the Executive Agreement, authorized by the Security Treaty, was considered exclusively for the determination of the executive and legislative branches and it was not considered a concern of the Court. This was a procedural case, not a substantive one, since the provisions were already the law of the land as expressed in the Treaty. The question remained, however, concerning the content of the Treaty itself.

CHAPTER VII

Uses of International Agreements in the Kennedy Administration

The use of the International Agreement was not diminished in the Kennedy Administration in spite of the Bricker Movement. First of all, there was a further reorganization of the Aid Program. The Foreign Assistance Act of 1961 created the Agency for International Development (AID) on November 4, 1961. AID combined the economic and technical assistance operations of the International Cooperation Administration, the loan activities of the Development Loan Fund, and the local-currency lending functions of the Export-Import Bank. It also had responsibility for the coordination of economic and military assistance and for the overseas operation of the Food for Freedom program. As a consequence, from 1961 on, all aid programs were implemented under AID through Executive Agreements of Class II.

There were also several new programs of farreaching change. On September 22, 1961 the Peace Corps Act was passed by Congress and as a result Executive Agreements of Class II were made with underdeveloped countries throughout the world.

On August 17, 1961 all members of the Organization of American States (OAS), except Cuba, signed the Charter of Punta del Este, a Treaty establishing the Alliance for Progress.[1] It was a program of action to bring accelerated economic progress and broader social justice within the framework of Operation Pan America. It provided measures to accomplish growth of per capita incomes; to make benefits of economic progress available to all citizens; to bring about balanced diversification in national economic structures; to accelerate the process of rational industriali-

1. *Current History*, Current Documents, January, 1964, pp. 39-46.

zation; to raise the level of agricultural productivity; to eliminate adult illiteracy; to increase life expectancy at birth; to increase the construction of low-income houses; to maintain stable price levels; to strengthen existing agreements on economic integration; to develop cooperation programs to prevent harmful effects of excessive fluctuations in the foreign-exchange earnings from exports of primary products; and to adopt measures necessary to facilitate access of Latin American exports to international markets. The United States promised to assist the countries whose Development Programs established self-help measures, economic policies, and programs consistent with the goals and principles of the Charter. Many Executive Agreements of Class II followed. The O.A.S., the United Nations Economic Commission for Latin America, and the Inter-American Development Bank also strengthened their agreements for coordination.

On October 11, 1962 President Kennedy signed the Trade Expansion Act of 1962, which conferred on the President new authority to enter into trade agreements.[2] The European Economic Community (EEC) had come into existence and it was thought highly desirable for the United States to negotiate while it was in its formative stages. The act authorized the President to reduce duties with any other country by 50%; and to enter into a trade agreement with the European Economic Community (EEC) reducing as far as zero tariffs on industrial products where 80% of free world trade was conducted by the EEC and the United States. In case of agricultural products the President could reduce tariffs as far as zero without reference to the 80% criterion, if he determined that such action would help maintain or expand United States exports of like articles. The President could reduce or eliminate duties on tropical agriculture and forestry commodities, which were not produced in significant quantities in the United States, if the EEC would take comparable action; and he could eliminate tariffs on products where the duty was 5% or less. In all cases except tropical agriculture the reductions would have to be made no more rapidly than in five equal annual stages. Negotiations were to be on an across-the-board basis and the most-favored-nation principle was to be applicable.

According to the Trade Expansion Act advance public notice was to be given so that the public could make its views known.

2. *ABC's of Foreign Trade, U.S. Trade Policy in Brief* (Washington: Government Printing Office), pp. 29–32.

The President was to seek the advice of the Tariff Commission and other government agencies and the President's Special Representative for Trade Negotiations was to be the chief United States representative for each trade agreement negotiation and was to head the interagency organization, which would participate in the trade agreements program, i.e. the Departments of Agriculture, Commerce, Defense, Interior, Labor, State and Treasury.

The President could also deal with unreasonable foreign import restrictions by denying the benefits to the offending country or imposing restrictions on its products. In case serious injury would be caused the President, as in previous legislation, could impose import restrictions, i.e. increased tariffs or quotas in retaliation. There could also be trade adjustment assistance to firms in an industry in the form of technical assistance, loans or special carryback of operating losses for Federal income tax purposes. Individual firms could also have adjustment assistance.

As a result of this act the United States proposed to the contracting parties to GATT that there be a new round (the 6th) of multilateral trade negotiations. For various reasons these negotiations did not get started until May 4, 1964 but they were to accomplish a whole panoply of agreements merged into one, called the Kennedy Round.

The most outstanding motivation for the foreign policy of the United States during the Kennedy Administration, however, was to be anti-Communism. The deterrence policy continued wherever Communism posed a threat to the free world. Activities began with a fiasco in Cuba in 1961.[3] By 1960 President Eisenhower had been convinced that Castro of Cuba was an agent of international Communism, and the Central Intelligence Agency (CIA) was enjoined to support and train Cuban exiles in the United States so that they could free Cuba from Communist control. After President Kennedy's election, the new President had been briefed by Allen Dulles, the head of the CIA, on the training program and he had sanctioned its continuance. There was a sharp difference of opinion among President Kennedy's advisers, however, after he took office and the liberal ones won their point for non-involvement. By last minute compromises the Bay of Pigs operation on April 19, 1961 was doomed to failure.[4]

3. Mario Lazo, "At Last the Truth about the Bay of Pigs," *Reader's Digest*, September, 1964, pp. 243-272.
4. The United States had no fact-finding agencies on which to base its foreign policies until during World War II the Office of Strategic Services (OSS) was brought

The failure led directly to the Soviet Union's decision to move into the Western Hemisphere in force, with both men and missiles. In 1962, there were many warnings that Soviet forces were being landed in Cuba but they were disregarded until on October 16, 1962 there were photographs taken by the CIA's U-2 planes that could not be ignored. On October 22, 1962 President Kennedy ordered a blockade and demanded removal of existing missiles with on-site inspection. The free world voiced approval of this commitment of American strength, but the President's advisers insisted that the dispute be handed to the United Nations. In the end there was no insistence on inspection; the Cuban exiles were prohibited from further harassing actions; and the United States became committed to a no-invasion policy.[5] The Cuban question remained. The whole experience, however, emphasized the menace of Communism.

After the Cuban missile crisis of 1962 had demonstrated the need for urgent and direct contact to avoid military misunderstanding and miscalculations, the United States on June 20, 1963 negotiated an Executive Agreement of Class IV with the Soviet Union for "a hot line" between Moscow and Washington.[6] This went into operation August 20, 1963 and seemed necessary to both parties.

A Treaty also marked an accomplishment in the restriction of nuclear power. On October 10, 1963 a Multilateral Treaty banning nuclear weapon tests in the atmosphere, in outer space and under water became effective for the United States.[7]

Meanwhile the Southeast Asian situation continued as a problem. The SEATO Treaty, in 1954, had in a special protocol included Cambodia, Laos, and Vietnam as beneficiaries. The government of Laos had suffered changes and had come under attack by the Communist Pathet Lao, supported by the North Vietnamese. The United States guaranteed Thailand against attack and established bases close to the Laos border for a contingent of 5000 United States troops and air support by Executive Agreement of Class I with the Thai Government. The United States

into existence. When this was disbanded after the war, the Central Intelligence Agency (CIA) was established in 1947 by the National Security Act, which was generally to coordinate domestic, foreign and military policies relating to national security.

5. James Daniel and John G. Hubbel, "While America Slept", *Reader's Digest*, March, 1963, pp. 60–66, 239–286.
6. *New York Times*, June 21, 1968.
7. 14 UST 1313; TIAS 5433; 480 UNTS 43.

moved to support a Geneva Conference in 1962 (convened by Great Britain and the U.S.S.R.) that resulted in the neutrality of Laos. The withdrawal of United States forces from Laos followed and was arranged for by an Executive Agreement of Class I.

The commitment in Vietnam was extended during the Kennedy Administration. From the beginning these promises were made because the United States believed that the security of the states of Southeast Asia was related to the security of the United States and the future security of all of the free nations in the Asia-Pacific area.

On May 13, 1961 an agreement in principle on measures to increase and accelerate United States assistance to Vietnam took the form of a joint communiqué issued at Saigon by President Diem of the Republic of Vietnam and Vice-President Johnson of the United States. Its commitment constituted an Executive Agreement of Class IV. These representatives recognized that the independence and territorial integrity of Vietnam were violated by Communist agents and forces from the north and stated that it was clear to both governments that action must be strengthened and accelerated to protect the legitimate rights and aspirations of the people to choose their own way of life. The United States, it was stated, was conscious of its responsibility and duty, in its own self-interest as well as in the interest of other free peoples, to assist Vietnam. "It has no other motive than the defense of freedom." [8]

The joint communiqué agreed in principle on the means to accomplish the joint purpose, subject to prompt finalization and implementation. Regular armed forces of the Republic of Vietnam were to be increased and the United States military assistance would extend to an additional number of Vietnamese forces. The two governments would collaborate in the use of military specialists to assist and work with Vietnamese armed forces in health, welfare, and public works activities in the villages of free Vietnam. A group of highly qualified economic and fiscal experts would meet in Vietnam to work out a financial plan on which joint efforts should be based. Also new economic and social measures to accompany anti-guerrilla efforts and a longer range economic development program including further progress in fields of agriculture, health, education, fisheries, highways, public ad-

8. *American Foreign Policy, Current Documents, 1961* (Washington: Government Printing Office), p. 1043.

ministration and industrial development would be discussed.

The presence of teams of the Control Commission, appointed after the Geneva Conference of 1954, helped to preserve peace but the Report of the Commission on September 18, 1961 emphasized the lack of cooperation of both sides. The Commission tried to be a forum and link for both sides and to play the role of a catalyst but complaints were registered of breakdown of vehicles, conditions of road transports, the want of water transports for teams, and violations of the Geneva Accords restrictions on "time notices for controls" of the mobile elements of the fixed teams. The Commission had to contend with the tendency of the parties to differ with its interpretation of some of the provisions of the Geneva Accords and to refuse to accept and implement the Commission's recommendations and decisions.

On October 11, 1961 President Kennedy announced that he had asked General Maxwell D. Taylor, his military representative, and others to go to Saigon to discuss with the President of Vietnam ways in which the United States could better assist the Government of Vietnam and on October 24, 1961 President Kennedy sent a letter to President Diem saying: "Let me assure you again that the United States is determined to help Viet-Nam preserve its independence, protect its people against Communist assassins and build a better life through economic growth." [9] This commitment was that of an Executive Agreement of Class I. General Taylor's mission to Southeast Asia lasted from October 15 to November 3, 1961 but he was in South Vietnam from October 18 to 25, 1961. On November 16, 1961 President Kennedy in line with the report of General Taylor decided to step up deliveries to Saigon, including weapons not previously sent.

While these consultations were going on there was an acceleration of deliveries under the defense assistance program, through Executive Agreements of Class II. Changes in the type of equipment delivered and in the nature of the United States military advisory and training program seemed to be required.

On December 7, 1961 President Diem of the Republic of Vietnam sent a letter to President Kennedy saying "We must have further assistance from the United States if we are to win the war now being waged against us." [10]

9. *Ibid.*, p. 1049.
10. *Department of State Bulletin,* January 1, 1962, pp. 13–14; *American Foreign Policy, Current Documents,* 1961 (Washington: Government Printing Office), pp. 1053–1054.

On December 9, 1961 the Liaison Mission of the Republic of Vietnam sent a report to the International Commission for Supervision and Control in Vietnam that the Government of the Republic of Vietnam had requested the Government of the United States to intensify the aid in personnel and material which the latter was already granting. It was justified, the Mission said, as the right of self-defense is an attribute of sovereignty and the Government felt constrained to exercise this right and to request increased aid.

On December 14, 1961 President Kennedy replied to President Diem's letter. The United States, although not a party to the Geneva Accords, had declared that it "would view any renewal of the aggression in violation of the agreements with grave concern and as seriously threatening international peace and security." "In accordance with that declaration and in response to your request," the President said, "we are prepared to help the Republic of Viet-Nam to protect its people and preserve its independence." [11]

On February 7, 1962 President Kennedy sent two United States Army air support companies totaling 300 men to Saigon. This addition brought United States personnel to 4000. On April 22, 1963 Secretary Dean Rusk said that the United States role would continue to be "limited and supporting."

During 1963 there were many Buddhist troubles and accusations against the CIA of the United States were numerous. President Kennedy said on September 2, 1963 that the Diem Government had gotten out of touch with the people and on November 1, 1963 President Diem and his brother were assassinated.

On November 15, 1963 the United States headquarters in Saigon announced that 1000 United States servicemen, now totaling 16,575, would be withdrawn from South Vietnam beginning on December 3, 1963 because of progress made in the training of the Vietnamese. Later that month, however, on November 22, 1963, President Kennedy was assassinated.

---

11. *Department of State Bulletin*, January 1, 1962, p. 13; *American Foreign Policy, Current Documents*, 1961 (Washington: Government Printing Office), pp. 1056–1057.

CHAPTER VIII

International Agreements and Their Aftermath in the Johnson Administration

Section A—Defense versus Communism

President Johnson, when he was precipitated into the Presidency in 1963, inherited the Vietnam War that had been stepped up by both military and economic aid. The United States had become increasingly involved by Executive Agreements of Classes I and II. There were also, at this time, several allied contingents in the armed forces as a result of commitments of the SEATO Treaty.

February 4-6, 1964 the Vietcong opened an offensive and in May, 1964 a United States aircraft transport ship sank in Saigon Harbor. The real provocation, however, came on August 2-4, 1964 when two American destroyers were reported to be attacked in international waters off the North Vietnamese coast by North Vietnamese torpedo boats. President Johnson then ordered action against the torpedo boats and their bases.

The next day, August 5, 1964, the President asked Congress for a resolution expressing support "for all necessary action to protect our armed forces and to assist nations covered by the SEATO Treaty," and ordered reinforcements to the Tonkin Bay area. Both houses passed the Southeast Asia Joint Resolution on August 7, 1964.[1]

By February 7, 1965 in retaliation for guerrilla attacks on Pleiku, United States bombers struck targets in North Vietnam for the first time. At this date the United States forces numbered 23,000. By February 28, 1965 continuous limited air strikes against North Vietnam were decided upon by the President to force nego-

1. *Current History*, Current Documents, January, 1968, p. 49.

tiations. On April 7, 1965 President Johnson in his speech at Johns Hopkins University stated: [2]

"Armed hostility is futile—our resources are equal to any challenge—because we fight for values and we fight for principle, rather than for territory or colonies, our patience and our determination are unending.

"Once this is clear, then it should be clear that the only path for reasonable men is the path of peaceful settlement.

"Such peace demands an independent South Vietnam—securely guaranteed and able to shape its own relationships to all others—free from outside interference—tied to no alliance—a military base for no other country.

"These are the essentials of any final settlement.

"We will never be second in the search for such a peaceful settlement in Vietnam.

"There may be many ways to this kind of peace; in discussion or negotiation with the governments concerned; in large groups or in small ones; in the reaffirmation of old agreements or their strengthening with new ones.

"We have stated this position over and over again 50 times and more to friend and foe alike. And we remain ready with this purpose for unconditional discussions. . . .

"We will use our power with restraint and with all the wisdom that we can command.

"But we will use it."

As a part of this program for peace in Southeast Asia the President on June 1, 1965 sent a special message to Congress requesting additional United States funds for use in the economic and social development of Southeast Asia. This request was subsequently incorporated into the Foreign Assistance Act of 1965 and was implemented by Executive Agreements of Class II. It was authorization for help in water and power resources in the Mekong basin, for electricity in small towns, for importation of materials for homes and factories, for clinics and doctors for rural areas, for training of people for construction of roads and other projects. Most of the assistance was for Vietnam but the program was to extend to Thailand and Laos. (Economic aid to Cambodia had been discontinued in November, 1963.)

Meanwhile, however, on May 6, 1965 two marine divisions were

2. *Patterns for Peace in South East Asia*, Department of State Publication 7872 (Washington: Government Printing Office).

sent to Vietnam as the first combat troops. On May 19 bombing against North Vietnam was resumed after a five day moratorium. By June 7, 1965 military personnel of the United States in Vietnam had passed 50,000. At that time, June, 1965, Brigadier General Nguyen Cao Ky headed a military regime in South Vietnam. In July President Johnson announced that the United States military force would be increased to 125,000. By November, 1965 the contingent had reached 160,000 men and it was announced that by March, 1966 the fighter bomber force would be increased from 550 planes to 1200 or 1300.

All of these executive military acts reflected Presidential power to make Executive Agreements of Class III with South Vietnam supported by the Joint Resolution of Congress or Executive Agreements of Class I because of the SEATO Treaty.

Another instance of the use of armed troops on order of the President took place in the Western Hemisphere. On April 28, 1965 the United States had sent 450 Marines by helicopter to Santo Domingo to secure an area for an airlift evacuation of Americans and others citizens of foreign nations on the day when it was feared that there was danger of a Communist seizure in a political and military revolution. These Marines were followed by 2000 troops of the 82nd Airborne Division on April 30, 1965, arranged for by an Executive Agreement of Class IV. The troops stayed for several months in peace-keeping roles until in September a provisional government was set up through the assistance of United States and OAS diplomats.[3]

This episode, as in Vietnam, represented the role of the President, acting on his own responsibility to use troops after an Executive Agreement, and recalled the "interposition" arguments of a former era. On September 15, 1965 Senator Fulbright in a speech published in the *Congressional Record* criticized this continuing "intervention" in the Dominican Republic.

Meanwhile there was an attempt to have the United Nations play a part in restoring peace in Vietnam. There had always seemed to the layman that there should be a possibility of having the Security Council of the United Nations enter the picture. As early as November 17, 1961 Secretary Rusk had said that the question of the threat to peace posed by the situation in Vietnam would come to the United Nations at some stage.

---

[3] Kenneth O. Gilmore, "The Truth about Santo Domingo," *Reader's Digest*, May, 1966, pp. 93-98.

In 1964 the United States suggested to the Security Council that an observation group be put at the Cambodian border to establish conditions caused by the Vietcong there, after Cambodia had registered a complaint to the United Nations. A fact-finding mission of the United Nations was sent to the Cambodian border and suggested that an observer group would be useful but Cambodia changed her mind and none was sent.

In August, 1964 after the Tonkin Bay incident the United States supported the Security Council in an invitation to the Hanoi Government to discuss the incident. The North Vietnam Foreign Minister replied that the Vietnamese problem was not within the competence of the Security Council as North Vietnam was not a member of the United Nations.

In June, 1965 President Johnson at San Francisco, upon the twentieth anniversary of the signing of the Charter of the United Nations, "appealed to members of the United Nations, 'individually and collectively, to bring to the table those who seem determined to make war.' "[4] On July 28, 1965 he expressed the same appeal to the United Nations Secretary General Thant. Ambassador Goldberg about this time sent a letter to the members of the Security Council reminding them of their responsibility to seek the peace and of the desire of the United States to collaborate unconditionally.

On September 23, 1965 the United States laid a new bid for Vietnam peace before the United Nations; and on January 31, 1966 the United States formally requested that the United Nations consider the problem. She proposed a draft resolution in the Security Council that called for immediate unconditional discussions to arrange a conference looking toward the application of the 1954 and 1962 Geneva Accords and the establishment of a durable peace in Southeast Asia. The resolution recommended a cease-fire, supervision, the provision for arbitrators or mediators, and the assistance of the Secretary-General as appropriate.

The Security Council voted, with a majority of nine, on February 2, 1966 to place the Vietnam problem on its agenda.[5] France and three African states abstained and the Soviet Union and Bulgaria opposed the proposition. The Security Council adjourned immediately after the vote for private consultations among the

---

4. Lincoln P. Bloomfield, *The U.N. and Vietnam* (New York: Carnegie Endowment for International Peace, 1968), pp. 7 and 8.
5. *New York Times,* September 8, 1967.

members to determine whether and how the Council might assist in moving the conflict to the conference table. On February 26, 1966 the Council President reported that the differences of opinion had "given rise to a general feeling that it would be inopportune for the Council to hold further debate at this time"; [6] but on December 19, 1966 the United States appealed to the Secretary-General to "take whatever steps are necessary (to) bring about the necessary discussions" that would lead to a mutual cessation of hostilities.[7]

Meanwhile the war dragged on!

On September 3, 1967 there were elections for President in Vietnam and the voting seemed the culmination of a long commitment to the introduction of constitutional processes in South Vietnam. The United States was satisfied by "observers" that the elections were fair, under the circumstances of the war. There were also new possibilities that peace negotiations might be initiated by the Vietnamese themselves.[8]

On August 7, 1967 Senator Mike S. Mansfield (Dem.) and Senator John Sherman Cooper (Rep.) urged the Administration to resume an initiative to engage the United Nations Security Council in a Vietnamese debate. On September 8, 1967 Secretary of State Dean Rusk said in a news conference, "We believe that the United Nations has a responsibility under its Charter to deal with any situation affecting international peace and security, and we would

6. Lincoln P. Bloomfield, *The U.N. and Vietnam* (New York: Carnegie Endowment for International Peace, 1968), p. 8.
7. *Ibid.*
8. Under President Ngo Dinh Diem in 1956 the first General Assembly was elected. A second Assembly was chosen in 1959 but because of Vietcong insurgency the third election was put off until 1963. The members largely represented Diem-ist parties. President Diem ran for reelection in 1962 and both President Eisenhower and President Kennedy, in spite of supplying military and economic aid, followed a "get-along-with-Diem" policy. President Diem was ousted on November 1, 1963 and was assassinated on November 3, 1963.

From 1963 to 1965 there were eight changes of Government as rival cliques of army generals vied for power. Toward the end of 1964 under intermittent pressures from the United States, and Buddhist street demonstrations, the military tried out a short-lived series of civilian Premiers. By June 15, 1965 Lieutenant General Nguyen Van Thieu became Chairman of the National Directory (Chief of State) and on June 19, 1965 Air Vice Marshal Nguyen Cao Ky took over as Premier. Soon the Buddhists agitated for the overthrow of this government and for elections as well. Finally, because of United States pressure, General Thieu on April 14, 1966 announced that elections would be held for an Assembly that would frame a constitution. On September 11, 1966 the 117-member Constituent Assembly was elected with no militant Buddhists included. This Assembly produced an acceptable constitution on April 1, 1967 and on September 3, 1967 the military candidate for President, Lieutenant General Nguyen Van Thieu, was elected and Nguyen Cao Ky was chosen as Vice President.

welcome any contribution which the United Nations can make toward peace in Southeast Asia." [9]

In the first week of September, 1967 Ambassador Goldberg queried the allies of the United States at the United Nations on a course of action by the Security Council to obtain a cease fire and peace negotiations in Vietnam. The main idea was that the Council call for a conference for peace in Southeast Asia like the 1954 and 1962 conferences. He conferred with the representatives of Great Britain, France, Japan, Argentina, Brazil and Denmark, all of whom were on the Council. The American view was that if the U.S.S.R. took a negative position, this action would spike an expected Communist propaganda barrage on Vietnam in the General Assembly, which was to open in two weeks. Ambassador Goldberg, also the previous week, had discussed plans for a negotiated peace with Secretary-General Thant, who had held similar views.

On September 12, 1967 Senator Wayne Morse introduced a resolution in the Senate calling upon the President to request an emergency meeting of the Security Council "to consider all aspects" of the war in Vietnam and "to act to end the conflict." According to the resolution the United States would pledge in advance "to accept and carry out any decision on the matter by the Council." [10] This meant that if the majority called on the United States to end the bombing in North Vietnam, the United States would not exercise its veto, even though it opposed the decision. This resolution was rejected by the Senate.

On September 21, 1967 Ambassador Goldberg told the United Nations Assembly that the United Nations has "the most explicit right and duty to concern itself with this question" and that the United States "continues to seek the active participation of the United Nations in the quest for peace in Viet-Nam." [11]

All of this time the Security Council was paralyzed by a potential Soviet veto. Senator Fulbright on October 11, 1967 said that the United Nations was deterred from taking action by the failure of the United States to encourage it to act; while Secretary Rusk denied this and said that Hanoi, Peking, and Moscow were preventing the key to the problem to be found. Secretary Rusk hoped that other means and procedures would appear. The U.S.S.R. took the position that since neither Communist China nor North Viet-

9. Lincoln P. Bloomfield, *The U.N. and Vietnam* (New York: Carnegie Endowment for International Peace), p. 9.
10. *New York Times*, September 13, 1967.
11. Lincoln P. Bloomfield, *The U.N. and Vietnam* (New York: Carnegie Endowment for International Peace), p. 9.

nam were members of the United Nations, the proper place for negotiations was a reconvened Geneva Conference, although as one of the co-chairmen she had persistently refused to join Great Britain, the other chairman, in calling for a new meeting.

Fifty-four Senators concurred in a resolution introduced by Senator Mansfield on October 25, 1967 that it was the sense of the Senate that the President take appropriate initiative to assure that the United States resolution of January 31, 1966 or any other resolution of similar purpose be brought before the Security Council. This resolution passed the Senate by a vote of 82 to 0 on November 30, 1967.[12] Moreover Ambassador Goldberg on November 2 had told the Senate Foreign Relations Committee for the first time that the United States would accept the Vietcong as a party to discussions of Vietnam in the Security Council or at a new Geneva Conference.[13]

About this time there came to fruition an episode that had begun the latter part of September when an official inquiry was made of Ambassador Goldberg by a member of the Secretariat (later admitted to be Secretary-General Thant) as to whether the United States would agree to the arrival of two or three representatives of the Vietcong and whether visas would be granted for them. Further information was requested by the United States and a vague answer came early in November to the effect that names were not yet available but that the representatives would want to stay for one year and perhaps two. The United States then replied to the Secretariat that visas would be granted "in connection with any United Nations business as required by and in conformity with" the applicable part of the Headquarters Agreement.[14] This Executive Agreement of Class II obligates the United States to admit persons invited to the United Nations headquarters on official business and to issue visas to them. No request for visas followed.

About the middle of November, 1967 President Johnson offered to have peace talks "on a neutral ship in a neutral sea" but Hanoi gave a negative response.[15] The Rumanian delegation in mid-December, 1967 requested the United Nations to circulate a document that purported to be a presentation of the National Liberation Front but the document had nothing new within it.

On December 10, 1967 Ambassador Goldberg conferred with

12. *Ibid.,* p. 5.
13. *Ibid.,* p. 6.
14. *New York Times,* December 8, 10, 23, 1967.
15. *Ibid.,* November 15, 1967.

Secretary General Thant on a possible Security Council meeting on Vietnam, as he had been sounding out the opinion of other diplomats. By December 23, 1967 it was being said by East European diplomats that a new effort would be made in the near future to establish a National Liberation Front "presence" at the United Nations. It was said that either France or the Soviet Union might issue the invitation. The Front would explain its views on the conditions for a settlement in South Vietnam where the Front sponsored the guerrillas, and would offer a channel of communication between the United States and the Front's leaders. The Front had contended that it operated independently of the North Vietnamese Government and that it had the authority to make peace in Vietnam through the formation of a coalition government. The United States had consistently rejected the concept of the Front's independence of Hanoi, but the Front was encouraged by President Johnson's statement in a televised interview on December 19, 1967 of interest in talks between the South Vietnamese Government and representatives of the Front; and on December 22, 1967 in a communiqué from Canberra, Australia from President Johnson and President Nguyen Van Thieu, President Johnson "stated the intent of the United States to continue its support for this policy of national reconciliation.[16]

While Ambassador Goldberg was frustrated in his many efforts to have the United Nations consider the Vietnamese problem, other means and procedures were being pursued. On February 8, 1967 President Johnson had sent a letter to President Ho Chi Minh in which he said that he would halt the bombing of the North and stop the buildup of American forces in the South as soon as he had assurances that the North Vietnamese had stopped their infiltration of the South. This was followed by an extensive series of face-to-face official contacts between American and North Vietnamese diplomats in Moscow; there was also an attempt in Saigon to arrange for peace talks in Warsaw.[17]

New and softer terms for a total halt of bombing were relayed secretly to North Vietnam by an American and two Frenchmen, in the summer of 1967. The American discussed the plan with Ambassador-at-Large W. Averell Harriman, the President's personal representative for peace negotiations, in July and briefed the two Frenchmen on the American position. The two Frenchmen

16. *New York Times*, December 23, 1967.
17. *Ibid.*, March 26, 1967.

arrived in Hanoi on July 21, 1967 for a four day visit and discussion about the North Vietnamese views of establishing peace. Their report was relayed to the State Department and apparently there was "something interesting" in Hanoi's position. There seemed to be "some hint of North Vietnamese flexibility that led State Department officials to suspect that Hanoi might be willing to respond positively if the United States did not publicly demand advance assurances on a halt in infiltration of the South before a bombing cessation." [18] This report led to a new formulation of conditions which was handed to a North Vietnamese representative in Paris on August 25, 1967 and about a month later, September 29, 1967, was announced by President Johnson as a new formula at San Antonio. The new statement was: "The United States is willing to stop aerial bombardment of North Vietnam when this will lead promptly to productive discussions. We would assume that while discussions proceed, North Vietnam would not take advantage of this cessation or limitation." [19]

On January 26, 1968 Secretary of Defense Clark M. Clifford amplified the President's San Antonio formula, saying: "I do not expect them to stop their military activities. . . . Their military activity will continue in South Vietnam, I assume, until there is a cease-fire agreed upon." [20]

On March 31, 1968 in the speech in which he declined to be a candidate for reelection, President Johnson announced a "curtailment" in the bombing of North Vietnam. Three days later Hanoi said that it was ready to send representatives to talk to the United States about "the unconditional cessation of the United States bombing raids and all other acts of war against the Democratic Republic of Vietnam so that talks may start." [21] Then came a month of sparring over a site for the talks until finally Paris was chosen and the date of the opening of the talks was to be May 10, 1968.

The negotiations continued throughout the summer of 1968—and the war also continued. The United States had increased her forces to 540,000 and South Vietnam had launched an expansion program designed to increase her armed forces by 135,000 men by the end of 1968. There were pauses in the activity of the North Vietnamese but the end was not in sight. Secretary Rusk insisted

18. *Ibid.*, April 9, 1968.
19. *Ibid.*, August 2, 1968.
20. *Ibid.*, January 27, 1968.
21. *Ibid.*, April 1, 1968.

on a "responsible, authoritative" statement from Hanoi concerning Hanoi's response to the curtailment of bombing on the part of the United States, "not just for today, but for tomorrow, next week, next month!" On August 19, 1968 President Johnson reiterated his position that deescalation would not be by the United States alone, but on October 31, 1968 he announced that he was ordering a complete halt to all American air, naval and artillery bombardment of North Vietnam as of 8:00 a.m. on November 1, 1968, in the hope of wider talks on November 6, 1968.[22]

Each request for appropriations by Congress for the Vietnam War was met, for no member of Congress wanted the soldiers in Vietnam to be deprived of the best support possible. In Vietnam the United States had military and agricultural commitments, made by a succession of Presidents. The Southeast Asia Resolution of August, 1964 was a blank check, for the resolution had wording so general that after the initial provocation was met it was made applicable for all future escalation of the war, whether it was undeclared or not, and the war brought more and more Executive Agreements of all Classes.

The Secretary of Defense, Mr. Robert S. McNamara, in the middle of 1967, in his desire for an answer to the question of how the United States became involved in the Vietnam War, commissioned a history to be written which was supposed to be top secret. It took a year and a half and tapped some secret documents, leaving many gaps in between. *The New York Times* published what came to be known as *The Pentagon Papers,* beginning on Sunday, June 13, 1971. Important as this study will be when more documents are available, the main issue of motivation became clouded by the quarrel over the Freedom of the Press and the right of individuals to make documents available to the Press, especially if the enemy would profit. Light has been thrown on the desultory classification and declassification of documents; and legal action has been taken against those who provided documents from the files. These cases were still in the courts in 1973. The results of these developing issues, important as they were, did not contribute to the controversy between the Executive and the Congress, or help the people to understand why the involvement of the United States in the Vietnam War could take place.

22. *New York Times,* August 20, and November 1, 1968.

Section B—Executive Agreements for Trade

The Kennedy Round of tariff discussions, which was the sixth forum under the General Agreement on Tariff and Trade (GATT) and which had been instigated by the Trade Expansion Act of 1962, had finally gotten under way in 1964 with fifty-three nations participating. It was preceded by discussions concerning the items to be included in the package since it was to be reduction across the board, and also concerning the size of the cuts to be offered. The United States Tariff Commission and the new Trade Information Committee held hearings from December 2, 1963 to March 27, 1964 and heard testimony from 500 individuals, before 6300 items were decided upon as the list to be considered. It was the first time that the European Economic Community (EEC) was to bargain as a unit. The United States insisted that agricultural duties be included in the bargaining but there was delay because of the struggle over a uniform farm policy in the EEC itself. Finally, just before the time limit of the authorization of the Round, on May 15, 1967 the negotiations were concluded. The results were cuts of about 35% over the next four years on some 60,000 industrial and agricultural products; a food-aid program providing underdeveloped nations with wheat and other grains annually over the next three years; a liberalization of trade in fruits, vegetables and many other non-cereal farm products; mutual trade benefits that would go into effect if Congress would repeal the "American Selling Price" system of customs valuations applied to some chemicals and a few other products; and an antidumping agreement.[23]

This was a most imposing large-scale Executive Agreement of Class II with fifty-two other nations; and the first tariff reductions went into effect January 1, 1968.

The possibility of increasing exports from the United States and the keeping of the markets of the EEC open in the formative stage of that Community were important for the United States for there was a recent unfavorable balance of trade for the United States. The inclusion of the agricultural items in the tariff reductions was a reflection of a new policy of the United States.

In the summer of 1967 there was a conference in Rome the pur-

23. James B. Shuman, "Giant Step toward Freer Trade," *Reader's Digest*, February, 1968, pp. 83–87.

pose of which was to translate the GATT cereals agreement into a new International Wheat Agreement. This was done by a Multilateral Treaty and a Food Aid Committee was set up to supervise its implementation.

Section C—Changes in Agricultural Aid

Mention has been made of the passing of the Agricultural Trade Development and Assistance Act in 1954, called Public Law 480.[24] This act brought into being the first United States food aid program and was made effective by many Executive Agreements of Class II. At that time the United States had a surplus of 42 million tons of wheat. In 1953 the Mutual Security Assistance Program had introduced the idea of selling surpluses for local currency and the PL480 in 1954 made the idea a systematic policy. The Act brought forth Executive Agreements of Class II throughout the world. From 1956 to 1963 PL 480 aid accounted for 40% of the whole aid program of the United States. By 1964–1965 PL 480 provided over half of the grain imports of the underdeveloped world.

There were three titles to the Act. Title I channeled the food through the commercial market. The grain did not necessarily reach those most in need but the process disposed of United States surpluses and the amount might vary each year. Three-year Executive Agreements of Class II with Brazil and Pakistan were arranged in the mid-fifties and four-year Executive Agreements of Class II were negotiated with India in 1960 and with Pakistan in 1961. President Johnson then reverted to one-year Executive Agreements of Class II in order to bring pressure for self-help on the recipient country. Payment was made in local currency of which about a quarter was reserved by the United States for embassy costs, sales to its own tourists, loans to its own businessmen, educational and cultural program costs, sales promotion activities for United States farm products, common defense costs, and internal security expenditures. The recipients paid the shipping costs and since the United States required at least 50% of aid supplies to be shipped in United States flag vessels, this meant that 50% of the shipping cost was in dollars. By 1966 the local currency accumulations in Burma, Ceylon, Guinea, India, Israel,

---

24. David R. Wightman, "Food Aid and Economic Development," *International Conciliation*, No. 567, pp. 36–39 (March, 1968); and *Current History*, Current Documents, July, 1966, pp. 46–47, 54.

Pakistan, Poland, Tunisia and the United Arab Republic were beyond foreseeable requirements.

Title II of PL 480 provided for food aid as donations for famine and disaster relief and for programs to combat malnutrition. The very poor profited by it. In 1960 Title II included also development projects for which payment in food-wages could be made.

Title III provided for food aid as donations to voluntary welfare agencies such as CARE, Catholic Relief Service, Church World Service; and to UNICEF and the United Nations Relief and Works Agency for their relief and work programs. Under this Title food was bartered for strategic materials for United States stockpiles but due to criticism of exporters this practice was discontinued in 1957.

In 1959 a Title IV was added which allowed dollar sales to governments on long term credit. After 1962 credit could be extended to private foreign traders also.

AID, which was brought into being in 1961, saw in PL 480 a means to encourage economic development so development loans were made from the local currency accumulations under Title I.

Disposing of surplus food by the United States brought repercussions from other food exporting countries but there developed a consultation procedure and PL 480 became a vital instrument of foreign policy. It was used to combat Communism; moreover it was advantageous, for some recipients soon became commercial customers, such as Greece, Israel, Poland, Spain and Taiwan. Economic self-interest, humanitarianism, cold war diplomacy—all could justify the program.

Surplus disposal caused discussion in foreign forums such as the Food and Agriculture Organization (FAO), an organization associated with the United Nations, for it affected the stability of international markets. In 1954 "FAO drafted a set of Principles of surplus disposal, or a code of conduct, which countries were asked to accept. By the end of 1967, fifty-one countries had done so. In addition, an FAO Consultative Sub-Committee on Surplus Disposal (CSD) was set up in Washington as the guardian of the Principles." [25] In 1968 it comprised forty-one member countries. The CSD heard complaints; and after 1958 Congress directed that consultation with third parties had to take place and provided that "Title I supplies must be additional to the usual marketings

25. *Ibid.,* pp. 39–40.

of friendly countries as well." Surpluses in the future were to be used to raise food consumption.

One of the effects of PL 480 was the lack of encouragement of recipient countries to put more resources into their own development. Industry and mining received the greatest share of development loans from the receipts of Title I.

Between 1961 and 1967 United States wheat stocks fell. By the mid-sixties surplus stocks had disappeared. There were unexpected demands for wheat from the U.S.S.R., Communist China, East European countries and India. There was a great population growth in underdeveloped countries also. The United States had been paying the farmers not to raise crops but now it was clear that food had to come from planned production. In 1966 the United States decided to encourage large sowings of wheat, rice, and soybeans and to revise the terms of the PL 480 program.[26] Commodities were no longer limited to surpluses. They also included "any commodity the Secretary of Agriculture decides should be made available or produced for food aid." Applicants in the future would have to demonstrate that they were making efforts to increase agricultural production themselves and improve storage and distribution facilities. Sales for local currency would be phased out by 1971 in favor of dollar cash and credit sales. The aim was to make the terms for food aid the same as those for development loans under the United States aid program.

The new PL 480 also retained food aid donations but combined the old Titles II and III into a single unit "covering disaster relief, school feeding, work recreation projects and voluntary agency relief."

The disposition to use food aid for political purposes seemed stronger under the Johnson Administration. The United Arab Republic and Algeria had aid discontinued. The new PL 480 forbade shipments to countries that do business with Cuba or North Vietnam and at the beginning of 1967 deliveries to Yugoslavia were discontinued on this account.

In 1963 the United States also took part in launching a World Food Program under joint United Nations and FAO auspices, for an experimental period of three years. The United States wanted to get other countries to share the costs and difficulties of food

26. David R. Wightman, "Food Aid and Economic Development," *International Conciliation*, No. 567, pp. 36–39 (March, 1968); and *Current History*, Current Documents, July, 1966, pp. 43–45.

aid. The basic idea was to use the food "as subsistence capital, or a wages fund, to finance labor intensive projects such as rural public works, road building, minor irrigation, afforrestation and community development." [27]

The WFP would rely on voluntary pledges of food, cash and shipping services. There were seventy-one contributors but the United States contributed 50% of the total. The food contributions were to be in wheat, coarse grain, or their cash equivalent and would be sold for local currency. The cash would be paid for administrative overhead and shipping costs. In 1965 at the end of the experimental period the United Nations and FAO decided to continue the World Food Program indefinitely. The WFP is supervised by an Inter-Governmental Committee which meets twice a year at its headquarters in Rome. There is an Executive Director, a secretariat of fifty professional officers and eighty-one secretarial, clerical and technical staff members. There is also a field staff. There was a third pledging conference in January, 1968 and there was prospect for an enlarged multilateral program. The WFP gave promise of being a successful experiment.

It is, therefore, clear that the United States trade in food comprises commercial sales; the new PL 480 aid program; and participation in the World Food Program. All methods required Executive Agreements of either Class I or Class II.

Section D—Balance of Payments

The crucial issue during the Johnson Administration was the climax to which the international financial problem had come. The Balance of Payments began to be perilously jeopardized by the Vietnam War and military expenditures abroad, in general; by the expenditures for Foreign Aid; by tourism abroad; and by foreign investment. Gold was being drained from the country since World War II and the gold stock in the country dropped from $25 billion in 1949 to less than $11 billion in 1968, with potential claims of more than $30 billion against the gold that was left. In March, 1968 there was a run on the dollar in Europe. To deter this drain of gold on March 17, 1968 the United States joined with the United Kingdom, the Netherlands, West Germany, Belguim, Italy and Switzerland and suppliers of gold to the London market, in an Executive Agreement of Class IV not to

27. *Ibid.,* pp. 46-55.

sell any more gold to private individuals or to other governments that resell gold to the public.[28] For the first time since 1934 the American dollar was no longer fully convertible into gold.

For many years the promise of the United States to buy and sell gold at $35 an ounce, and the pegging of the currencies of other countries to the dollar gave fixed rates of exchange among world currencies. For many years also the gold stock of the United States was two-thirds of all the world's currency-backing gold. For years the United States dollar was acceptable abroad instead of gold which was hard to store, but now the countries demanded gold.

Under President Kennedy foreign aid had been "tied" to purchases in this country and he had asked for voluntary controls over private American investment in Europe. Soon European nations began to attack United States private investment in their economies. President Johnson asked for voluntary curbs on tourism and private investment abroad; expenditures for aid were reduced by Congress to the lowest level since the aid program began; but appropriations for the Vietnam War were not curtailed and the defense budget was the highest ever passed.

The March meeting of nations agreed to suspend further private sales of gold and to supply massive new lines of credit to help support the British pound. At the same time short-term credits were extended to support the dollar. This meant that the price of gold could fluctuate on the market according to private supply and demand with the floor no longer at $35 an ounce.

This was a temporary expedient and it was thought that domestic inflation had to be stopped in the United States by the 10% rise in income tax and a curtailment of spending by the United States amounting to $6 billion in the 1968–1969 budget.

Meanwhile in 1968 the International Monetary Fund proposed an international reform. There was need for an international monetary unit to supplement gold and the dollar. At the annual meeting of the International Monetary Fund organization in Rio de Janeiro a new plan known as paper gold was approved.

There would be an annual creation of an amount of Special Drawing Rights. The Special Drawing Rights could be used only to settle accounts between nations and would not enter the ordinary trade between individuals or corporations. Voting strength

---

28. James Daniel, "A New Program to Solve the Gold Problem," *Reader's Digest*, June, 1968, pp. 171–176.

was to be based on member nations' gold and currency contributions to the "already-in-existence" loan fund which helps members over temporary "dips" of their balance of payments. A nation could transfer its drawing rights as credits instead of gold or dollars to a creditor country. At least sixty-five countries with 80% of the Fund's weighted vote would have to approve. A country would be obliged to accept from other countries up to three times its own quota.

The United States passed an act of Congress to comply and sent it to the White House on June 7, 1968. Thus there were two forms of gold transactions: the private one for industry, jewelry makers, dentistry, and private hoarders, which buys on the market and causes gold to fluctuate in price; and the paper gold ones of the IMF between nations. It remained to be seen how this monetary arrangement would meet the problem of the Imbalance of Payments.

Section E—Criticism of the Vietnam War

The continuation of the Vietnam War and its consequences in the financial world brought once more a question concerning the policy itself. Were the commitments by Treaty and Executive Agreements, which expressed the purpose of fighting against territorial aggression and which gave the legal basis for our concern in Southeast Asia, the only explanation of our being there or were there additional reasons for keeping the Straits of Malacca open for the new trade of Japan, Formosa, the Philippines, Australia, New Zealand, etc.? Was it a practical confrontation as well as an ideological one? If the policy had been succeeding, if the costs had not been soaring, would thought have been given to the policy itself?

As the statistics of casualties mounted and as the cost of the Vietnam War increased, condemnation of the war had become more vocal. At a televised hearing of the Senate Foreign Relations Committee in February, 1966 General James Gavin, former Ambassador George F. Kennan and others offered ways of seeking to solve the Vietnamese problem. It was emphasized that the war had become a policy war and that the commitment, not made by a formal declaration of war, was *assured* by the reiterated, simplistic explanation of helping a small nation check aggression and determine its own destiny and also by the explanation of furthering the aim of the cold war by containing Communist expansionism in Asia.[29]

It was on February 8, 1966 that President Johnson of the United States and the Chief of State and the Prime Minister of the Republic of Vietnam concluded a three day discussion at Honolulu and issued the Declaration of Honolulu.[30] They had reviewed the efforts for peace undertaken by the United States and made note of the absence of interest on the part of the Government of North Vietnam and they reviewed the diplomatic situation of early 1966 in the United Nations and decided to continue diplomatic efforts for peace.

The Honolulu Declaration in its formal announcement amounted to an Executive Agreement of Class III to give continued emphasis (1) to efforts to build democracy in the rural areas; (2) to the design of rural construction work; (3) to concentration of resources in priority areas to protect rural construction against destruction by the enemy; (4) to the removal of agricultural know-how—i.e. new species of productive rice and corn and vegetable seed—to the farmer in the field; (5) to intensification of programs in health and education; (6) to care for refugees from the north who were prepared to resume a useful role in society; and (7) to a policy of growing military effectiveness and of still closer cooperation between the military forces of Vietnam and those of the United States.

The purposes of the Vietnam Government were set forth as including the formulation of a democratic constitution in the months ahead, including an electoral law; the taking of that constitution to the people for discussion and modification; the seeking of its ratification by secret ballot; and the creation, on the basis of elections rooted in that constitution, of an elected government.

The United States declared its purposes to be (1) to prevent aggression; (2) to be pledged to the principles of self-determination of peoples, and of government by the consent of the governed; and (3) to give special support to the work of the people of Vietnam—to build, while they fight, to stabilize the economy, to increase the production of food, to spread education, to stamp out disease, and to press the quest for peace.

29. *New York Times*, February 13, 1966.
30. "The Pledge of Honolulu," February 8, 1966 (White House Press Release, Honolulu, Hawaii, dated February 8, 1966).

On April 18, 1966 at a televised Foreign Relations Committee hearing (referred to as a teach-in) Secretary Rusk was asked to set forth the Administration's arguments on the legality of the commitment, and again on May 9, 1966 at another televised hearing of the same committee on the question of Aid to Vietnam he was put on the defensive. The Secretary reiterated the explanation that the United States was justified both by the SEATO Treaty and by other considerations, such as the principle of collective defense stated in the United Nations Charter.

By July, 1967 the Chairman of the Foreign Relations Committee, Senator J. W. Fulbright, was dealing with the Vietnamese problem as a constitutional issue, and a challenge to the Senate to reclaim its constitutional responsibilities of "advice and consent." He did not think that there was a willful usurpation of Congressional power by the Executive or a conscious surrender of power by Congress, but he said that the situation was the result of "an entire era of crisis in which urgent decisions have been required . . . of a kind that the Congress is ill-equipped to make with what has been thought to be the requisite speed." [31] He said that he suspected that the Executive often exaggerated the need for quick action and thus made mistakes that "might have been avoided by greater deliberation" within the Senate. By the device of the Congressional Joint Resolution, giving advance approval to actions that the Executive might deem necessary, Congress had given away that which was not theirs to give, the constitutional right to declare war.[32]

On July 31, 1967 Senator Fulbright introduced a resolution to prevent the Executive Branch from making national commitments to other nations without legislative approval. It was to provide a basis for the September hearings of the Fulbright Committee. The resolution, if approved, would have no force other than to express the sense of the Senate.[33] At a news conference on August 18, 1967 President Johnson challenged Congress to withdraw its support of the Tonkin Bay Resolution if it thought "we have acted unwisely or improperly" in exercising the authority it granted him.[34]

31. *New York Times*, July 20, 1967.
32. Previously in January, 1955 Secretary of State John Foster Dulles used the so-called "Formosa Resolution," which gave the President the right to defend the off-shore islands of Quemoy and Matsu; and in 1958 President Eisenhower used the Joint Resolution on the Middle East (1957) when he landed marines in Lebanon.
33. *New York Times*, August 1, 1967.
34. *Ibid.*, August 22, 1967.

In the Senate Committee hearings Nicholas deB. Katzenbach, Under-Secretary of State, took the position that the Executive had the power to do what he had done—it was an Executive Power; and that the SEATO Treaty and the Southeast Asia Resolution together gave the President authority equivalent to what he would have under a Congressional declaration of war, as provided in the Constitution. The rescission of the Resolution would not prevent the President from continuing to exercise his authority but would bring a division between the President and the Congress which would be reflected in lack of appropriations by Congress of funds to support the forces in Vietnam. The real issue, as he saw it, was the support of the President by Congress and their acting in a unified manner.[35]

Senators testified, however, as to the intention of Congress at the time the Tonkin Resolution was passed and felt that the President had exceeded Congressional intent at the time; and reviewed the assurances given at the hearings on the SEATO Treaty by Secretary John Foster Dulles that it was not the policy of the United States to build up "a large local force" of ground troops on the Asian mainland but to "rely upon the deterrent power of our mobile striking force." [36] The Senators had their impressions and their memories! Did a sense of guilt prompt their questionings? Should they have made the wording more specific so that the Resolution could not be effective after the immediate episode?

What was brought out by the whole discussion, however, was that it was the Vietnam policy itself that was widening the breach between the President and the Congress and that fear of failure of the policy and its high cost had made the Senate take refuge in an argument over constitutional practice, and the controversy between the Executive and the Congress. It was the current counterpart of the Bricker Movement of the 1950's. It was clear that in the world-wide civil war with the Communists, traditional diplomatic procedures, such as declarations of war and peace treaties, had lost their old meanings. Communists did not declare war or sign peace treaties; nor had the United States given diplomatic recognition to two of the recent enemies, North Korea and North Vietnam, which precluded declarations of war. It was pointed out that in these changed circumstances, there had developed in the United States an informal practice of bipartisan consultations with

35. *New York Times,* August 22, 1967.
36. *Ibid.*

the leaders of both Houses and the ranking members of the committees dealing with Foreign Affairs and Military Affairs. Not to get authority but to impress the enemy of solidarity in the United States did the President occasionally ask for Joint Resolutions. Mutual confidence was required; but since the policy itself was doubted, the mere record of the Senate discussion indicated that it wanted to be consulted in advance and not just told in a briefing about decisions already made.[37]

To the legislative debate there was soon added the voice of the Supreme Court in November, 1967. In Case No. 401 three soldiers, who had refused to go to Vietnam because no war had been declared by Congress, were denied an appeal by the Supreme Court.[38] The importance of the case was in the fact that Justice Potter Stewart and Justice William O. Douglas filed dissenting opinions which raised anew the constitutional questions. Draft resistance was a subject of great interest to young people of the 1960's.

The one thing that was clear at this time was the fact that the Vietnamese War was a policy war. The Administration had not made clear its rightness or its necessity, and had not explained to the citizens how the war was an expression of national need and sentiment to which they could respond wholeheartedly.

On February 11, 1968 Secretary Rusk appeared before the Senate Foreign Relations Committee on behalf of the Foreign Aid Program. The questions were mainly on Vietnam and in answering the Secretary sounded like a broken record. The same clichés were given. Senator Fulbright put his questions in an evaluation framework: "Can we afford the horrors which are being inflicted on the people of a poor and backward land to say nothing of our own people? Can we afford the alienation of our allies, the neglect of our own deep domestic problems and the disillusionment of our youth? Can we afford the loss of confidence in our government and institutions, the fading of hope and optimism and the betrayal of our traditional values?" [39]

As a followup of this appearance of Secretary Rusk he was prevailed upon by Senator Fulbright to submit to questioning on the Vietnamese War, at hearings on March 11, 1968. It was pointed out that the national objectives were not clear. At this time there were reports that the Administration was considering a substantial

37. *Ibid.,* August 23, 1967.
38. *Ibid.,* November 14 and 18, 1967.
39. *Ibid.,* February 12, 1968 and March 7, 1968.

increase in the American troop strength, perhaps by 200,000 men; so Senator Fulbright decided before Secretary Rusk's appearance to voice his concerns in a speech on the Senate floor on March 7 as a last effort to re-establish communication with the Administration. This speech touched off a spontaneous debate in the Senate. Senator Fulbright pleaded with the Administration to consult with Congress, and many Senators participated in the debate.[40] Many words were spoken; emotions prompted many assertions; but no new ideas were advanced.

Section F—Relations with the U.S.S.R.

While the Vietnam issues were uppermost in popular attention there were evidences during the Johnson Administration before the fall of 1968 of a detente between the United States and the U.S.S.R. There were several Treaties and Executive Agreements which acted as a barometer of Soviet-American relations.

A Consular Convention between the U.S.S.R. and the United States, effective on July 13, 1968, included provisions that persons from the United States would have the right to have access to American consular authorities within four days of arrest and the United States would be notified of the arrest within three days.[41]

A Treaty on the principles underlying the activity of states in exploring and using outer space banned nuclear weapons in outer space, and covered the safe return of astronauts. On October 10, 1967 there were ceremonies in Washington, Moscow and London putting the space treaty into effect.[42]

The draft Nuclear Non-Proliferation Treaty was approved by the General Assembly of the United Nations on June 12, 1968 and in the United States was referred to the Senate.[43] This was a multilateral treaty providing that nations with nuclear weapons were not to transfer arms or other nuclear devices to nations without such weapons; guaranteeing research, and production and use of nuclear energy for peaceful purposes to all nations with no nuclear weapons; and stating that nations with nuclear weapons would agree to pursue negotiations on effective measures relating to the cessation of the nuclear arms race and negotiations on a treaty on general and complete disarmament at an early date. The missile

---

40. *New York Times*, March 8, 10, 12, 14, 17, 1968.
41. *Ibid.*, July 14, 1968.
42. *Current History*, Current Documents, March, 1967, pp. 175 177.
43. *Ibid.*, February, 1968, pp. 107–109.

race between the countries with nuclear power was, therefore, not affected by the terms of the Non-Proliferation Treaty but the U.S.S.R. and the United States announced their willingness to enter into talks on missile curbs.

There were also Executive Agreements of Class IV with the U.S.S.R.: a Commercial Agreement, signed on May 6, 1968, paving the way for direct air flights between the United States and Moscow, which was made effective by the first flight on July 15, 1968; and a new Cultural Agreement, signed on July 15, 1968.[44] By the latter annual exchanges of university students were cut from 40 to 30 by each country and exchanges of professors for research were reduced from 15 to 10. Instead of five major performing arts groups the new Agreement called for exchange of three by each side. It provided for continuation of distribution of the journals *Amerika* in the Soviet Union and *Soviet Life* in the United States, and for exchanges of motion pictures, books, journals, and radio and TV programs. In science, technology, agriculture and medicine there was more encouragement. The new agreement provided for exchanges in weather control, treatment of industrial waste water, and air pollution information and for studies of solar eclipses. Delegations of doctors would study the progress in transplanting human organs.

Before the end of 1968 the detente was put in jeopardy. The interference of the U.S.S.R. in the affairs of Czechoslovakia on August 20, 1968 caused a changed climate of opinion in the United States concerning the U.S.S.R.

It was brought to the fore that the U.S.S.R.'s intercontinental and submarine-launched ballistic missiles had been increasing in number and the Pentagon had been wanting American escalation. The Soviet deployment of an ABM system around Moscow spurred the Washington political pressure that culminated in the Administrations's decision to create a "thin" American ABM system.[45] The Administration at first advanced the System as a defense against the emerging Chinese missile threat but later justified the step as a defensive move against the Soviet Union.

The competition was enhanced when on September 20, 1968 the U.S.S.R. in turn announced its latest achievement—a satellite's circling of the moon!

44. *New York Times,* July 16, 1968.
45. *Ibid.,* August 10, 1968.

Section G—World Changes

By 1968 the world had been altered greatly. Scientific, technical and cultural changes were multiple: airpower; atomic powered submarines and submarines that could stay under water almost indefinitely; atomic and hydrogen bombs; medium and long range missiles and antiballistic missiles that made conventional weapons secondary; new sites for missile bases that were not the same as those needed for the Strategic Air Command of the forties; [46] new defense mechanisms that must be distributed throughout the world; range and effectiveness of planes from aircraft carriers; logistical arrangements enabling vessels to remain at sea indefinitely without recourse to fixed bases; ever more ingenious weapons; projects for exploring outer space; new sources of war materials and new developments in synthetic substitutes that gave importance to different regions of the world; new sites for oil and natural resources; monstrous tankers that made former canals, such as Suez, and waterways inadequate for service, and obsolete; new scientific processes; new telecommunications; new communications by way of satellites that made the world shrink; new utilization of space; new food and resources from the bottom of the sea; constant travel abroad for business, recreation, and culture; increased investment in developing nations; greater growth of populations; new bigness and mergers in corporations; and new importance placed on the struggle for individualism and identity.

All of these changes were being experienced to a certain degree by other states as well as the United States. The United States was at first the only Great Power, because of peculiar circumstances after World War II, but now there were three Great Powers—the U.S.S.R., Red China, and the United States—and five with atomic and hydrogen weapons. Great Britain had withdrawn from her global imperialism and was sighting her goals in the direction of Europe. France was going through a metamorphosis in her relations to the European states. The United Nations had experienced a period of ineffectiveness because of the very growth of the number of states and the principle of one state one vote, of the shifting of Great Powers' interests, and of their use of the veto.

---

46. At the end of President Eisenhower's administration the United States had many bases around the world; in 1968, the United States had 140 or 150 such bases. The United States was committed to defend more than 40 different countries. Some bases were no longer needed. The relinquishment, in June, 1968, of an advanced radar and communications center in Turkey near Ankara and the return to Japan of the Bonin and Volcano Islands in July, 1968 had recently occurred.

All of these developments by 1968 were calling for International Agreements. Some Treaties and hundreds of Executive Agreements had already been made in the last decade. At the beginning of 1960 there were 4399 Treaties and Executive Agreements in TIAS. By September, 1968 there were 6533. This great increase was mainly in the area of Executive Agreements.

Many of the Executive Agreements were simply protocols of extension or amendment of previous Agreements. Many were extensions to the many new states in the world of the privileges, such as aid, already enjoyed by the older states.[47] The increase, however, was mainly in Group IV of the Executive Agreements, those executed by the President because of his Constitutional authority and not referred to Congress before they became effective. Some of these were oral declarations of the Chief Executive that amounted to promises, such as the statements made in Joint Communiqués after visits of foreign heads of state. The declaration of support at the Honolulu Conference in 1966 to the Head of South Vietnam and the last Agreement with President Thieu at Honolulu on July 22, 1968 [48] were of Class III. President Johnson was to renege on his statement that he would go anywhere at any time to confer with representatives of North Vietnam, when he found that the location of talks had some necessary conditions of environment and facilities.

Most of the Executive Agreements of Group IV that were not referred to Congress had to do with matters that the average citizen takes for granted and were the ones that make the "housekeeping" arrangements of government function smoothly and keep the everyday business of foreign relations in order.

A few examples of these categories of subjects that were dealt with by Executive Agreements of Class IV up to 1968 throw light on this modern, technological age: civil uses of atomic energy; aerial mapping programs; upper atmosphere research facilities; space research programs; tracking and communication stations when satellites are launched; air search and rescue operations; weather stations; fishing operations in various waters; waiver of

47. In October, 1968 there were 141 states in the world and of them 125 were in the United Nations.
48. President Van Thieu upon his return from Honolulu on July 22, 1968 reported to his people that President Johnson would strengthen the South Vietnam Army and support the war even after the November, 1968 elections. He said that the United States was opposed to a coalition government. "We agreed that there will be no cessation of bombing of North Vietnam unless the North Vietnamese respond with reciprocal action."

non-immigrant visa fees; financing of cultural exchange; preservation of temples of Abu Simbel from inundation of Aswan High Dam; copyright; exchange of official publications; cooperative programs of anthropological research and investigation; distribution and exposition of American motion picture films; patents; cooperative health and sanitation; relief from double taxation; investment guarantees; claims arising from traffic accidents; control of export of potatoes from Canada to the United States; temporary migration of agricultural workers from Mexico; cooperative rubber plantation investigations; winter maintenance of Haines Road with Canada; the inter-American highway; etc. . . . All of these Executive Agreements of Class IV and others made the American world function.

CHAPTER IX

International Agreements, 1968-1971

Section A—Challenge for Change

The Presidential Election of 1968 gave the victory to Richard M. Nixon by a small but sufficient margin to indicate that a change in both foreign and domestic policies was in order. The immediate post-World War II policies had escalated throughout four administrations to the point where they were being retained because of their historical reality rather than because of their appropriateness for the end of the sixties. Inspired by anti-Communism, after World War II, when aggression on the part of the Communists was visibly military, the United States in her relatively affluent condition had stepped in to revive the weak and to curb territorial expansion of opponents. In a quarter of a century, however, the world had changed. The old empire of the British was relinquished and replaced by the symbolic and spiritual bond of the voluntary Commonwealth. For survival and prosperity Great Britain looked to a European orientation and a link with the revived industrialization of western Europe. Even her bases east of Suez she announced she would give up in the early 70's, substituting big airlifts to Singapore and other Far Eastern destinations when necessary. France, also, yielded to the inevitable and held together her former possessions by voluntary association. Under De Gaulle she resorted to a revived nationalism. The alliance of fourteen non-Communist states of Europe and the United States (NATO) held the status quo in Europe against Communism but meanwhile the new trends toward industrialization had drawn Italy, France, West Germany, the Netherlands, Belgium and Luxembourg into a successful European Economic Community (the Common Market). Germany and Japan, defeated powers in World War II, had forged ahead and become prosperous; the military restrictions imposed upon them by the peace and security treaties had enabled them to emphasize internal development. The country, however, that still in the late 60's had commitments on the basis of the immediate post-World War II realism was the United States and anti-Communism was still an obsession. Internally, however, the people of the United States were impatient and wanted change. The Vietnam War, inflation, riots, lack of law and order, poverty problems, military spending, increased armaments, minority grievances—all spelled a mandate for change.

National security and national interest were still the goals of the United States and technological advances gave the opportunity for the country to function internationally in a different way. Should security still be geared to the use of conventional weapons only or could it be provided by missiles at greater distances from the potential aggressors? Because of the cultural changes of "One World," experienced by the United States and by other countries, did the national interest not dictate an understanding or accommodation not dreamed of in 1946–1948? Should commitments not be made to reflect the changes in the world? Would new Executive Agreements of all kinds not increase in number as expressive of new policies?

Section B—The Vietnam War

Many old problems had to be dealt with in a new way. The Nixon Administration took over with restraint. Any dramatic changes were avoided. Projects of study by new personnel were initiated as background for every problem that demanded attention and the public seemed glad to get its breath for the first few months. The Vietnam War, however, dominated thought, and became the symbol of everything that was wrong. It had to have priority. Already by April 3, 1969 there were 549,500 servicemen in Vietnam and over 33,641 had been killed, a number higher than the death toll of the Korean War.[1] Each week was bringing added casualties. Anti-war demonstrations and riots continued.

President Johnson had hoped to end the war during his administration. On March 31, 1968 he had announced that the United States would limit bombing of North Vietnam. An aidememoire of North Vietnam, however, dated April 5, 1968, de-

1. *U.S. News and World Report,* July 14, 1969.

manded that the United States release immediately "any citizens of the Democratic Republic of Vietnam now being illegally detained," "stop all arrogant acts," and respect the sovereignty, territory and security of the Democratic Republic of Vietnam.[2] The United States did not meet these demands but North Vietnam declared its readiness to appoint its representative to contact the United States to determine the unconditional cessation of the United States bombing raids and "all other acts of war against the Democratic Republic of Vietnam so that talks may start." After much jockeying concerning the place, as stated in Chapter VIII, talks did start at Paris on May 10, 1968. By October there was a breakthrough in these talks by Hanoi's favorable reaction to an American proposal for seating the Saigon Government and the National Liberation Front in the Paris negotiations. This seemed to assure an early start for substantive discussions. Hanoi had demonstrated a lull in the fighting in South Vietnam and President Johnson, who had been asking for an explicit assurance of future Communist military restraint, accepted this as a condition for a complete halt of the bombing of North Vietnam. On October 31, 1968 he announced that the halt would begin on November 1, 1968. He stated that on November 6, 1968 at Paris the talks would resume, with the Vietcong present and representatives of the Government of South Vietnam free to attend.[3] He added that this did not mean that the United States was recognizing the National Liberation Front. President Thieu refused to participate, however, demanding that Hanoi acknowledge the National Liberation Front as part of its delegation, and therefore as an instrument of North Vietnam, thus trying in advance to resolve the issue of legitimacy, status, and future relations of the National Liberation Front with the Saigon Government. This effort to stall the Paris peace talks in the belief that the newly elected President Nixon would be more sympathetic was wishful thinking, for President Nixon made it clear that he would not accept an invitation of President Thieu to visit South Vietnam unless President Johnson asked him to make the trip. This reinforced Mr. Nixon's campaign pledge to support President Johnson in respect to the peace talks, and his post-election statement of "assistance and cooperation" to the Johnson Administration on Vietnam.

2. *New York Times,* April 6, 1968.
3. *Ibid.,* November 1, 1968.

Meanwhile during the boycott by South Vietnam, it was thought that the United States and Hanoi could have fruitful private meetings concerning an agenda for discussion of the mutual withdrawal of troops, etc. The boycott precipitated the long discussion of the shape of the table and its relation to the question of the National Liberation Front's being a separate entity. This political issue was a challenge to the Thieu regime as to whether all the non-Communist elements supported President Thieu. Saigon in the meantime suggested that its government head an Allied Delegation but the United States rejected the proposition. The boycott was finally ended on November 26, 1968. South Vietnam was to have a major voice in affairs relating primarily to her interests but she was not to be chairman of the allied delegation.[4] The seating arrangements and the shape of the table were not resolved until the announcement of January 16, 1969 that the first expanded talks of the four parties would take place on January 18, 1969. There would be a round table at which each of the four parties would have fifteen delegates and there would be two rectangular secretarial tables on opposite sides, 18 inches from the circular table. The United States and Saigon could call this arrangement two-sided and the enemy could call it four-sided. At the meeting of January 18, 1969 procedural matters were discussed. On the same day President Thieu said that he and the United States would draft a program for withdrawal of not more than 50,000 United States servicemen.[5]

On January 20, 1969 the Nixon Administration took over with Henry Cabot Lodge as chief negotiator at Paris. The first plenary talks took place on January 25, 1969 and formal meetings occurred every Thursday. There were many secret conferences and finally on March 26, 1969 President Thieu announced that he was willing to allow members of the National Liberation Front to participate in South Vietnamese politics under an overall peace settlement.[6] It was on May 8, 1969 that the National Liberation Front offered a ten-point peace plan, providing for an unconditional unilateral withdrawal of United States forces, free elections in Vietnam, and an eventual coalition government. South Vietnam on the same date said she was ready to open talks privately or at Paris on exchange of prisoners of war, on restoring the de-

4. *New York Times*, November 27, 1968.
5. *Ibid.*, January 19, 1969.
6. *Ibid.*, March 27, 1969.

militarized zone between North and South Vietnam and on reinstituting the 1962 Geneva Agreements on Laos.[7]

Up to this time each side was adamant about its program but the National Liberation Front did not insist that its ten-point program was the only basis for a settlement. Among the new elements was a suggestion that the question of the withdrawal of North Vietnam "shall be resolved by the Vietnamese parties among themselves." It was suggested that the Front might agree to ask North Vietnam to go home for a similar request by Saigon to the United States. The National Liberation Front continued to insist on a coalition regime in the period between the cessation of hostilities and the holding of general elections, thus trying to ease Saigon's fears of a Communist takeover during the period. The questions were, therefore, mutual withdrawal of troops and the political relation of the Vietcong and the South Vietnam Government. The North said that the talk of the United States withdrawals was a trick to placate American opinion at home and to buy time. The theory of the United States seemed to be that the Communists might prefer an agreed peace, in which they would have some say, to a unilateral American withdrawal tied to the strengthening of South Vietnamese forces. There was fear in some quarters, also, of a blood bath in South Vietnam if there was a sudden withdrawal of United States troops.

On May 14, 1969 President Nixon made his first report to the United States public on the war in Vietnam and in his nationwide televised address outlined an eight point peace plan, suggesting that the United States and North Vietnam should schedule a phased mutual withdrawal of troops from South Vietnam over a twelve month period.[8] On May 20, 1969 it was announced that President Thieu and President Nixon would meet on Midway Island in the Pacific on June 8, 1969 for further clarification. On May 28, 1969 President Thieu said in a speech that any peace settlement had to conform to the present South Vietnamese constitution. He rejected an interim coalition government and special elections, both of which had been mentioned by the United States as possibilities for negotiation in Paris.[9]

On June 8, 1969 President Nixon and President Thieu met at Midway Island and President Nixon announced the Executive

7. *Ibid.*
8. *Ibid.*, May 15, 1969.
9. *Ibid.*, May 29, 1969.

Agreement of Class III that the United States was to withdraw 25,000 troops before the end of August, 1969 and that the responsibility for the war was to be gradually increased for the South Vietnamese.[10]

On June 10, 1969 the National Liberation Front announced the establishment of a "Provisional Revolutionary Government," representing a wider spectrum of political membership than the National Liberation Front and on June 14, 1969 this new organization was represented at Paris.[11]

In South Vietnam, as a result of new taxes imposed by the Premier, the House of Representatives on June 16, 1969 urged President Thieu to consider a vote of no confidence in the Cabinet and as a result a new Cabinet was installed, reflecting military and old Diem complexions. On June 22, 1969 President Thieu said his troops were ready to shoulder a major responsibility for the fighting of the war. On July 11, 1969, in a televised speech, he urged the Vietcong to participate in free elections to be supervised by an international body but on July 21 he said that at least two years would elapse before national elections could be set up to include the Vietcong. This proposal was called stupid by North Vietnam and "trickery" by the Provisional Revolutionary Government. On July 20, 1969 Ho Chi Minh said no free elections could be held in South Vietnam as long as any United States troops were in the country.[12]

Thus we see that by the end of July, 1969 the withdrawal of United States troops, to be replaced by South Vietnamese troops, and the political question of elections were the two main foci of interest. South Vietnam would not accept a coalition government but proposed national elections in the dim future. Up to this time the Vietcong had denied the legitimacy of the Thieu Government and demanded a coalition government from which President Thieu and other officials would be barred. President Thieu realized that the United States might demand an end to the war on less favorable terms than the announced withdrawal and North Vietnam seemed not to welcome a prolonged time during which the United States would supply aid to South Vietnam if the United States troops were pulled out. The United States did not know whether the North would rely on the possibility of the

10. *New York Times,* June 9, 1969.
11. *Ibid.,* June 11 and 15, 1969.
12. *Ibid.,* July 21, 1969.

collapse of the South Vietnamese Government and the American weariness with the war. However, the North adhered to its demands for the unconditional withdrawal of all American troops and the destruction of the current Saigon Government.

The announcement of the withdrawal of 25,000 United States troops was followed by North Vietnam's recalling several organized regiments into North Vietnam, reducing the infiltration into the battle zones, and releasing a few United States prisoners. The dilemma that followed was whether this mutual withdrawal would be interpreted as an opportunity for negotiations or a trap. Was either side, or were both, acting out of a condition of weakness? Would President Nixon take "risks for peace," as Secretary of State Rogers recommended? The reaction of North Vietnam was negative concerning mutual withdrawal, however, and Hanoi was adamant concerning unilateral withdrawal of United States troops. The military lull was punctuated during the summer by the revival of offensive action on the part of the North. Hanoi also questioned the fairness of the proposed elections and said they would be "under the menace of American bayonets." On July 27, 1969 President Thieu said that the election proposal was the final offer to the enemy and the peace talks reached a stalemate.[13] The Paris talks continued every Thursday with no new developments. Henry Cabot Lodge resigned as the United States representative and his place was taken by David Bruce, another experienced diplomat, but no real progress was made. On January 21, 1971 the 100th such meeting was held and all that could be said was that channels of communication and negotiation were kept open.

President Nixon in a statement on September 16, 1969 reviewed the position of the United States. He said: [14]

"We have denounced an imposed solution.

"We have proposed free elections organized by joint commissions under international supervision.

"We have offered withdrawal of the United States and allied forces over a twelve month period.

"We have declared we would retain no military bases.

"We have offered to negotiate supervised cease-fires under international supervision to facilitate the process of mutual withdrawal.

13. *Ibid.*, July 28, 1969.
14. *Dept. of State Bulletin*, LXI, No. 1580, p. 302.

"We have made clear we would settle for the *de facto* removal of North Vietnam forces as long as there are guarantees against their return.

"We and the Government of South Vietnam have announced that we are prepared to accept any political outcome which is arrived at through free elections.

"We are prepared to discuss the ten point program of the other side together with plans put forth by the other parties.

"The only item which is not negotiable is the right of the people of South Vietnam to determine their own future free of outside interference."

The former negotiators, W. Averell Harriman and Cyrus R. Vance, suggested that the United States at Paris call for a "cease fire in place." But halting the fighting entirely required prior agreement on the nature of the political settlement.

President Nixon had wanted an honorable solution and not just an end to the war in Vietnam. He had said early in his administration that he did not want to be the first president to face defeat in war. After a study by his advisers he was ready to travel to six Asian countries, Rumania and Great Britain for twelve days after July 22, 1969 to explain his new Asian Doctrine for the post-Vietnam War period. He desired a "lower posture" in Asia, but this would be dependent upon keeping the American commitment in South Vietnam. He wanted limited commitment. The pattern he sketched was conformity to all treaty commitments but he said, "Peace and progress in Asia must be shaped and protected primarily by Asian hands. . . . American contributions should come as a supplement to Asian energies and in response to Asian leadership." [15] Often economic rather than military aid could further Asian stability. The President said that the United States in no formal commitment is obligated to protect a country with combat troops against internal subversion or guerrilla insurgency. Nor when external invasions were involved was the United States obligated to play the primary role in defending nations that are incapable of mobilizing themselves for self defense. President Nixon stopped at Guam (a United States possession),[16] the Philippines, Indonesia, Thailand, South Vietnam, India, and Pakistan and then called at Rumania and Great Britain in Europe.

15. *New York Times,* July 23, 1969 and August 1, 1969.
16. The Nixon Doctrine that was the outcome of the Executive Agreement at Midway Island came to be known also as the Guam Doctrine because President Nixon explained the Vietnamization Doctrine to a group of newspaper reporters at Guam.

While President Nixon was enunciating the new Asian Doctrine he had Secretary of State Rogers visit Japan, South Korea and Taiwan to assure these countries that all treaties would be honored; and he had Senator Mike Mansfield, chairman of the subcommittee on Asian affairs of the Senate Foreign Relations Committee, make a followup trip in the same region to report on its reception. Senator Mansfield had a sixteen day trip to the Philippines, Indonesia, Burma, Laos and Cambodia and reported that the heads of state were generally pleased.[17]

The trip came immediately after the splashdown of Apollo 11 on July 24, 1969. Three American astronauts on July 20, 1969 were the first persons to arrive at the moon and two walked on its surface. This made a real occasion to capitalize upon the feeling of unity throughout the world that, even though momentarily, somehow transcended the attitudes of strife. The use of tracking stations throughout the world, arranged for by Executive Agreement of Class IV, seemed to hold the world together. The sharing of the experience of the moon flight with the people of the world through television emphasized the constructive side of foreign policy.

On September 5, 1969 it was announced that President Ho Chi Minh of North Vietnam had died. The Vietcong declared a three-day cease fire out of respect to the dead leader. What effect the death of Ho Chi Minh would have on peace negotiations and how the United States would react and respond only time would indicate. A new approach was increasingly urgent for the United States had never been as upset by any war as she was by the Vietnam War. Vietnam had become a symbol for everything that was wrong or vulnerable in the United States. It became a "token of the incomprehensible," for Revolutionary Warfare was a kind of conflict the United States did not fathom. In a nuclear age it seemed to be the kind of warfare that was realistically feasible, however.

On September 16, 1969 the United States announced, after a high level meeting had been held at the call of President Nixon in Washington on September 11, and after contacts with President Thieu had been made, that 35,000 more troops would be withdrawn by December 15, 1969;[18] and on April 20, 1970 it was announced that the withdrawal of an additional 150,000 Americans from Vietnam would take place within a year, bringing the total

17. *New York Times*, August 30, 1969.
18. *Ibid.*, July 16, 1969 and September 17, 1969.

of withdrawals to 260,000.[19] All of the arrangements for troop withdrawals were in the form of Executive Agreements of Class III with South Vietnam.

On September 18, 1969 President Nixon addressed the 24th General Assembly of the United Nations, giving special emphasis to the desire of the United States for cooperation of the 126 member states in making peace.[20]

Section C—Southeast Asia

The Nixon Policy of 1969 had repercussions throughout Southeast Asia. Withdrawals from Laos and Thailand, in addition to South Vietnam, were indicated for economy reasons as well as in response to anti-war agitation. The mood of the American people in 1969 was clearly for no more Vietnams.

The war in South Vietnam had involved Laos almost from the beginning, but this aspect was kept a "secret war." Laos had been recognized as an independent sovereign state by France in 1949, under the French Union; and the regime was recognized by the Communists in the cease-fire agreement with France, signed at Geneva July 21, 1954. There followed conflicts among the neutralist, Communist and conservative factions. Although Laos was to be neutral, rivalry between the Communist Pathet Lao movement in the northern third of the country, led by Prince Souphanouvong, and right-wing and neutralist factions prevented integration of the Pathet Lao into the royalist army. Armed conflict increased after 1960 with the arrival of Soviet arms and North Vietnamese technicians and troops. There was a cease-fire in 1961 and the three factions formed a coalition government in June, 1962 with Prince Souvanna Pouma as premier. A fourteen nation conference, that had begun at Geneva May 15, 1961, signed agreements July 23, 1962 guaranteeing the neutrality and independence of Laos. In 1964 the Pathet Lao had withdrawn from the coalition govern-

---

19. *Dept. of State Bulletin*, LXII, No. 1617, June 22, 1970.
20. *New York Times*, September 19, 1969.

On August 20, 1969 Ambassador Charles W. Yost, the United States delegate, asked the President of the Security Council of the United Nations for an early meeting of the fifteen-member committee formally to request that Secretary-General Thant place on the agenda of the 1969 General Assembly the item: "Creation of a category of associate membership." There were at that date 126 members. The Meldive Islands were a member with only 112 square miles of territory and 97,000 inhabitants. Talked of as a prospective member in 1969 was the Pacific Island of Nauru with 8.2 square miles and a population of 4,914! (See *New York Times*, August 21, 1969.)

ment, however, and with aid from North Vietnamese troops had renewed sporadic attacks on government positions. Both Laos and the United States planes also bombed Pathet Laos positions along the Ho Chi Minh Trail, supply line from North Vietnam to Communist forces in northern Laos and South Vietnam.[21]

Since 1967 the government had lost political control over provinces in the northeast. The cease-fire line of 1961 had divided the rightist areas of Laos from the neutralist and the Pathet Lao (Communist) areas, but if the North Vietnamese would penetrate into Vangvieng in the northwest, operating in the name of the Pathet Lao, the Laotian Government would be pushed behind the cease-fire line. This would give the Pathet Lao a military claim to dominance of Laos and a strong argument for dominance of the cabinet at about the time the Vietnam War might end.

The United States had supported the neutralist-rightist regime in the hope of keeping Laos a nominally neutral but basically anti-Communist country. The government had been totally dependent on American economic and military aid. In return the government had permitted the United States, as arranged by an Executive Agreement of Class III, to bomb the North Vietnamese routes through the Ho Chi Minh Trail, to use areas near the North Vietnam border to support bombing and spy missions against Hanoi, and to play an increasingly crucial role in the Laotian civil war.[22]

The Pathet Lao, on the other hand, became almost totally dependent on North Vietnamese troops, who actually did most of the fighting for the Pathet Lao. There had been a gradual erosion of the Government's position in the period since 1964. American arms, American supplies, American logistics, American bombing, American advice and Laotian soldiers had been a poor match for the modestly equipped but determined North Vietnamese infantry. The North Vietnamese were now in August, 1969 in a strong position to dislodge Government forces from two Laotian bases and to strike toward Vangvieng, the last major pro-Government neutralist position.

Because of the strictures of the Geneva Protocol of 1962 the United States faced a dilemma about disclosing its actions in Laos.[23] President Kennedy had established a branch of the United States AID mission in Laos, "staffed by retired military personnel

---

21. *Current History,* December 20, 1970, p. 327.
22. *New York Times,* August 25, 1969.
23. *Current History,* December 20, 1970, pp. 326–327.

in civilian clothes, under the name of the 'Requirements Office,' to handle military supplies," and President Johnson had announced in May and June, 1964 that "the United States reconnaissance planes were flying over Laos, . . . escorted by armed planes authorized to strike at antiaircraft batteries on the ground which were manned by Pathet Lao and North Vietnamese troops," and the large size of the military attachés office at the United States Embassy in Vientiane was publicly announced. Much else remained officially undisclosed, although it was written about by the press occasionally.

When the United States announced the Vietnamese Policy in the summer of 1969, the stakes behind intermittent fighting in August, 1969 were the makeup of the Laotian Government in the post-Vietnam War period and the foreign policy it would follow. In future talks aimed at reconstituting the three-way coalition of rightists, neutralists and the Pathet Lao, the Pathet Lao, it seemed, were intending to claim not only the four Cabinet seats that the old arrangement gave them, but also the eleven allotted to the neutralists.

During the summer of 1969 there had also developed a question of the relationship of the United States and Thailand. Thailand was a country that had never been conquered by a colonial power. After a bloodless revolution in 1932 a new constitution established a limited monarchy. Since World War II there had been several military coups and changes in government. On June 21, 1968 a new constitution provided for an appointed Senate, an elected House with limited powers and a Prime Minister. Sporadic Communist terrorism had occurred in the northeast and far south in 1968 and earlier.

In 1969 Senator J. W. Fulbright, Chairman of the Foreign Relations Committee, learned of a plan "worked out by the United States and Thailand in 1965 to cope, if necessary, with a major Communist invasion threat to Thailand through Laos. If Laos were invaded, the plan called for Thai and American forces to move into southern Laos to preserve the region as a buffer zone protecting Thailand. Senator Fulbright and others in Congress were concerned that the plan might envelop the United States in a Vietnam-type war in Thailand. They became particularly incensed when their efforts to get a copy of the plan were originally rebuffed by the Pentagon.[24]

24. *New York Times,* August 31, 1969.

On July 10, 1969 the Department of State confirmed that the United States had signed a secret defense pact, i.e. an Executive Agreement of Class III, with Thailand in 1965; and it was described as a "military contingency plan" within the framework of previous United States commitments to Thailand. There was senatorial criticism of the 1965 plan itself for it seemed that the United States forces might be under Thai control. Secretary of Defense Laird said that the plan did not have the approval of President Nixon and was not binding. This, of course, raised the old question of whether one Administration should be bound by the Executive Agreements of previous ones.

In 1969 about 49,000 United States servicemen, two thirds of them Air Force, were stationed in Thailand and air strikes against the Ho Chi Minh Trail in Laos were conducted from air bases constructed by the United States in Thailand. Also about 10,000 Thai combat troops served with the South Vietnamese in South Vietnam and were paid for by the United States. These arrangements had been made by Executive Agreements of Class III.

Out of pique over the senatorial criticism the Foreign Minister of Thailand asked for talks on American troop withdrawals. These were scheduled for September 1, 1969 in Bangkok but did not seem to represent a real desire on the part of either side for the withdrawal of the troops in Thailand, before the Vietnam issue was settled. The talks did represent to the world, however, the assertion of independence on the part of Thailand.

Section D—Congressional Criticism

In 1969 Senator Fulbright, chairman of the Foreign Relations Committee, reopened the issue of the conflict of relations between the Executive and the Congress, when he submitted Senate Resolution 85, the language of which duplicated that of Senate Resolution 151 of 1967.[25] The resolution was reported out on March 12,

---

25. In 1967 on July 31 Senator Fulbright introduced a broad resolution (Senate Resolution 151) declaring it to be the sense of the Senate that a United States commitment to a foreign power "necessarily and exclusively" resulted from affirmative action by the executive and legislative branches of the government and a commitment meant any kind of International Agreement. After consideration a new draft was evolved and was presented by Senator Fulbright, on November 20, 1967, as Senate Resolution 187. This one was confined to one type of commitment, i.e. the commitment of armed forces to hostilities on foreign territory. A commitment for purposes other than to repel an attack on the United States or to protect citizens or property would result from a decision made according to constitutional processes, i.e. Executive action plus Congressional action "specifically intended to

1969 and immediately brought a reaction from the State Department. On June 22, 1969 Senator Fulbright said on the American Broadcasting Company's program "Issues and Answers" that the Senate Foreign Relations Committee would open hearings on Vietnam and re-evaluate the American policy.[26]

On June 25, 1969, after five days of debate, the Senate approved by a vote of 70 to 16 Resolution 85 calling on the Executive Branch not to commit troops or financial resources to foreign countries without the express approval of Congress.[27] The resolution was not binding on the Executive but it did indicate that the Executive would be under pressure to give greater weight to Congressional opinions in its foreign policy decisions because of this resolution. The President was opposed to the resolution but the sponsors emphasized that the resolution was to restore the constitutional balance between the Executive Branch and Congress, especially in the use of the war power.

Congressional debate continued through the summer and fall of 1969. Its height coincided with the October 15th nationwide "Moratorium" anti-war demonstrations and to a lesser extent with the November 15, 1969 mass rally in Washington. Various amendments to current bills were introduced to limit activities in Laos and Thailand.[28] On August 12, 1969 an amendment to the Defense Procurement Bill (S2546), limiting United States aid to forces in South Vietnam and local forces in Laos and Thailand to $2.5 billion, became law. A related proposal, approved by the Senate on September 17, 1969, to limit such aid to material and equipment was abandoned in the bill's final version, however. On October 20, 1969 a special Senate Foreign Relations Subcommittee on United States commitments abroad began closed hearings on Laos. (These minutes were published with some deletions on April 17, 1970.) On December 15, 1969 the Senate approved an amendment to the Defense Appropriations Bill (HR15090) to prohibit the introduction of United States ground combat troops in Laos and Thailand and this bill became law. The House on December 2, 1969, by a 334–55 roll-call vote, passed a resolution supporting the President's efforts to achieve "peace with justice" and by the end of the year debate was again muted.

give rise to such a commitment." Congress took no action on Senate Resolution 187 after it was reported out of committee.
26. *New York Times*, June 23, 1969.
27. *Congressional Quarterly, Weekly Report,* January–February, 1970, p. 14.
28. *Ibid.,* January–February, 1970, pp. 11 and 14.

Section E—Developments in Southeast Asia in 1970

1970 was to bring developments in Southeast Asia which had bearing on the war and on United States commitments. On March 6, 1970 President Nixon made a statement for the first time revealing the United States' involvement in Laos.[29] He said that the United States had no ground troops in Laos and that there were no treaties but that at the request of the Royal Laotian Government the United States had provided logistical and other assistance to that government for the purpose of helping it to prevent the Communist conquest of Laos. Air power had been used to interdict the flow of North Vietnamese troops and supplies on that part of the Ho Chi Minh Trail that runs through Laos. Reconnaissance missions in North Laos had been flown in defense against North Vietnamese aggression and "some other activities" had been engaged in. This cooperation was by Executive Agreement of Class I. The policy of official silence about Laos was therefore ended.

In March, 1970 attention was directed to Cambodia. It was the third of the protocol countries in the SEATO protection. It was a country that had originally been a French protectorate, but in 1949, after World War II, it had become an associated state within the French Union. In 1953 it had declared its independence from France. On November 20, 1963 it had severed economic and military ties with the United States, charging United States interference in its affairs and in March, 1964 it had sent military missions to Communist China and the U.S.S.R. to purchase arms. Because of an attack on Cambodian villages by South Vietnamese planes Prince Sihanouk broke off diplomatic relations with the United States in May, 1965, accusing the United States and Thailand of border violations. The United States and South Vietnam charged that the Vietcong forces had attacked their troops from Cambodian soil. "The intrusion of United States troops into Vietnam in 1965–1966 and the intensified bombing of Laos and North Vietnam in 1966–1968 forced the Communists to use Cambodian territory first as a rest and staging area and later as their principal avenue of supply."[30] At this juncture Prince Sihanouk was convinced that the Communists would be the winners and he, therefore, permitted Cambodian rice and other supplies to pass into

---

29. *Department of State Bulletin,* LXII, No. 1605, March 30, 1970.
30. *Current History,* December, 1970, p. 334.

Communist hands through illicit channels. But the Communist victory was not a swift one and Prince Sihanouk began to have doubts.[31] In 1967 and 1968 he charged that Vietnamese and Thailand Communists were supplying arms to Cambodian insurgents, who were terrorizing remote villages and he contended that Communist China was behind these troubles.

By November, 1968 the Cambodian Government had been asking the International Control Commission, which had been established by the 1954 Geneva Conference to insure that the Geneva accords were carried out, to investigate and document the presence of North Vietnamese and Vietcong troops within its territory. This was a departure from the previous Cambodian attitude of asking the Commission to investigate only intrusions of American and South Vietnamese forces. The shifting attitude seemed to have been motivated by the fear that the North Vietnamese and the Vietcong troops that had been using the country as a springboard into South Vietnam might not be willing to quit Cambodian territory after a Vietnamese cease fire. It would seem, therefore, that there was a movement toward the United States once more and a desire to renew diplomatic relations. In 1969 Prince Sihanouk had begun to seek guarantees from the West and on June 11, 1969 the United States announced an agreement in principle, an Executive Agreement of Class IV, with Cambodia on the reestablishing of diplomatic relations, which had been interrupted in May, 1965.

In August, 1969 Prince Sihanouk abdicated a considerable portion of his power to a "government of salvation" under Lon Nol, Minister of Defense, aided by Prince Sihanouk's cousin, Sisowath Sirik Matak, an efficient administrator. At this point Prince Sihanouk was near a breakdown and in January, 1970 he left for medical treatment and rest in France. In February, 1970 a governmental fiscal manoeuvre rendered Cambodian currency held by the Vietnamese Communists temporarily worthless, thus making it impossible for them to purchase rice and other supplies from Cambodian peasants.[32]

In March, 1970 Prince Sihanouk started for home, stopping in Moscow and Peking to obtain guarantees against any more extensive North Vietnamese incursions.

On March 8, 1970 two days after President Nixon's statement

31. *Current History*, December, 1970, p. 334.
32. *Ibid.*, pp. 335–336.

on Laos, a series of events began that were to exert an influence on the war and on American involvement. "On March 8, 1970 villagers in the Cambodian province of Svay Rieng demonstrated against the Vietcong; on March 11, the North Vietnamese and Vietcong embassies in Cambodia were sacked; and on March 18, 1970 the Cambodian Chief of State, Prince Norodom Sihanouk, was deposed by unanimous vote of the Cambodian Parliament. Shortly afterward, the trade and payments agreement between Cambodia and the Vietcong government, under which the latter purchased supplies and held transit rights through Cambodia, was suspended by decision of the new Pnompenh government. . . . With their supply route by sea and air through Cambodia suddenly closed off, the North Vietnamese needed to make absolutely sure of the security of the Ho Chi Minh Trail through Laos and to increase its carrying capacity. . . ."[33] On April 30, Communist forces seized the town of Attopec in southeastern Laos, which had been in Royal Government hands continuously since the June 24, 1962 cease-fire."[34] On June 9, the Laotian provincial capital of Saravene fell to the Communists—"a violation of the 1962 cease-fire line," ostensibly "to foil American plans for introducing South Vietnamese and Thai troops into the region."[35]

After March 18, 1970 when the North Vietnamese saw that the new government of Cambodia was not willing to permit a continuation of the wide scope of misuse of its territory,[36] a decision was made by the North Vietnamese to expel the Cambodian Government presence from the border areas and to move militarily against the Cambodian army with the view of linking up all sanctuaries and the Port of Sihanoukville on the Gulf of Siam. This would have produced a unified and protected sanctuary from the Gulf of Siam to Laos with virtually unrestricted movement and unlimited supply access. From April 20th to the 30th the Communists launched a series of attacks against a number of key cities in central Cambodia.

33. *Ibid.*, p. 329.
A military tribunal soon condemned Prince Sihanouk to death if he should return to Cambodia (*Current History*, December, 1970, p. 337) and on October 9, 1970 Cambodia was declared a Republic (*Current History*, December, 1970, p. 373).
34. *Current History*, December, 1970, p. 329.
35. *Ibid.*
36. *Department of State Bulletin*, LXII, No. 1617, June 22, 1970:
"According to the Fifth Hague Convention of 1907 a neutral may not allow belligerents to move troops or supplies across its territory, or to regroup forces on its territory. A neutral is obliged to take positive action to prevent such abuse of its neutrality, either by attempting to expel the belligerent forces or to intern them."

This threat provoked the United States and the South Vietnamese, without first getting the permission of Cambodia, to move in and destroy the sanctuaries in May and June, 1970.[37] The mission was successful, according to President Nixon; the contingents were withdrawn the end of June, 1970; and a whole new chapter of Congressional agitation was started.

President Nixon explained that the United States could have obtained advance permission from Cambodia but in that case the neutrality of Cambodia would have been compromised and the United States would have moved closer to a situation in which the United States was committing its armed forces to help Cambodia defend itself against North Vietnam's attack. He emphasized that the United States was not in Cambodia to defend the Cambodian Government but to help defend South Vietnam and the United States troops in South Vietnam from continuing North Vietnamese attack. The United States did not wish to see Cambodia become a cobelligerent along with South Vietnam and the United States. Such a procedure, President Nixon said, was consonant with his Vietnamization Doctrine, which he had restated on November 3, 1969 and on February 18, 1970.[38]

Since the President had announced on April 20, 1970 the withdrawal of an additional 150,000 Americans from Vietnam within a year, bringing the total to 260,000, he stated in June, 1970: "If the enemy took advantage of this by increased attacks in Cambodia, Laos or South Vietnam in a way that endangered the lives of our men remaining in South Vietnam, I would, in my capacity as Commander-in-Chief of our Armed Forces take strong action to deal with that threat." [39]

This rationalization of the action of the United States presented a new line of reasoning. Up to 1970 the legal basis for the Vietnam War was the Tonkin Bay Joint Resolution (78 Stat. 384) with the ensuing Executive Agreements, and the responsibilities under the SEATO Treaty. Senatorial hearings and debate had emphasized these two sources. The new assertion of the President was consonant with the reply, dated March 12, 1970, of the Department of State to a letter from Senator Fulbright of the Senate Foreign Relations Committee, sent December 11, 1969, in which it was

37. *Department of State Bulletin*, LXII, No. 1617, June 22, 1970:
"According to the Fifth Hague Convention of 1907 a neutral may not allow belligerents to move troops or supplies across its territroy, or to regroup forces on its territory. A neutral is obliged to take positive action to prevent such abuse of its neutrality, either by attempting to expell the belligerent forces or to intern them."
38. *Ibid.*, LXII, No. 1617, p. 766.
39. *Ibid.*, LXII, No. 1617, p. 761.

stated that the Nixon Administration had not relied on or referred to the Tonkin Bay Resolution of August 10, 1964 as support for its Vietnam policy. However, it was pointed out in this reply that repeal of the Resolution might create a wrong impression abroad.[40]

The Senate still felt the Tonkin Bay Joint Resolution to be important. On June 24, 1970 that body in an amendment to the Military Sales Bill (HR 15628) had voted for its repeal and again on July 10, 1970 a Senate Concurrent Resolution was passed by the Senate. This second effort was due to the fact that a Concurrent Resolution requires passage of both houses but does not require the President's signature.

The incursion into Cambodia precipitated a reaction in Congress expressed in an avalanche of proposed bills and resolutions on the war-making powers of the President. These ranged from the suggested repeal of the Tonkin Bay Joint Resolution to the limitation of the number of United States troops by specific dates; to limitation of the use of funds; to prohibition of the use of draftees in South Vietnam, Laos or Cambodia unless they had volunteered for such duty or had voluntarily extended their enlistment; to a split of a prized destroyer contract among two shipyards; to delay of authorization of arms to Israel; to the Cooper-Church Amendment to the Military Sales Bill (HR 15628).

This Cooper-Church Amendment was adopted on June 30, 1970 by the Senate and it read originally as follows: "In concert with the declared objectives of the President of the United States to avoid the involvement of the United States in Cambodia after July 1, 1970, and to expedite the withdrawal of American forces from Cambodia, it is hereby provided that unless specifically authorized by law hereafter enacted, no funds authorized or appropriated pursuant to this act or any other law may be expended after July 1, 1970 for the purpose of (1) retaining United States forces in Cambodia; (2) paying the compensation or allowances of, or otherwise supporting, directly or indirectly, any United States personnel in Cambodia who furnish military instruction to Cambodian forces or engage in any combat activity in support of Cambodian forces; (3) entering into or carrying out any contract or agreement to provide military instruction in Cambodia, or to provide persons to engage in any combat activity in support of Cambodian forces; or (4) conducting any combat activity in the air above Cambodia in direct support of Cambodian forces.

40. *Department of State Bulletin*, LXII, No. 1606, April 6, 1970, p. 470.

"Nothing contained in this section shall be deemed to impugn the constitutional power of the President as Commander-in-Chief, including the exercise of that constitutional power which may be necessary to protect the lives of United States armed forces wherever deployed.

"Nothing contained in this section shall be deemed to impugn the constitutional powers of the Congress including the power to declare war and to make rules for the government and regulation of the armed forces of the United States." [41]

On October 8, 1970, in a televised address to the nation, President Nixon outlined what he termed "a major new initiative for peace" in Indochina. He made five specific proposals as follows:

"First, I propose that all armed forces throughout Indochina cease firing their weapons and remain in a position they now hold. This would be a cease-fire in place. It would not in itself be an end to the conflict, but it would accomplish one goal all of us have been working toward; an end to the killing. . . .

"A second point of the new initiative for peace is this: I propose an Indochina peace conference. . . .

"The third part of our peace initiative has to do with the United States forces in South Vietnam. . . . We are ready now to negotiate an agreed timetable for complete withdrawal as part of an overall settlement. . . .

"Fourth, I ask the other side to join us in a search for a political settlement that truly meets the aspirations of all South Vietnamese. . . .

"Finally, I propose the immediate and unconditional release of all prisoners of war held by both sides. . . ." [42]

All of the attempts to reaffirm the power of Congress were incomplete as the 91st Congress was ending in December, 1970, due in large part to an extensive use of filibustering and the slow movement of bills through conference committees. At the last minute before the adjournment of Congress there was a spurt of activity. On December 22, 1970 the Senate passed the Foreign Aid Bill (HR 19911) and incorporated into it an abbreviated version of the Cooper-Church Amendment preventing the President from using any funds to introduce ground troops or military advisers into Cambodia and stipulating that the military aid program did

---

41. *Congressional Quarterly, Weekly Report,* July to September, 1970, pp. 1674, 1777–1779, 2170–2173.
42. *Current History,* December, 1970, p. 362.

not constitute a defense commitment to the Cambodian Government. The Senate provision was accepted by conferees of the House Foreign Affairs Committee and was incorporated into the compromise foreign aid legislation, which authorized $525-million in supplementary foreign aid for countries in Asia ($255-million for Cambodia) and the Middle East. This aid legislation was sent to the House, where it was adopted by a voice vote and sent to President Nixon for signature.[43]

A deadlock in the House-Senate Conference on the Military Sales Bill (HR 15628) had lasted since July, 1970 because of the Senate-adopted Cooper-Church Amendment on June 30, 1970 and the Amendment Repealing the Tonkin Bay Resolution on July 10, 1970. The acceptance of the Cooper-Church Amendment in its condensed form in the Foreign Aid Bill opened the way for the Senate supporters of such restrictions to relinquish their insistence on its inclusion in the Military Sales Bill, thus finally clearing the way for action on HR 15628. On December 31, 1970 the House-Senate Conferees filed a report on HR 15628 and among other items in this report there remained the agreement to the Senate Amendment repealing the Tonkin Bay Resolution. (The Senate Resolution (S Con Res (64)) had never been reported out by the House Foreign Affairs Committee where it was tied up as a result of the Cooper-Church Amendment.) The House Conferees now on December 31, 1970 stated that "recent legislation and Executive statements made the 1964 resolution unnecessary for the prosecution of United States foreign policy," and accepted the Conference Report. The Senate by voice vote accepted the Conference Report on the Military Sales Bill on January 2, 1971 and the way was cleared for the President's signature to HR 15628, financing credit sales of United States military materiel to foreign countries. It was made clear in the Bill that appropriations for military sales should not be made without prior authorization by Congress.

This action ended, for the time being, a long Congressional debate over the issue of imposing Congressional restrictions on the President's war-making powers. The aid legislation, containing a modified version of the Cooper-Church Amendment, the Military Sales Bill, containing the amendment repealing the Tonkin Bay Resolution, and the Amendment to the Defense Appropriations Bill of December, 1969 (HR 15090) to prohibit the introduction

43. *New York Times,* December 23, 1970.

of United States ground combat troops in Laos and Thailand, all take their place with the National Commitments Resolution of the Senate on June 25, 1969 in reaffirming, if not reestablishing, the powers of Congress against commitment by Executive Agreement. Congress had reasserted its control over monies used to finance the war in Asia and was rediscovering its legitimate weapon against Executive prerogatives.

Section F—The Pacific

By 1970 the Nixon Policy was recognizing realities and finding its expression in new Executive Agreements in the Pacific. The independent nations of Pacific Asia had grown in strength and confidence and the Nixon Policy was to support and encourage them in combating insurgency; was to respect the commitments of the United States; and was to have the United States remain a Pacific power.

In the many cases in which the United States had commitments of assistance it was only in the Mutual Defense Treaty with Japan that the use of United States troops was assured. According to the Constitution of Japan after World War II, Article IX stipulated that "land, sea and air forces, as well as other war potential, will never be maintained." The Constitution did provide, however, for Japanese "self-defense" forces and these grew to number 250,000 in 1969.

The United States–Japan Mutual Security Treaty of September 8, 1951 expressed the hope that Japan would increasingly assume responsibility for her own defense but Japan was under no obligation to defend any territory of the United States. The treaty stated that the United States had the right to dispose its land, sea and air forces in and about Japan and that these forces might be used not only to protect Japan from external attack but also "to contribute to the maintenance of international peace and security in the Far East." Japan could not grant bases or military facilities to a third power without United States consent.[44] The treaty was renegotiated later and on January 19, 1960 a revised Security Treaty was signed. This treaty provided that any attack against territory under the administration of Japan would be considered dangerous and each party would act to meet the common danger "in accordance with its constitutional processes." Article IV gave

---

44. *Current History*, August, 1969, pp. 94 ff.

Japan the right to assent to the disposition of land, sea and air forces of the United States in and about Japan and Japan was not denied the right to make similar concessions to a third power. This treaty was to expire January 19, 1970.

The bases of the United States in Japan covered 98,000 acres and were manned by 39,300 American servicemen. In the late 60's there was a reaction in Japan against the United States' having bases in that country and against her having nuclear power there. The largest opposition group was the Socialist Party, which advocated a national policy of unarmed neutrality. Early in June, 1969 a United States Phantom jet fighter plane, attempting to land at the Itazuke Air Base, crashed into a computer center under construction on the campus of Kyushu University. The crash triggered violent demonstrations. There were also controversies about the establishment of a United States hospital for soldiers wounded in Vietnam on the outskirts of Tokyo because, it was stated, it would interfere with schools.[45] The Japanese felt that some of the bases could be merged and others could be eliminated entirely. Japan had prospered and the 98,000 acres represented valuable housing and land for industrial expansion. One solution was to relocate the bases on sparsely populated areas but alternate sites were hard to find.[46]

Certain islands taken from Japan in World War II were retained by the United States as possible military bases with the understanding that they would eventually be returned to Japan. On June 26, 1968 the following islands were returned to Japanese control and administration by Executive Agreement of Class I: the Bonin Islands with an area of about 40 square miles, south of Japan; the Volcano Islands, south of the Bonins, including Iwo Jima (about eight square miles), scene of the famous World War II battle; and Marcus Island, about one square mile east of the Volcanoes. In 1968 agreement provided that the United States would continue the use of navigational stations on Iwo Jima and Marcus.[47]

Another problem with Japan was the continued United States administration of the Ryukyu Islands, including Okinawa. Since American servicemen living on Okinawa were subject to American laws and not Okinawa's the Japanese thought of Okinawa as

---

45. *New York Times*, June 23, 1969.
46. *Ibid.*
47. *World Almanac of 1970*, p. 679.

occupied territory. Many Japanese wanted the installations at the air and naval bases to be subject to the same restrictions that were imposed on American bases in Japan by the Mutual Security Treaty. Under these rules the United States would not be able to keep nuclear weapons on the Ryukyu Islands and she could not use her forces that were based there for operation against other countries without Japan's consent.

Okinawa was a major supply depot for the Vietnam War, a repair shop, and a staging area. It was used as a base for bombing raids against North Vietnam. If war broke out in Korea, Okinawa would be vital for air strikes and supply operations. Also the Ryukyus were a shield between mainland China and the Philippines, Indonesia and the rest of Southeast Asia. Okinawa was a base for a variety of nuclear weapons for use if necessary against China or elsewhere.[48]

Although Okinawa was a financial burden and received about $17 million in economic aid each year and although the United States had long acknowledged the "residual sovereignty" of Japan over Okinawa, that island was regarded so vital to the defense of East Asia that the United States declined to set a time limit for revision until her military requirements were guaranteed. Premier Eisaku Satu was scheduled to have conferences in the United States in November, 1969 concerning these problems. Meanwhile the Okinawa issue was attaining crisis level in Japan.

On December 21, 1970 the United States announced the long-awaited plans to take most of the combat forces out of Japan, reducing personnel by 12,000, to a total of 28,000 by mid-1971. A high-level consultative committee, meeting under the United States–Japanese Security Treaty, had announced an Executive Agreement of Class I for reductions as a result of worldwide reassessment of American military forces, in response to the Nixon Doctrine "to lower the American profile" but also as a result of the need to reduce over-all defense costs.

F-4 Phantom fighter-bombers would be deployed to bases in South Korea and Okinawa. The United States Seventh Fleet headquarters would be moved from Yokosuka naval base near Yokohama to Sasebo in southern Japan. The Yokota base west of Tokyo would remain an important military air transport facility and Misawa in the north would become little more than a housekeeping operation. The Marine Air Station at Iwakuni in south Japan

48. *New York Times,* June 23, 1969.

would be retained to support Marine ground troops, all of whom were based on Okinawa. The United States would retain one drydock at Yokosuka—the only Navy-controlled drydock west of Pearl Harbor that could repair large aircraft carriers.[49]

It was also announced on December 21, 1970 that American forces in Okinawa numbering 40,000 would be reduced by 5,000 as several Air Force and Army facilities would be closed down. The island was to be returned to Japanese rule by 1972. Ten thousand Japanese employees and 2,800 Okinawans would lose their jobs as a result of these moves. The talks concerning Okinawa were not complete at this time but full agreement was expected by mid-1972. A list of American built and American utilized facilities had been drawn up for desired reversion. One was the Naha military port, the largest protected port in Okinawa. Others were the Naha airfield as well as the Naha-Machinato housing area of 1179 housing units, or 41% of the available Army quarters on Okinawa. Part of the White Beach area, across the island from Naha Harbor, was also desired, as well as a petroleum storage area near Naha known as the Yogi tank farm and a billeting area with barracks and officers' quarters near Naha port. The United States' position was that if such transfers would take place the Japanese would have to provide similar facilities at no cost to the American taxpayers.[50]

The Fifth Japan–United States Conference on Cultural and Educational Interchange was held on March 18–23, 1970 at Tokyo. A comuniqué at the end served as an Executive Agreement of Class IV.

Korea also had attention in announced shifts. President Park Chung Hee of the Republic of Korea made an official visit to the United States from August 20 to 24, 1969 and he and President Nixon, on August 22, 1969, made a joint statement constituting for the United States an Executive Agreement of Class I.[51] It was agreed that the forces of Korea and the United States in Korea must remain strong and that the United States and Korea would meet armed attack from North Korea in accordance with the Mutual Defense Treaty. President Park expressed agreement with the proposals of President Nixon in his address to the American nation on May 14, 1969 and President Nixon expressed appreciation for the contribution of Korean troops in Vietnam. The

---

49. *Ibid.*, December 22, 1970.
50. *Ibid.*
51. *Department of State Bulletin*, LXI, No. 1577, September 15, 1969.

United States was to continue to extend technical cooperation, would invest in Korea and would cooperate in having joint, mutually beneficial ventures. The two heads of state agreed on strengthening existing organizations and institutions for East Asian and Pacific regional cooperation, for it was stated that Asian countries were contributing to the security of the East Asian and Pacific region, as well as to their own security.

As part of a series of steps ordered by the Department of Defense to "consolidate activities, improve efficiency and achieve cost savings in operations" of the American forces in the Pacific and East Asian area, two Air Force units would be moved from Japan to Korea by June, 1971.

In the summer of 1970 the Nixon Administration announced that the authorized United States troop strength of 64,000 in Korea would be reduced by 20,000. Since then, however, the State Department's officials argued that further cuts in the near future might give Asians the impression that the United States was making a hasty retreat from the Far East despite its pledge to fulfill its commitments there. President Nixon, therefore, directed the Defense Department to delay indefinitely plans for withdrawals from South Korea beyond the 20,000 men scheduled to be removed by June, 1971.[52]

In the Philippines in 1970 the United States had the Subic Naval Base, the Sangley Point Naval Base and the Clark Air Base. In December, 1970 the United States Ambassador announced through an Executive Agreement of Class I that in 1971 Sangley Point Naval Base was to be returned to the Philippines. President Marcos had instructed his Foreign Affairs Department to request this in a diplomatic note of November 3, 1970. The note said that the Philippine Navy and Coast Guard needed the installation. The note was followed by a Philippine request for immediate renegotiation of the Military Bases Agreement of 1947. The move was made after weeks of protest over a series of jurisdictional disputes involving the killing of Filipinos within United States bases. There had been 35 Filipinos killed inside the bases since 1947 and in no case had the Philippines obtained jurisdiction. Students and politicians took to the streets. The Government, however, would have to find jobs for the 25,000 Filipinos employed in the main

52. *U.S. News and World Report*, December 28, 1970, p. 20 and *New York Times*, January 3, 1971.

United States base but some complained that the Government had made no preparation for the change-over.[53]

In Taiwan the forces of the United States were reduced from 10,000 to 9,000 in 1970 in keeping with the general policy of Vietnamization.[54]

Section G—European Adjustments

The European scene also called for negotiation rather than confrontation under the Nixon Administration. For several years there had been a movement for better relations between the Soviet Union and the United States but the Soviet military aggression against Czechoslovakia in August, 1968 and her renewed militancy had interrupted the détente. The United States maintained that the Czechoslovakia incident was a violation of the United Nations Charter but avoided deliberate provocation. Cooperation did seem to be necessary on such issues as disarmament, the Middle East and Vietnam. There was also need for improved markets and political ties of the West with East Europe, for bridges to the East were a necessary part of the Nixon program. NATO was also weighing approaches to Moscow for a mutual reduction of armed forces and for peace in East Europe. In March, 1969 the U.S.S.R. had proposed in Budapest a European Security Pact, and the Soviet Union had quietly improved relations with her neighbors, offering to extend a pipeline from Soviet oilfields across Poland and East Germany to West Germany.

The Nixon Administration reported on June 26, 1969 that a five-man team to negotiate on missile limitation with the U.S.S.R. had been chosen;[55] these negotiations, suggested in the Non-Proliferation Treaty, were expected to start in the late summer or fall. Mr. Gromyko in his address to the Supreme Soviet, as reported on July 10, 1969, welcomed the approach of negotiations. These Strategic Arms Limitation Talks, called SALT, were started at Helsinki in November, 1969. They were continued at Vienna, then back at Helsinki in 1970 and were to continue at Vienna on March 15, 1971. The first sessions were devoted to a preliminary agreement and assessment of the course to be taken. Both the

---

53. *New York Times*, December 25, 1970.
54. *U.S. News and World Report*, December 28, 1970, p. 21.
55. *New York Times*, June 27, 1969 and July 23, 1969.

United States and the U.S.S.R. were motivated by the same desire for economy and for survival.

The status of limitations expressed by treaties and accepted by both the United States and the U.S.S.R. when the talks began can be summarized as follows: [56] a treaty banning military activities in Antarctica; a treaty banning the orbiting of weapons of mass destruction in outer space and prohibiting the establishment of military installations on the moon or other celestial bodies; and a treaty prohibiting the testing of nuclear weapons in the atmosphere, under water and in outer space.

Already at Geneva at the Disarmament Conference of the United Nations there were signs of the ability of the United States and the U.S.S.R. to work together. They were able to agree on adding six countries to the group increasing the membership to 26. The Conference had started in 1962 with 18 members and two more had been added in May, 1969. The ideological balance of the Conference was kept by the new additions, with the United States and four allies and the U.S.S.R. and four allies, plus non-aligned members. France had boycotted the talks from the start and some western members had remonstrated that the increase in membership converted the Conference of 18 into a debating society.

On March 18, 1969, when the 17 nation Disarmament Conference had reopened after a seven month recess, the Soviet representatives had submitted a draft treaty to outlaw nuclear weapons and military installations from the seabed and the ocean floor beyond the twelve mile offshore territorial limit.[57] On March 25, 1969 the United States delegate told the Conference that the United States rejected the Soviet proposal for demilitarizing the ocean floor as "simply unworkable"; [58] but on August 22, 1969 the Soviet Union was ready to accept the United States proposal to ban nuclear weapons and other weapons of mass destruction from the seabed and to shelve for the present its demand for complete demilitarization of the ocean floor.[59] A draft of a new treaty on prohibition of emplacement of nuclear weapons and other weapons of mass destruction on the seabed and ocean floor and in the subsoil thereof was presented at the Conference of the Committee on Disarmament at Geneva by the United States and the U.S.S.R. on October 7, 1969 and a revised joint draft was pre-

56. *Department of State Bulletin*, LXI, No. 1588, December 1, 1969, p. 466.
57. *New York Times*, March 19, 1969.
58. *Ibid.*, March 26, 1969.
59. *Ibid.*, August 23, 1969.

sented on October 30, 1969.[60] This treaty was signed by the United States on February 11, 1971.

A subcommittee of the Committee on the Peaceful Uses of Outer Space, a committee of the United Nations, met on June 8 and by June 27, 1969 the United States, the U.S.S.R. and 26 other nations had agreed in principle that international, rather than national, law should be used to determine liability for damage caused by spacecraft.[61] The subcommittee was working on the legal aspects of a proposed convention on liability for damage caused by space vehicles but whether to fix a ceiling on damages was still to be decided.

United States–U.S.S.R. cultural relations had been maintained in spite of the break in the détente when Czechoslovakia was invaded. A University of Minnesota band, a Duquesne University performing arts group, and an educational exhibit were sent to tour the U.S.S.R., having been arranged for by Executive Agreements of Class IV; and an art exhibit was sent by the U.S.S.R. to the State University of New York at Binghamton in 1968. Expanded cultural relations were due for negotiations later in 1969. An Executive Agreement of Class IV on new chancelleries for the respective embassies was reached after years of trying and on July 22, 1969 the United States accepted in principle, by Executive Agreement of Class IV, a Soviet proposal for opening a Soviet consulate in San Francisco and a United States consulate in Leningrad.[62]

There were also signs of stronger bonds in Central Europe that affected the attitude of the United States. With the growing doubt that the United States as a member of NATO would risk a nuclear war with the Soviet Union by defending Western Europe from a Soviet attack, the Assembly of the Western European Union, meeting in Paris the weekend of June 21, 1969, advocated the need for a more closely integrated defense effort and discussed the pros and cons of an independent nuclear deterrent based on existing British and French nuclear forces.[63] Europe's interest had been increasing because of the possible effect on Europe of an agreement between the United States and the Soviet Union in the projected strategic arms limitation talks (SALT) of the fall and winter of 1969. If in the potential agreement there were a provision for a military dis-

60. *Department of State Bulletin*, LXI, No. 1584 and 1588.
61. *New York Times*, June 28, 1969.
62. *Ibid.*, July 23, 1969.
63. *Ibid.*, June 22, 1969.

engagement in Central Europe that would reduce American conventional forces in Germany, there was thought to be strong reason for a European nuclear force. Since European members of NATO had consistently failed to meet the conventional force levels set by the Organization, the only alternative was said to be a tactical European nuclear force capable of deterring Soviet aggression. The France-Britain nuclear cooperation would help admit Great Britain to the Common Market but questions remained. Would the United States accept a French-British agreement giving France access to nuclear information that originally came to Great Britain from the United States? Meanwhile the claims for the cost of moving United States and NATO installations from France, totaling $600 million, were submitted to France on June 18, 1969. The claims generally covered the cost of airfields, barracks, pipelines and other permanent installations that had to be abandoned in 1966 and 1967 at President de Gaulle's request. The claims were split into two broadly equal parts, one representing purely American interests, the other those of all of the NATO members including the United States.[64]

President Nixon early in his administration reaffirmed the American commitment to NATO. In 1970 he decided not to withdraw any American forces because a sudden or major withdrawal would have a distinctly destabilizing effect on the European scene. Other members might be tempted to withdraw, if American troops were reduced in number.[65]

On July 9, 1969 the United States and West Germany had a new agreement, an Executive Agreement of Class I, for offsetting foreign exchange costs of American forces in Germany for United States fiscal years of 1970 and 1971. It provided for inflow of foreign exchange to the United States in the amount of $1.52 billion. This would be achieved by $925 million of procurement of United States goods and services and $595 million of financial measures.[66]

The United States had also been building bridges to Eastern Europe for some time. In 1964 the United States and Hungary had arranged by Executive Agreement of Class IV to elevate their diplomatic missions from legations to embassies and to exchange ambassadors for the first time since Hungary was overrun in 1956.

---

64. *New York Times*, June 20, 1969 and *American Journal of International Law*, July, 1968, pp. 577–640.
65. *Department of State Bulletin*, LXI, No. 1571 and LXII, No. 1598; and *New York Times*, December 25, 1970.
66. *Department of State Bulletin*, LXI, No. 1571, August 4, 1969.

On August 15, 1969 the United States and Hungary announced a four point understanding, which was an Executive Agreement of Class IV. It provided: "1) for the establishment of a Hungarian trade office in New York to increase Hungarian trade with the United States; 2) for a means of payment for Hungary's surplus-property debt to the United States; 3) for the increased staffing of the two countries' respective embassies to 32; and 4) for a start of American Social Security pension payments to some 300 beneficiaries in Hungary.[67]

In May, 1964 the United States and Rumania had agreed to take a series of steps to give a new and friendly tone to their relations. A Joint Communiqué, an Executive Agreement of Class IV, the first week of June, 1964 provided for the elevation of the countries' diplomatic missions from legations to regular embassies and established terms for an expansion of trade, especially the sale of modern equipment to Rumania under commercial credits guaranteed by the United States Government.[68] The Executive Agreement provided for a series of future negotiations on still unresolved questions. The Agreement also provided that the Export-Import Bank would underwrite normal commercial credits by Americans for terms up to five years. The Rumanians wanted equipment, synthetic rubber factories and even whole atomic power plants but the deterrent was the relatively small market for Rumanian exports. That same year (1964) Rumania made informal contacts for inclusion in the General Agreement on Tariffs and Trade. There were precedents among the Soviet satellites, for both Poland and Yugoslavia had links with GATT although they were not full members. Czechoslovakia was one of the 62 full members but her role dated from before she came under Communist rule.

On November 22, 1969 the United States and Rumania signed an Executive Agreement of Class IV to exchange information on the peaceful uses of atomic energy.[69] This Executive Agreement would be in effect until 1971. It provided for the exchange of scientific delegations, the assignment of Rumanian graduate students to American laboratories and Universities, and the exchange of unclassified technical literature and films. This was the first such pact concluded with any Eastern European nation and it was a re-

67. *New York Times,* June 20, 1969.
68. *Ibid.,* May 27, 1964.
69. *Ibid.,* November 23, 1969.

assertion of Rumania's basic insistence that "every Socialist country is entitled to full sovereignty and freedom of action."

There were also other readjustments for the relations of the United States and Europe. On September 23, 1969 the Executive Agreement of Class II of 1953 with Spain concerning bases expired. Congressional leaders questioned the usefulness in the missile age of bases built essentially for bombers in the mid-nineteen-fifties, but finally an arrangement was renewed for two years from September 26, 1968 to September 26, 1970 by a new Executive Agreement of Class II. In the renewed Agreement Spain would receive $50 million in military aid and would receive Export-Import Bank credits up to $35 million for further military purchases. The United States would have the use of four military bases—two airbases that were then inactive, Moron and Zaragoza; a third airbase still in use but of diminishing importance at Torrejon; and a fourth, a submarine base at Rota near Cadiz. The new Agreement retained the statement: "A threat to either country, and to the joint facilities that each provides for the common defense, would be a matter of common concern." [70] The two years' extension gave the two governments time to consider Spanish proposals for a broader agreement for cooperation in various civilian fields as well as in defense. If not renewed again, the pact gave the United States until September 26, 1971 to evacuate forces and equipment.

In the meantime Senator Fulbright of the Senate Foreign Relations Committee had contended that a new Executive Agreement, calling for a continuation of a defense agreement, should be an Executive Agreement the terms of which should be aired in public, or there should be a treaty. He wanted to avoid the ambiguity of the Tonkin Bay Joint Resolution by having public hearings. Secretary Rogers, as early as March, 1969, had told the Foreign Relations Committee that extension beyond September 26, 1970 would entail no added defense commitments to Spain and the Committee would be briefed before renewal. Public hearings would be discussed by Secretary Rogers and Senator Fulbright. On August 5, 1970, however, Secretary Rogers told Senator Fulbright that the next day, August 6, 1970, a new Agreement of Class II would be signed. This provided for military assistance to Spain, including loans from the Export-Import Bank to purchase 36 used Phantom jets, grants for modernization of an aircraft-warning

70. *New York Times*, June 24, 1969.

network, and the loan of 16 United States naval vessels. Despite the signing, the Senate Foreign Relations Committee voted to hold a public hearing on the subject on August 26, 1970. Two of the witnesses were the Deputy Secretary of Defense and the Under-Secretary of State for Political Affairs, the latter of whom stressed at last that support of Spanish defense by the United States is subject to Congressional control in the authorization and appropriations processes.[71]

Section H—Latin American Problems

The Nixon Administration in its first months was urged to undertake a comprehensive political, military and economic policy for the Caribbean. The recommendation was made in a confidential report, prepared during the last year of the Johnson Administration by Milton Barall, a career Foreign Service officer.[72] The growing number of Soviet nuclear-powered submarines operating off the northern coast of South America, plus the growing number of Western tankers sailing around Africa, since the closing of the Suez Canal in 1967, pointed up the importance of United States military facilities in that Sea. Among the most important of these facilities were the sensitive tracking and monitoring devices at Caribbean sites. These were said to enable the Pentagon to track and identify almost instantly Soviet submarines moving westward across the Atlantic, crossing successive underwater detection systems as they approached the United States. The Soviet Union, in turn, had been said to have submarines constantly trying to find these devices and to analyze their work and frustrate them by electronic countermeasures. Important Executive Agreements seemed to be ahead for the Caribbean region.

The Nixon Administration was confronted with the need of giving high priority to hemisphere problems as a whole and to reevaluate the Alliance for Progress. This, as previously stated in Chapter VII, was initially a ten-year program to speed up economic growth and social reform in Latin America and was based on a formal inter-American Agreement, the Charter of Punta del Este, Uruguay, adopted in 1961. The United States gave about $1 billion each year in public development aid to match Latin-American "self-help" efforts to increase domestic resources, plan economic growth, and carry out reforms in education, agriculture,

71. *Department of State Bulletin,* LXI, No. 1567, p. 15.
72. *New York Times,* May 4, 1969.

housing and income distribution. The common effort was supposed to strengthen democratic institutions in the nineteen participating Latin-American countries. The United States also agreed in the Charter to cooperate in relieving Latin America's foreign trade and external debt problem. President Johnson had extended by Executive Agreement of Class II the United States commitment in 1965 for as long beyond 1971 as was necessary to reach the specific targets of the Charter and in 1967 he pledged increased United States support for a Latin-American Common Market.[73]

The Alliance for Progress was subject to criticism, however, almost from the beginning.[74] In April, 1966 an eight member economic advisory panel responsible for reviewing national development plans for the Alliance resigned, with the charge that there was too much reliance on bilateral agreements between the United States and individual countries in Latin America. Washington, it seemed, was the chief culprit in bilateralism over multilateralism. Some countries fared better than others. The United States had promised to assist all of its partners but a major share of aid had gone to those who demonstrated a capacity for making good use of it. The Johnson Administration agreed to write a commitment for economic assistance into a revised Charter of the Organization of American States but the United States could not fulfill this desire, for two reasons. Understanding with the Senate Foreign Relations Committee had broken down when the Tonkin Bay Resolution was having priority in discussion and the United States wanted only a general reference to the obligation to provide assistance while the Latin Americans wanted specific revisions of the Charter.

The Latin-American Foreign Ministers meeting at Vina del Mar, Chile the end of May, 1969 and the first week of June drew up a 6000 word document, which was critical of how the United States had carried out its commitments and which called for "a more effective form" of inter-American cooperation.[75] This document was presented to President Nixon about June 11, 1969. The main preoccupation of the document was with economic growth, which in most of the Alliance period had not met the regional target of 2.5 per cent net annual increase in production of goods and services. On social development, the document said that the

73. *New York Times*, June 5, 1969.
74. *Ibid.*, April 27, 1966.
75. *Ibid.*, June 5, 1969.

Alliance targets, such as six years of schooling for all children after 1970 and general agrarian reform, were beyond the financial capabilities of most countries without massive outside aid. Large sections of the memorandum referred to trade and foreign capital transfers, both in the form of aid and of private investment. Among the measures proposed were the following: effective compliance with commitments to halt any new measures restricting exports from Latin America of basic products and manufactures; negotiation of schedules for elimination of customs and non-tariff restrictions on Latin American products "of special interest," such as Brazilian and Colombian cotton textiles, or Argentine and Central-American beef exports; modification of United States policies that encourage uneconomic domestic production of basic products that keep out Latin-American commodities such as beef and sugar, or compete with Latin-American exports in world markets, such as cotton; systematic consultation to prevent "the disruption of Latin-American trade" caused by requirements that United States aid loans be used to buy United States goods that are not competitive in price, or by "dumping" of surpluses; and adoption by the industrial countries of a system of preferences in favor of manufactures and semimanufactures from developing countries. On aid financing, the proposals covered elimination of "special conditions" requiring United States purchases, use of United States ships to transport aid-financed goods, and other devices arising out of the United States balance-of-payments problems. The document did not want private foreign investment to be considered as assistance or computed as part of financial cooperation for development. The role of foreign investors, it said, should be to generate export income, make a technological contribution and "participate as a supplementary element of national investment, preferably associated with it." [76] The Latin Americans felt that their best hope was in expanding exports and they felt that their action had far-reaching importance for the United States, for the Chilean Foreign Minister said to President Nixon, "Never before has your country encountered a Latin America united on its own definition." [77]

76. *Ibid.*
 Foreign investment had become a major issue in Latin America. The seizure of a United States owned oil company in Peru, oil companies in Colombia and Ecuador, and copper companies in Chile illustrated the problem of negotiating new contracts more favorable to the governments of those countries. Venezuela was also seeking new service contracts for oil concessions that were soon to expire.
77. *New York Times,* June 5, 1969.

On June 21, 1969 the United States agreed to work through a special inter-American committee to establish "new bases and instruments of action" for economic cooperation with Latin America.[78] This special committee was set up by the heads of delegations of 22 hemisphere republics participating in the sixth meeting of the Inter-American Economic and Social Council of the Organization of American States, meeting at Port of Spain, Trinidad. The committee was to begin its work on October 20, 1969 and present its recommendations to the hemisphere ministers before the end of 1969. This decision was a compromise agreement that postponed for four months an intensive discussion of Latin-American complaints.

Meanwhile Governor Rockefeller with twenty specialists accompanying him had made four separate trips throughout Latin America from May 11 to July 6, 1969.[79] His report was submitted to President Nixon on September 3, 1969; and "was to play a vital part," according to President Nixon, "in the construction of sensitive new concepts and programs." [80]

It was not until the eighth Special Meeting of the International American Economic and Social Council at Caracas, Venezuela, February 3–6, 1970, however, that the United States committed herself by Executive Agreement of Class IV to a new program. President Nixon said he would press for generalized preferences applicable to all less developed countries.[81] The United States would thus have a two-tiered-favored-nation policy, one applicable to more developed countries and one applicable to less developed ones. The President also said that he would take steps to stimulate exports from hemisphere countries and that he wanted multilateral mechanisms within the inter-American system to be given increased responsibility for operations and decisions. He made a grant to the Inter-American Committee on Alliance for Progress and said he would submit programs to the CIAP. The United States was also to cooperate in the study of the debt service problem. The AID loan dollars after November 1, 1969 were to be untied to permit procurement not only in the United States but anywhere in Latin America; and in relation to procurement under AID loans made in Latin America there would be a 50-50 test of origin instead of 90-10. President Nixon also approved removal of special

78. *New York Times*, June 22, 1969.
79. *Ibid.*, September 8, 1969.
80. *Ibid.*, September 4, 1969.
81. *Department of State Bulletin*, LXII, No. 1601, p. 255.

letter of credit procedures applicable to dollars used for local cost procurement by AID and the Fund for Special Operations of the Inter-American Development Bank.

In November, 1969 it had been stated that the United States intended to expand technical assistance in establishing national and regional capital markets and in easing access to American capital markets; and in 1970 the United States was willing to expand its program of financial support to the local private sector in Latin America.

The United States reiterated its offers of financial assistance to the Andean Group, the Caribbean Free Trade Association, the Central American Common Market and to the eventual Common Market of Latin America when necessary steps would have been taken.

The United States, therefore, no longer imposed limitations on the exports of similar commodities in the negotiation and implementation of PL480 sales agreements with Latin America.

Military assistance would continue to include furnishing technical advisers, supplying some grant materiel, and sponsoring formal training. This training had been supplied to 17 countries and grant materiel had been given to 11 countries. In the early sixties the United States program in Latin America had been shifted to strengthening national capabilities to counter Communist sponsored insurgency movements.

President Nixon's Latin American policy became known as "Action for Progress"—action that could realistically be implemented. The United States was to contribute, not dominate. In keeping with the principle and spirit of the Vietnamization Policy there should be a community of independent, self-reliant states linked together in a vital and useful association.

Legislation had also been submitted on December 20, 1969 that would create the position of Under-Secretary of State for Western Hemisphere Affairs, a suggestion of Governor Rockefeller.

The International Committee of the Federal Council for Science and Technology established a Latin American Subcommittee in December, 1969. Provisions were being worked out to make the United States Government-owned patents accessible to development of the hemisphere. Latin American specialists were to be trained; support of the United States was to be given to regional programs of science and technology, to science teaching and to research.

In March, 1970 it was announced that President Nixon would appoint a broadly representative Commission on International Trade and Investment Policy to examine and make recommendations on the major international economic issues facing the country in the 1970's.[82]

Section I—Miscellaneous International Agreements

As the first Nixon Administration neared its half-way point, there were other commitments expressive of foreign policy that were discussed. The United Nations Committee on the Peaceful Uses of the Seabed and Ocean Floor Beyond the Limits of National Jurisdiction had met from August 11 to 29, 1969. To this committee in the summer of 1970 President Nixon and the Under-Secretary of State Richardson made a proposal combining narrow limits of national sovereign rights over seabed resources with a pragmatic division of royalties and administration of the resources of the continental margin and assuring orderly development in the exploration and use of seabed resources beyond the continental margins. The concept of an international trusteeship for coastal states was a new one.

The treaty establishing the international regime would contain the general legal rules regarding exploitation of seabed resources beyond the 200-meter limit, including rules relating to matters such as preventing unreasonable interference with other uses of the ocean, protecting the ocean from pollution, etc. Substantial mineral revenues from the exploitation of this entire area would be used for international community purposes.[83]

President Nixon also asked the consent of the Senate to two Conventions drawn up in Brussels at the International Legal Conference on Marine Pollution Damage, in 1969: an International Convention Relating to Intervention on the High Seas in Cases of Oil Pollution Casualties; and the International Convention on Civil Liability for Oil Pollution Damage.[84]

President Nixon soon after taking office directed a comprehensive study of the United States' chemical and biological defense policies and programs and finally in 1970 submitted to the Senate, for advice and consent to ratification, the Geneva Protocol of 1925, which prohibits the first use of "asphyxiating, poisonous or

---

82. *Department of State Bulletin*, LXII, No. 1603, March 16, 1970.
83. *Ibid.*, LXI, No. 1579 and LXII, No. 1616, June 15, 1970, p. 740.
84. *Ibid.*, LXII, No. 1616, June 15, 1970, p. 756.

other gases and of Bacteriological methods of warfare."[85] The United States had repeatedly affirmed its renunciation of the first use of *lethal* chemical weapons but she now extended this renunciation to the first use of *incapacitating* chemicals. She now added the renunciation of the use of *lethal* biological agents and weapons and *all other methods* of biological warfare. Biological research in the future would be confined to defensive measures, such as immunization and safety measures. Existing stocks of bacteriological weapons would be disposed of.

President Nixon also presented the Trade Act of 1969, which was to be applicable in 1973.[86] While it was not passed by the end of the 91st Congress it projected new discussions on items with international implications. It was realized that world economic interdependence had become a fact; that a number of foreign countries were now competing fully with the United States in world markets; and that the traditional surplus in the United States balance of trade had disappeared. A departure from the approach to freer trade would invite disaster for the less developed countries need improved access to the markets of the industrialized countries if their economic development is to proceed satisfactorily; and the need to restore the trade surplus of the United States emphasizes that other nations must lower their trade barriers, which deny fair access to their markets. The new Trade Act of 1969 restored the authority needed by the President to make limited tariff reductions; it took concrete steps toward lowering non-tariff barriers to trade; it recognized the very real plight of particular industries, companies and workers faced with import competition and provided for readier relief in these special cases, for the assistance programs of the Trade Expansion Act had not worked. It strengthened GATT by regularizing the funds of the United States participation, which had been financed previously by general contingency funds. The United States proposed to eliminate the American Selling Price System of customs evaluation, which had applied to benzenoid chemicals mainly. This had had severe opposition abroad for in other items valuation was based on actual prices of foreign products and not on the price of competing American products. The removal of the American Selling Price System, it was thought, would bring a reduction in foreign non-

---

85. *Congressional Quarterly, Weekly Report*, October 2, 1970 and *Department of State Bulletin*, LXI, No. 1590, December 15, 1969.
86. *Department of State Bulletin*, LXI, No. 1590, December 15, 1969, p. 557.

tariff barriers, such as European road tariffs which discriminate against the large automobiles of the United States. Opposition to the new Trade Act was voiced by the textile and shoe industries and it remained for the 92nd Congress to work out a trade act that would further the movement toward freer trade.

There were also many Executive Agreements of Class IV in the first half of the first Nixon Administration. Diverse agreements were reached, concerning such matters as weather stations and the meteorological program; cash contributions of Japan concerning mutual defense assistance; coverage of Philippine citizens employed by United States AID, the Joint Military Advisory Group, and the Peace Corps in the Social Security System of the Philippines; financing of the exchange programs; arrangements for seismic observations; air transport services with Czechoslovakia; fishing operations in the Northeastern Pacific Ocean; customs regulations in reference to containers (tanks, vans, etc.); maritime load line marks; meat imports; air transport services; sales of agricultural commodities; claims relating to the GUT Dam (Canada); alien amateur radio operators; surplus property rescheduling of payments, with Indonesia; relief supplies and packages; loan of vessels; earth surveys; double taxation; lifting of the ban on credit sales of arms to Peru and Eucador (in a one sentence communiqué); etc. There was also discussion in July, 1969 concerning how much Bonn should pay to effect the costs of American troops in West Germany.[87] This list illustrated the variety of Executive Agreements that were taken for granted in the daily routine of government. By February 1, 1971 International Agreements, as published in TIAS, had reached 6985, an increase of 5484 since 1946, most of which were Executive Agreements.[88]

Section J—The End of an Era

The first half of the first Nixon Administration had been concerned with foreign relations that outlined problems and clearly indicated that new policies were in order. In foreign affairs at the end of twenty-five years since World War II the United States was still playing the role of international leadership. She was recognized as a power and she had commitments of assistance around the globe. At the peak of her influence she had 2000 military installations in various countries, of which 400 were of a major

87. In TIAS.
88. TIAS, No. 6985.

nature. She had Mutual Defense Treaties with 45 nations, implemented by hundreds of Executive Agreements; had military Executive Agreements, that were published, with 21 more countries; and had secret arrangements with other nations that were of a classified nature. She had about a million and a quarter American troops throughout the world.[89]

In the first half of the first Nixon Administration, as has been said, there was a quantitative reduction of troop consignments around the world and some bases were relinquished but the principle of leadership was not diminished. The first alterations were due to the Vietnamization Policy as well as to other factors such as a ten percent cut for economy reasons in 1969, recommendations for changes in overseas bases in light of bigger transport planes and improved weapons, and demands in Congress for greater outlays to alleviate domestic problems, at the expense of military spending.

The goals of national interest and national security were constants always. The policy of the United States for twenty-five years had been to resist aggressive Communism and to try to demonstrate the success and tenacity of democracy in resisting Communism, by aiding the weak and underdeveloped countries to help themselves. In that way, the United States felt, her own interests were served, and national security was maintained.

By the 70's, however, it was a new interrelated world. Imperialism was almost gone; there were many new independent countries. New sources of food, new types of transport, new routes by ship and air, new means of communication, new technology, new products, new ventures—even to the moon, and new organizations for international cooperation existed. The United States had extended aid—economic, food, military and technical—to both developed and underdeveloped countries but now, it was thought, other countries could help to a greater degree. National defense had changed from participation in major wars to cooperation with the United Nations and other groups, to extension of military aid to individual states, to sponsorship of or membership in regional alliances. There was also development of weaponry and atomic power to the point of need for non-proliferation among the states. The United States found herself no longer the sole possessor of atomic power but had four competitors. She was challenged to keep her position of being first and having the greatest potential,

89. *U.S. News and World Report,* July 21, 1969.

or to accept through negotiation the fact that quantitative superiority is not salvation and the fact that retaliatory atomic power can be just as devastating as the initial offensive.

As has been seen, International Agreements had reflected all of these developments and the number of published TIAS Agreements had risen by the thousands. Most of these were Executive Agreements. Since Executive Agreements are only implementation of policies, their substantive contents varied as crises and circumstances changed and they merely reflected the times. They were, however, still authorized by treaties, or legislation, or joint resolutions or declaration of war or they expressed Executive authority alone.

To keep up with change, Executive Agreements usually have provisions stated within them for termination or possible renewal; but if there is no such provision and if both sides seem to be agreeable, some just live on after the crisis is over. If only one side wants the implementation to continue, there can be complications. An example of this last situation was the termination of France's being willing to have NATO headquarters on her soil, although she wanted to remain a member of NATO. Not one of the pertinent agreements spelled out the procedure for the termination and the change was made with great cost to NATO and to the United States.[90]

90. *American Journal of International Law*, July, 1968, pp. 577–640.
The importance of exact wording of an Executive Agreement is illustrated by the five Executive Agreements between France and the United States that were entered into consequent upon the North Atlantic Treaty which brought NATO into existence.
On February 21, 1966 General de Gaulle announced his withdrawal from the measures that were taken to apply the treaty but not from the treaty itself. The United States had Agreements concerning an Air Depot; certain Air Bases and Facilities in Metropolitan France; a System of Communications and Depots of the United States Army in Metropolitan France; the Construction, Operation and Maintenance of a Pipeline; and Headquarters of the Deputy Commander, Allied Forces in Europe.
The unilateral action of France was based upon her fear of being drawn into a war that she did not want and had reference to the concept of integration of forces. Integration was of limited scope and did not extend to nuclear weapons. NATO does have access to a nuclear arsenal, made available by the United States to the NATO forces on the continent and in the United Kingdom, and remaining under the "double-key" system, which is based on bilateral Agreements and assures ultimate American control. No nuclear weapons may be released without a special determination by the President of the United States or the Prime Minister of the United Kingdom.
After the U.S.S.R. acquired nuclear power the United States abandoned the Dulles doctrine of massive, immediate, atomic retaliation, and launched the new United States strategic doctrine of "controlled" or "flexible response." First there would be a resistance by conventional forces; nuclear weapons would be brought into

Other ways by which Executive Agreements may be terminated, if there is no specific provision for renewal or termination, are the changes of circumstances that make of no consequence the authority for the implementation, i. e. the Treaty, or the legislation, or the joint resolution or the declaration of war. An example was the Eisenhower Middle East Joint Resolution which recognized the possibility of assistance against external aggression of Communists. The Resolution soon lost its relevance, and the Foreign Assistance Act took its place.

Again the authorization by Treaty, or legislation or joint resolution may be vague and not refer to specific crises. As authorization, however, the document remains and all kinds of implementations can ensue. An example was the Tonkin Bay Joint Resolution and its application to the Vietnam War.

The interpretation of authorization in the last instance led to controversy between Congress and the Executive. The recriminations seemed to imply that the Executive was at fault and the Congress would have made better decisions if asked for advice in advance. The answer to such implications was that Congress has always had powers. It has the power of legislation, it has the power of passing resolutions, and it has the power of making appropriations. These, Congress was reminded, are real and potent. Congress, however, in the Vietnam question, always voted money to

play on a graduated scale by subtle escalation and only as a last resort. General de Gaulle took the position that no country will jeopardize its own survival for another and, therefore, each country must have its own nuclear arsenal to defend itself against attack while leaving all other countries to their fate. The concept of integration of NATO was, therefore, obsolete. Sovereignty is the crucial operative principle.

The members of NATO have adjusted to France's demands by placing SHAPE (Supreme Head Allied Powers Europe) in Belgium, the NATO Defense College in Italy, and AFCENT in the Netherlands.

The relocations cost money and thus far France had not been willing to make any contribution. Moreover the question of compensation for the NATO buildings and installations taken over by France had to be faced.

When France denounced the five bilateral Agreements with the United States she offered to begin bilateral negotiations for the settlement of "the practical consequences" of the decisions, which involved, first, the use by the United States of military facilities in France, and, second, the financial responsibility of France in connection with American installations left on French soil. The only negotiations that led to agreement were the ones arranging for a peacetime use of a 390-mile pipeline system across France, under the management of a French contractor. The discussion for the reactivating of military facilities in France for use by the United States in war was deadlocked; and the claims arising for the forced relinquishment of United States financed military installations were not presented until June 18, 1969.

The wording of the five bilateral Executive Agreements was silent as to the procedure a party was to follow in order to obtain termination or modification!

finance the war, as the members did not want their constituencies to think the soldiers were neglected. The trouble was that Congress usually became alarmed too late and did not demonstrate foresight. More careful framing of legislation, joint resolutions, declarations of war, Treaties and Executive Agreements, so that semantic difficulties could not occur, as experience pointed out, was long overdue. Vague, general, ambiguous language—when specific crises should be mentioned—were not worthy of responsible, elected members of Congress in the 70's; and Congress was alerted to prevent future ambiguities.

Foreign affairs during the quarter of a century after World War II were the interest and concern of organizations and professional groups mainly, but now in 1971 and 1972 there was emerging more and more a concerned citizenry. The times demanded a greater education of the electorate toward an understanding of the policies and the need for frequent reevaluation of those policies. The times demanded also a greater refinement and precision of the instruments that would express these policies.

Senator Stuart Symington, chairman of the Senate Subcommittee on Security Agreements and Commitments, referring to his two-year report on "creeping commitments" of the United States, stated to a news conference on December 11, 1970: "The basic thrust of the report is the people's right to know—what are the facts?" [91] In 1971 and 1972 then the beginning of a new era was evident.

91. *Congressional Quarterly Service—Weekly Report.* 1971, p. 22.

CHAPTER X

The New Era

Section A—Philosophy for the Seventies

The year 1971 was a watershed. The United States stopped reacting on the basis of yesterday's habits and started to deal with realities of "today" and the opportunities of the future. New conditions required fundamental changes in the world role of the United States.

Since Agreements are not an end in themselves, they had to contribute a structure for peace, which all countries would wish to preserve. International life, therefore, had to have a new dimension.[1] The Nixon Doctrine expressed this new philosophy. It was an enlargement of Vietnamization. The United States had to remain strong but she had to become a participant with other strong states in the world. She had to have multilateral understandings. She had to command respect, and to honor her agreements with others. She had to expect other restored countries to do their part in bringing about a better age. She had to see that peace was more than anti-Communism, and accept the solutions of negotiations and not just of confrontation. She had to accept reasonable "give and take" arrangements concerning monetary and trade relationships, even with Communist countries; she had to recognize the contributions of science and technology and accept the ease of mobility in travel, and the profit of cultural exchange. She had to show new leadership.

As has been shown, immediately after World War II the United States had been the preeminent economic power in the world and

1. *Weekly Compilation of Presidential Documents*, Vol. 8, No. 7 (Washington: Government Printing Office), p. 237.

assumed primary responsibility for the economic viability and security of much of the non-Communist world. The United States had launched the Marshall Plan, had helped Japan, and had encouraged European Economic Cooperation. The International Monetary Fund (IMF), the General Agreement on Tariffs and Trade (GATT), and the World Bank were new arrangements and institutions to govern the international economic system in this period.[2] Since these institutions had been established, the world economy had undergone major structural changes. The industrial capacities of Japan, Europe and Canada had grown rapidly and each was now a strong trading and financial power. New realities needed to be reflected in foreign economic relationships and international institutions.

The Bretton Woods Conference in 1944 had given to the United States the lead in creation of a new international monetary system.[3] This system allowed parity adjustments, which were expected to be used when countries were in fundamental balance of payments disequilibrium. Countries could draw on a pool of currencies established in the IMF to supplement their own gold and foreign exchange reserves. There was economic expansion. The United States' reconstruction assistance and persistent balance-of-payments deficits provided substantial liquidity to countries whose reserves had been depleted. Their holdings of gold and dollars increased substantially. This enabled countries to support a large flow of imports required for their reconstruction.

In the 1960's, however, the international monetary system showed increasing strain.[4] There were persistent United States deficits, which led to an increasing imbalance between the United States' liquid assets and her liabilities. A supplementary source of reserves was clearly needed and the agreement was reached in the International Monetary Fund in 1969 to create an alternative source of international liquidity in the form of Special Drawing Rights (SDR's) (See Chapter VIII). This reform did not deal with other sources of stress, however. The pressure to adjust problems did not apply equally to all countries. Those countries with a significant balance of payments surplus and undervalued currencies felt little pressure to increase the value of their currencies. They wanted to increase their trade surpluses in order to enhance the

2. *WCPD*, Vol. 8, No. 7, p. 286.
3. *WCPD*, Vol. 8, No. 7, p. 287.
4. *WCPD*, Vol. 8, No. 7, p. 288.

rates of their domestic economic growth and employment and to protect their external financial positions. Countries with overvalued exchange rates, however, had to devalue to correct their balance of payments deficits and halt the drain on their reserves. During the 1960's changes in the value of other currencies tended to push higher the exchange value of the dollar.[5] This aggravated a relative loss of American economic competitiveness as foreign countries completed their post-war reconstruction, achieved high levels of productivity, and proved adept at developing export markets. Then a crisis in currency markets brought mass purchases of gold by speculators. The gold reserves were being drained until introduction of a two-tier system in March, 1968 isolated private gold trading from international monetary transactions.

In 1970 after several countries had had to revalue their currencies, a major crisis was avoided, but there was a decline in United States interest rates relative to rates in major European countries and large amounts of dollars abroad complicated European attempts to achieve domestic monetary stability. The situation worsened in 1971. There was a deficit in the United States' balance of trade and dollars flowed abroad in record amounts. By August, 1971 it was clear that the dollar was overvalued, while the currencies of certain of the United States' trading partners were undervalued. Strong unilateral measures were required to address the immediate crisis and the fundamental structural problems of the system.[6] On August 15, 1971 the United States suspended convertibility of the dollar into gold and other reserve assets. The United States also imposed a temporary 10% surcharge on dutiable imports to raise their price and thereby reduce their level. The United States faced an international problem requiring a multilateral solution.

In mid-September, 1971 Secretary Connally at the London meeting of the Group of Ten—the Finance Ministers and Central Bank Governors of the major industrialized nations of the free world—spelled out the United States' objectives and stressed the necessity for action.[7] Afterward at the Group of Ten Meeting in Rome in early December, 1971, possible avenues for resolving the immediate problems were clarified and developed. Participation of all of the major industrialized nations was desired. The

5. *WCPD*, Vol. 8, No. 7, p. 288.
6. *WCPD*, Vol. 8, No. 7, p. 289.
7. *WCPD*, Vol. 8, No. 7, pp. 290–291.

participation of France was especially important and in mid-December President Pompidou and President Nixon reached an Executive Agreement of Class I, in principle, on their joint contribution to an overall solution.

At the Group of Ten Meeting at the Smithsonian Institution on December 18, 1971 a new Treaty was arrived at.[8] It covered a new pattern of exchange rate relationships, involving both revaluations and devaluations. The United States devaluated the dollar in terms of gold. The group recognized that trade arrangements were important to assure a new and lasting equilibrium in the international economy. The United States, in an Executive Agreement of Class I, also agreed to remove the import surcharge and the "buy American" provisions of the Job Development Credit. President Nixon announced the implementation of this decision at his meeting with Prime Minister Heath of the United Kingdom at Bermuda in December, 1971. The Smithsonian Agreement, unlike the arrangements at the Bretton Woods, when the United States was the predominant nation, was fashioned by relatively coequal economic powers. It was the first time in history that nations had negotiated a multilateral realignment of exchange rates. This December, 1971 realignment decreased the price in foreign currencies of American exports making them more competitive in foreign markets. It raised the price of foreign imports in the United States' domestic market. This was eventually to help to improve the United States' balance of trade and payments position and it was to help stimulate domestic employment. This realignment was the first step.

The other relations which were the fundamental ingredients of most of the Executive Agreements of 1971 and 1972 had to do with trade. Since the 1930's the United States' policy had been to remove barriers to the free exchange of goods in the international market.[9] Tariffs of industrialized countries had been reduced to roughly one-third of their immediate post-war level and between 1950 and 1970 United States exports quadrupled. United States workers had gained greater access for their products in world markets, and Americans had had a wider variety of products brought in from other countries. The post-war prosperity of the United States and its allies was enhanced by the trade between them and was an underpinning of strong political bonds.

8. *WCPD*, Vol. 8, No. 7, pp. 291-292.
9. *WCPD*, Vol. 8, No. 7, p. 293.

In recent years international trading relationships had changed.[10] The European Community and Japan were new centers of economic power and were strong international competitors. Discriminatory trading arrangements were assuming greater importance; additional trade barriers had been erected; and past reductions in tariffs had exposed other barriers to trade. The productivity of the United States' labor and industry had not increased as rapidly as that of some of the important trade partners; inflation had been high; and the dollar had been overvalued. The balance of trade in 1971 for the first time since 1893 eroded to being a trade deficit. In 1971 the United States had to take strong measures to reverse the declining trade of the country, focused international attention on the fundamental problems confronting the world trade system, and moved ahead with a major effort to improve the United States' competitive position.

The objectives in 1971 were: to curb inflation and realign exchange rates; to remove specific barriers to United States exports; to set the stage for further international negotiations; to strengthen the export competitiveness of American industry; to facilitate adjustment of domestic industries to the pressures of excessive rapid-import increases and to cushion the impact of these pressures; and to broaden and increase opportunities for trade with Communist countries.[11] There was growing realization in the United States that international trade is important to domestic economy. Particularly worrisome were new preferential trading arrangements entered into by the European Community, which encouraged the development of a world divided into discriminatory trading blocs. This weakened the multilateral basis of international economic relations and raised the risk of political tensions. Trade, like monetary issues, is a multilateral problem.[12] The European Community, Japan and the United States and other nations maintained trade barriers other than tariffs, which adversely affected each other's exports. Bilateral negotiations alone could not solve these issues. The Organization for Economic Cooperation and Development (OECD) in Europe could consider how best to deal with world trade problems. The time had come to begin moving toward a major series of international negotiations for reduction of trade barriers. The United States saw also that there must be an

---

10. *WCPD*, Vol. 8, No. 7, p. 293.
11. *WCPD*, Vol. 8, No. 7, p. 292.
12. *WCPD*, Vol. 8, No. 7, p. 295.

increase in its productivity and progress using new technologies in the future.

In 1971 the United States: [13]

—negotiated a voluntary textile restraint, by Executive Agreement of Class II, mainly for woolen and man-made textiles, with the four major textile exporters in the Far East: Japan, Korea, Republic of China, and Hong Kong;

—invoked the multilateral Long-Term Arrangement on Cotton Textiles, an Executive Agreement of Class II;

—negotiated an improvement of the Voluntary Steel Arrangement, by an Executive Agreement of Class II, in order to limit exports of steel mill products from Japan and members of the European Community to the United States;

—enforced anti-dumping laws to protect American industries from being injured by unfair pricing by foreign competitors;

—made available adjustment assistance in the United States, which provided financial and technical aid, to individual firms and workers injured by imports.

In 1971 opportunities for trade with Communist countries were also increased. They were seen to be an important potential market for the products of the United States. The United States supported Rumania's accession to GATT, by an Executive Agreement of Class II; supported the extension of the most favored nation tariff treatment to Rumania by an Executive Agreement of Class II; and extended the facilities of the Export-Import Bank for credits for exports to Rumania by an Executive Agreement of Class II.[14]

Also in April, 1971 the United States relaxed the currency controls which had prevented the use of dollars in transactions with the People's Republic of China, by Executive Agreement of Class II.[15] At the same time restrictions on provision of fuel to ships and aircraft going to and from the People's Republic of China were relaxed and United States vessels were permitted to carry Chinese cargoes between non-Chinese ports. On June 1, 1971 trade controls on a wide range of non-strategic United States products, to permit their export to the People's Republic of China without a license, were removed.[16] On November 30, 1971 a three-year ban on government-backed credits to Communist bloc coun-

13. *WCPD*, Vol. 8, No. 7, p. 296.
14. *WCPD*, Vol. 8, No. 7, p. 297.
15. *Ibid.*
16. *Ibid.*

tries ended when President Nixon authorized the Export-Import Bank to fund the sale of United States goods to Rumania.[17]

President Nixon announced on July 15, 1971 that he and Mrs. Nixon would visit Communist China beginning February 21, 1972. The President thus initiated a new phase in the United States policy toward mainland China.[18] The Shanghai Communiqué, an Executive Agreement of Class IV, on February 27, 1972 at the end of the trip was in three parts, each side stating its point of view in one part and then both stating what they agreed upon in the third.[19] The effect of this action was to remove the embargo on direct trade with the People's Republic of China. Diplomatic recognition could await further developments.

The economic negotiations in their technical aspects which were negotiated by the United States were parallel with the growing direct trade between United States business concerns and foreign agencies, for which licenses were granted.

Communist China in 1970 had bought four British Tridents, second-hand, from Pakistan; in 1971 she had ordered six Hawker-Siddeley planes from Great Britain; and on August 8, 1972 she ordered six British Trident airliners. On September 10, 1972 she signed a contract believed to be worth $150 million for ten American-built Boeing 707 airliners.[20] The Chinese also agreed to send five crews for training on the aircraft, possibly in the United States. In July, 1972 the United States Government had given Boeing an export license to sell the ten airliners at an average cost of $10-million each. Including spare parts the final cost of the planes was $150-million. Peking also ordered three British-French Concorde supersonic airliners.[21] Two weeks later, in 1972, the United States Commerce Department approved a license to the McDonnell-Douglas Aircraft Corporation to demonstrate its DC-10 airliner in China. This airliner carried 250 to 300 passengers instead of less than 200 and cost about $17-million each.[22] On September 15, 1972, through the Louis Dreyfus Corporation, the New York branch of a big Paris-based commodities trading organization, China National Cereals, Oils and Foodstuffs Import and Export Corporation, Peking bought about 500,000 metric

17. *New York Times*, September 15, 1972.
18. *Current History*, September, 1972, p. 143.
19. *Ibid.*
20. *Current History*, September, 1972, p. 143 and *New York Times*, September 11, 1972.
21. *Current History*, September, 1972, p. 140.
22. *New York Times*, September 11, 1972.

tons of United States wheat, the first such purchase by the mainland Chinese in more than twenty years.[23]

There was, also, a large increase in licenses for American exporters wishing to export to the Soviet Union and to Poland. On November 5, 1971 a sale of approximately $136-million of corn and other livestock feedgrains to the Soviet Union was concluded.[24] In July of 1972 another sale of $750-million of wheat for the next three years was made to the Soviet Union.[25] These transactions carried out Executive Agreements of Class II. The number of goods requiring licenses without weakening effective control over the export of strategic commodities was also reduced.

Congress on December 20, 1970 had cleared for the Preesident a bill extending the International Coffee Agreement Act.[26] This bill continued until June, 1971 the authority of the President to restrict entry into the United States of coffee imported from countries not participant to the Agreement and to prohibit entry of coffee shipments from participating members that were not accompanied by certificates of origin or of re-export. The original International Coffee Agreement, which had been a Treaty entered into in 1962, was to prevent major fluctuations in the world coffee market by stabilizing world prices at the 1962 level. In 1968 President Nixon had signed a new International Coffee Agreement, another Treaty, which extended the earlier Agreement with modifications for five years—through September 30, 1973. Although the Treaty was extended for five years, Congress had authorized the United States to continue to participate in the Agreement only for two years, by Executive Agreement of Class I, through September 30, 1970. The new bill of December, 1970 cleared the Agreement until June 30, 1971.

Export incentives were carefully considered. Legislation was passed late in 1970 and adopted in conference that made 50% of a Domestic International Sales Corporation (DISC)'s export-related profits subject to taxation when distributed to shareholders, but permitted deferral of the federal taxes.

In 1970 President Nixon had proposed parts of a new trade bill and "reluctantly" supported its textile import quota provision.[27] He opposed the footwear quota provision and on July 20, 1970 he

23. *New York Times,* September 15, 1972.
24. *Current History,* January, 1972, p. 62.
25. *New York Times,* September 15, 1972.
26. *Congressional Quarterly Almanac,* 1970, Vol. XXVI, p. 716.
27. *Congressional Quarterly Almanac,* 1970, Vol. XXVI, p. 105.

threatened to veto the bill if it contained quotas on imports other than textiles. In 1969 the President had sought to assist textile industries by trying to negotiate Executive Agreements of Class II with Japan and European textile-producing countries to limit their textiles by voluntary exports, but the approach for voluntary cooperation had not been successful. The new bill permitted the President to impose import quotas when there was injury to domestic producers, it provided for some favorable tax treatment of chemicals, but it did not include rubber-soled footwear.[28] The Trade Expansion Act of 1962 had contained authority to reduce United States tariffs. This provision lapsed in 1967 during the Kennedy Round but the other provisions remained in force. In 1971 the United States agreed with other industrial nations by means of Executive Agreements of Class II to institute a system of generalized tariff preferences for imports from the lower income countries.[29] The European Community, Japan, and the United Kingdom and others had already instituted their generalized preferential arrangements.

On May 6, 1972 voluntary curbs on sales to the United States were accepted by the European Common Market, Japan and the United Kingdom steel producers.[30] Quotas apply to about 85% of all foreign steel sold in the United States. There had been complaints concerning foreign electronic gear, cameras, machinery and similar parts. Executive Agreements of Class II were to be for 1972–1974. Imports into the United States were not to increase faster than capacity of American steelmakers increased. So imports were 2.5% instead of 5% in 1971. Importers agreed to limit shipments on a wide range of special products that proved highly competitive in recent years. Cutbacks were to occur for the first time in levels of stainless, tool and other alloyed steels permitted into the country. These had returned higher profits. Cutbacks were also on steelbars and finished structural steel. Foreign producers were not to ship unusually large quantities to any special section of the country where they might be able to compete most effectively.[31] Trade exports of the United States were greatly increased by 1972.

Assistance (AID) had to be continued but it, too, took on a new focus. Bilateral Agreements were to be coordinated with mul-

28. *Ibid.*
29. *WCPD*, Vol. 8, No. 7, p. 302.
30. *WCPD*, Vol. 8, No. 17, p. 823 and *Congressional Digest*, May 22, 1972, p. 70.
31. *Ibid.*

tilateral. The bilateral ones were to be concentrated on countries in which the United States had special interest. Since developing nations were increasingly able to set their developing priorities and plans, and to determine their most urgent assistance needs, the United States could play a less direct role and decrease the number of persons stationed abroad for that purpose. Other donors were also to be coordinated with AID. AID was separating economic security assistance programs from developing ones; AID's technical assistance program was concentrating on major developing priorities; AID was strengthening its population and humanitarian assistance; and AID was launching a systematic effort to engage American private organizations in application of scientific and technical capabilities.[32] Since 1969, however AID's staff had not been reduced. Congress in 1970 (December) passed supplemental assistance legislation for FY 1971, which represented a major step in implementing the security assistance component of the Nixon Doctrine, and Executive Agreements of Class II were entered into with Israel, Jordan, Cambodia, Vietnam and Korea. By the 70's then President Nixon was advocating a set of reforms, including two new developing institutions: one to provide capital developing loans and the other to provide technical assistance.[33]

On September 15, 1970 President Nixon proposed a major transformation in the bilateral foreign assistance program. To achieve this program reform he submitted two bills—the International Security Assistance Act and the International Development and Humanitarian Assistance Act. Separate organizational structures would be for security, and for development and humanitarian assistance. The various security assistance efforts (except those in Southeast Asia, which were funded in the Defense Budget) would be combined into one coherent program, under the policy direction of the Department of State, and would support the Nixon Doctrine. A United States International Development Corporation and a United States International Development Institute would replace the Agency for International Development. This change would enable the United States to reform her bilateral assistance programs to meet the 1970's.[34]

The new United States Bilateral Assistance Program of 1971 for Development Assistance therefore proposed: an International

32. *WCPD*, Vol. 8, No. 7, p. 300.
33. *Ibid.*
34. *WCPD*, Vol. 7, No. 17, pp. 667–669.

Development Corporation (IDC) to provide loans to finance development projects and programs in the lower income countries; and an International Development Institute (IDI) to seek research breakthroughs on the key problems of development and to administer the technical assistance programs. These two would join the two organizations created by the 91st Congress in 1970: the Overseas Private Investment Corporation (OPIC) to promote the role of private investment in the development process; and the Inter-American Social Development Institute (ISDI) to provide special attention to the social development needs of Latin America. The United States would also work through the international organizations more often, for the international development institutions had continued their progress toward leadership in the international development process—the World Bank; the United Nations Development Program; and the World Health Organization.

A new Coordinator of Development Assistance would be in the State Department, responsible directly to the President and Chairmen of the Boards of the IDC, IDI, and OPIC. He would also chair an Executive Coordinating Committee composed of the chief executive officer of each of these institutions and ISDI. The Secretary of State would provide policy guidance for all components of the new assistance program. Coordination among the three major components of the assistance program and between them and the national security policy would be handled through the National Security Council.[35]

By 1971 many of the industrial countries had agreed on comparable systems of tariff preferences for imports from the lower income countries. This action expanded the export earnings of these countries. The European Community put its plan into effect on July 1, 1971 and Japan on October 1, 1971. Progress toward the untying of bilateral development loans on a fully reciprocal basis was to be expected. A fair and equitable basis for competition had been worked out by the Organization for Economic Cooperation and Development. Also President Nixon had established a Council on International Economic Policy to coordinate all aspects of United States economic policy, including development assistance. He wanted Congress to vote additional funds for the Inter-American Development Bank and the Asian Development Bank and he wanted contributions to the doubling of the re-

35. *WCPD*, Vol. 7, No. 17, pp. 667 ff.

sources of the International Development Association, the soft loan affiliate of the World Bank. The United States was working for a soft loan window for the African Development Bank, also. President Nixon also transmitted legislation to authorize United States participation in the system of general tariff preferences for developing countries.

On June 2, 1971 President Nixon sent to the Senate for ratification a Treaty that was formulated at the United Nations Wheat Conference in Geneva in the spring of 1971. The Agreement was in two parts: the Wheat Trade Convention and the Food Aid Convention. Before accepting the Wheat Trade Convention on July 12, 1971 the Senate passed a resolution that the President should call an international conference at the earliest "practicable" date to establish world price standards. No price standards were included in the 1971 Treaty although they were in the 1967 Agreement.[36] The new Treaty retains the International Wheat Council, established in the 1949 Wheat Agreement, and created an Advisory Sub-Committee on Market Conditions, which was to review current market conditions and make prompt reports to the Executive Committee of the Council concerning the existence or the threat of market stability. The Council might then be convened to review the situation.[37]

The Food Aid Convention continued the commitment under the 1967 Food Aid Convention whereby parties contribute specified amounts of wheat, coarse grains, or products derived therefrom, or the cash equivalent, to developing countries.[38]

Before the first session of the 92nd Congress came to a close there were indications of other developments reflecting the Nixon Doctrine. On November 18, 1971 the Commerce Department approved the licensing of $5-billion worth of heavy equipment for possible sale by United States companies to the Soviet Union for the construction of a truck factory. A total of $1-billion in export licenses was issued for a factory to be built 600 miles south of Moscow;[39] and on November 17, 1971 President Nixon signed the bill ending the ban on the importation of Rhodesian chrome, as of January 1, 1972, but he said he would take no action during the current negotiations between Great Britain and Rhodesia.[40]

36. *Congressional Quarterly, Weekly Review,* Vol. XXIX, No. 29, p. 1516.
37. *WCPD,* Vol. 7, No. 23, p. 852.
38. *Ibid.*
39. *Current History,* January, 1972, p. 62.
40. *Ibid.*

From May 20, 1972 to June 1, 1972 President and Mrs. Nixon visited the U.S.S.R. and the President signed resultant documents. Besides those relating to security there were the following that were Executive Agreements of Class IV: [41] an Agreement on Cooperation in the Field of Environmental Protection between the United States and the U.S.S.R. on May 23, 1972 to reduce pollution and enhance environmental quality; an Agreement between the Government of the United States and the U.S.S.R. on Cooperation in the Field of Medical Science and Public Health, particularly in the conquest of cancer and heart disease, on May 23, 1972; an Agreement between the United States and the U.S.S.R. concerning Cooperation in the Exploration and Use of Outer Space for Peaceful Purposes, on May 24, 1972, to begin with Congressional funding and to result with a joint orbital mission of an Apollo vehicle and a Soviet spacecraft in 1975; an Agreement between the Government of the United States and the Government of the Union of the Soviet Socialist Republics on Cooperation in the Fields of Science and Technology, on May 24, 1972; an Agreement between the Government of the United States of America and the Government of the U.S.S.R. on the Prevention of Incidents On and Over the Sea, on May 25, 1972; and an Agreement between the United States and Soviet Navies aimed at reducing dangerous incidents between the United States ships and aircraft at sea, on May 25, 1972.

There was also another Executive Agreement of Class IV, a Communiqué Regarding a Joint United States-U.S.S.R. Commercial Commission, on May 26, 1972.[42] To promote development of mutually beneficial commercial relations between the two countries, Soviet leaders and President Nixon agreed to establish such a Commission. The first session was to be in Moscow in July, 1972 and sessions were to be held alternately in Moscow and Washington. The Commission was to negotiate: 1) an overall trade agreement, including reciprocal most favored nation treatment; 2) arrangements for the reciprocal availability of government credits; 3) provisions for the reciprocal establishment of business facilities to promote trade; and 4) an agreement establishing an arbitration mechanism for settling commercial disputes. The Commission was also to study possible United States-U.S.S.R. participation in the development of resources and the manufac-

41. *Ibid.*
42. *WCPD*, Vol. 8, No. 23, pp. 917-922.

ture and sale of raw materials and other products; and to monitor the spectrum of U.S.S.R.-United States commercial relations, identifying and, when possible, resolving issues that may be of interest to both parties, such as patents and licensing.

The first meetings of the Commission in Moscow and then in Washington in September, 1972 gave hope that a comprehensive trade agreement with the Soviet Union would be signed by the United States before the end of 1972.[43]

On June 26, 1972 President Nixon also disclosed a temporary suspension of the meat import quota for the rest of 1972, as a means of increasing the United States' supply of meat.[44] The meat import quota had been set at about 1.2 billion pounds for 1972 and applied to beef, veal, mutton, and goat meat, which was used mainly for commercial hamburgers and frankfurters. The exporters had acted voluntarily and were from Australia, New Zealand, Mexico, Ireland, Central America and several other areas. The temporary removal of the import quota was not expected to affect the problem of scarcity immediately as there was a world shortage.

Thus it was seen that there were new approaches to problems relating to monetary matters, trade, AID, tariffs and quotas. These reflected changes of policies and set the pattern for the era ahead. Many Executive Agreements and Treaties had already been signed, the TIAS grouping already showing 7314 by August 1, 1972.

On September 13, 1972 Henry A. Kissinger, President Nixon's national security adviser, and Soviet leadership reached an understanding concerning Moscow's outstanding World War II debt, i.e. the World War II Lend-Lease debts, which was an important preliminary to an over-all Soviet-American Trade Agreement. On October 18, 1972 the United States and the U.S.S.R. achieved this Trade Agreement, an Executive Agreement of Class II, which provided for payment to the United States of $722 million in World War II Lend-Lease debts and the extension of United States government-backed credits for sales to the Soviet Union. (The United States was on record as being against the Agreement if the Soviet Union would not lift the exit fees imposed on Jews desiring to emigrate from the Soviet Union.)

43. *New York Times*, September 15, 1972.
44. *Ibid.*

Section B—The Nixon Doctrine, 1971–1972

The American role in Vietnam had to be reshaped so that it contributed to world peace. The Vietnam War was the United States' most difficult war, and the end of the involvement had to come in a way that would not destroy the trust in the United States that other countries had through Agreements with the nation.[45] Major steps, it was seen, had to be taken for peace, steps which were dependent on partnership; and each nation involved in the Vietnam War had to have a stake in the preservation of that peace.

The Vietnam Policy, announced in 1969, had already provided for United States pullbacks of 25,000 on June 8, 1969; of 35,000 on September 16, 1969; of 50,000 on December 15, 1969; of 150,000 on April 20, 1970. Further pullbacks were announced for the next two years: 100,000 on April 7, 1971; 45,000 on November 12, 1971; 70,000 on January 13, 1972; 20,000 on April 26, 1972; 10,000 on June 28, 1972; and 12,000 on August 29, 1972. The President announced that by December, 1972 the troops in Vietnam would number 27,000. Combat activities by May 1, 1972 had been turned over completely to the Vietnamese and there were no active United States ground troops in Vietnam. All of the withdrawals that had taken place were the result of Executive Agreements of Class III or Class I between President Nixon and President Thieu.[46]

The United States wanted the conflict to end for the Vietnamese and their allies as well as for the United States. Since August, 1969 the United States pressed for negotiations with the representatives of Hanoi. The United States hoped that the steady success of South Vietnam and the prospect of South Vietnamese self-reliance would give the other side an incentive to negotiate. For Hanoi, however, negotiations were not a compromise with opponents but a continuation of the military struggle by other means. A long series of measures were suggested to launch meaningful negotiations but each move on the part of the United States brought fresh demands by the Communists. Genuine negotiations never took place. After each withdrawal of troops more withdrawals were required. The removal of all troops was then required. The United States offered to remove all troops as part of

---

45. *WCPD*, Vol. 8, No. 7, p. 326.
46. *U.S. News and World Report*, September 11, 1972, p. 28.

an overall settlement but Hanoi wanted the United States to do so unconditionally. Next the United States offered an immediate ceasefire throughout Indochina but there was no response to this suggestion.

These offers were unilateral measures on the part of the United States, but publicly at the negotiation table in Paris the United States and South Vietnam made a series of proposals. On May 14, 1969,[47] the United States and South Vietnam had proposed that all outside forces be removed from South Vietnam and that the Vietnamese be permitted to choose their future through internationally supervised elections. On July 1, 1969 President Thieu had offered elections with all parties, including the National Liberation Front, to participate and to sit on a Mixed Electoral Commission. On April 20, 1970 the United States had proposed a "fair" political settlement that would reflect the will of the South Vietnamese people, and would allow them to determine their own future without outside interference. The solution was to reflect the existing relationship of political forces within South Vietnam and the United States would abide by the outcome. On October 7, 1970 an overall settlement had been suggested: an internationally supervised ceasefire-in-place throughout Indochina; an Indochina Peace Conference; the withdrawal of all United States forces from South Vietnam on a schedule to be worked out as part of an overall settlement; a political settlement in South Vietnam based on the principles outlined on April 20, 1970; and the immediate unconditional release of all prisoners of war on both sides.[48]

In addition to these public proposals at Paris, after no progress was registered in ten months, a private, secret channel of communication was set up. This was with full knowledge of President Thieu. Ambassadors Lodge, Bruce and Porter were a succession of negotiators. Dr. Henry A. Kissinger,[49] President Nixon's Assistant for National Security Affairs, on twelve occasions between August, 1969 and September, 1971 met with high members of political leadership and the head of the North Vietnamese delegation in Paris, also. On May 31, 1971, for example, the United States offered a total United States withdrawal in return for a prisoner of war exchange, leaving the other issues for settle-

47. *WCPD*, Vol. 8, No. 7, p. 329.
48. *Ibid.*
49. *WCPD*, Vol. 8, No. 7, p. 330.

ment among the Vietnamese themselves, but the North Vietnamese argued that political questions had to be incorporated in any settlement. On June 26, 1971 the North Vietnamese tabled their own Nine Points, a program in which it was demanded that the Government of South Vietnam had to be removed as part of any settlement. The United States as a consequence agreed to deal with political as well as military issues. In effect the Nine Points became the basis of negotiations. Five days later, on July 1, 1971, the North Vietnamese publicly at Paris presented another set of proposals—The National Liberation Front's Seven Points. The NLF Plan focused on issues pertaining to South Vietnam, while Hanoi's secret proposal dealt with all of Indochina. On July 12, 1971 and on July 26, 1971 the United States tried to shape an agreement in principle which both sides could sign and on July 12, 1971 asked the North Vietnamese whether they wanted to address the Nine Point Proposal or the Seven Points. This choice would then be introduced into the public talks as a basis for a detailed negotiation of a final agreement. In pursuance of this goal the United States had to propose a new Eight Point Proposal on August 16, 1971.[50]

The United States on August 16, 1971 offered to withdraw all United States and allied forces within nine months of the date of an agreement. The United States suggested August 1, 1972, provided an agreement was signed by November 1, 1971. The United States proposed: 1) a total United States neutrality in Vietnam elections; 2) acceptance of the outcome of their results; 3) limitations on foreign military aid to South Vietnam if North Vietnam would accept similar restrictions; 4) non-alignment of South Vietnam and the other countries of Indochina; and 5) reunifications on terms for the North and the South to work out. President Nixon also offered to ask Congress for a five-year reconstruction program for Indochina immediately after the signing of the agreement. At the next secret meeting, on September 13, 1971, Hanoi turned down the United States' proposal. It was stated that the interval before total withdrawal was too long and the United States had not made clear what was meant by total withdrawal. They also said the political proposals were insufficient, for they wanted the replacement of the Thieu Government.

President Thieu was informed and consulted about all developments and Executive Agreements of Class III and Class I were to

50. *WCPD*, Vol. 8, No. 7, pp. 330–331.

be the commitments for the proposals to North Vietnam. On October 11, 1971 the United States conveyed a new proposal—a meeting on November 1, 1971 with an appropriate North Vietnam political leader and the Minister Xuan Thuy, head of the North Vietnam delegation in Paris.[51] The North Vietnamese wanted the date of November 20, 1971 and the United States accepted it. On November 17, 1971 the North Vietnamese said the political representative, Mr. Le Duc Tho, was unable to attend the meeting and the United States replied that her representatives would meet any time with any chosen leaders. To February 14, 1972 there was no response from Hanoi.

The United States Government then made public to the American people the course of the negotiations, private and public, and revealed the Eight Point Proposal made by the United States and President Thieu, through an Executive Agreement of Class I, on January 25, 1972 and presented at the Paris Peace Talks on January 27, 1972.[52] Its main elements were that within six months of an agreement there would be a complete withdrawal of all United States and allied forces from South Vietnam; an exchange of all prisoners throughout Indochina; a cease-fire throughout Indochina; and a new presidential election in South Vietnam. The proposal also called for respect for the Geneva Accord of 1954 and the Laos agreements of 1962; settlement by the Indochinese parties themselves of problems existing between them, including the role of North Vietnamese forces; international supervision, as necessary, of the Agreement; and an international guarantee which could involve an international conference. The United States also reaffirmed her willingness to undertake a reconstruction program for Indochina, including North Vietnam.

As far as the South Vietnam presidential election was concerned the following would be respected: [53]

The election would be organized and conducted by an independent body representing all political forces in South Vietnam, including the NLF. This body would begin its work the day the agreement was signed.

One month before the election President Thieu and Vice-President Huong would resign. The Chairman of the Senate would assume the administrative responsibilities of the Government except for those pertaining to the election.

51. *WCPD,* Vol. 8, No. 7, p. 331.
52. *Ibid.*
53. *WCPD,* Vol. 8, No. 7, p. 332.

The election would be internationally supervised.

All United States troops would be out of South Vietnam before election. The United States would remain neutral and support no candidate in the election. The United States would abide by the result or the outcome of any other political process shaped by the South Vietnamese themselves.

The United States offered to begin troop withdrawals and prisoner exchanges upon signature of an Agreement in principle and to complete that process within the specified six month period, provided final agreement had been reached on the other aspects of an overall settlement. Alternately the United States would be willing to settle only the military issues and leave the political issues to be settled separately as suggested in May, 1971. By this the United States would withdraw all United States troops and allied forces within six months in exchange for an Indochina-wide ceasefire and the release of all prisoners. The choice was up to Hanoi. The United States and South Vietnam would listen to additional suggestions from Hanoi.

The new elements of the United States' proposal were, therefore: [54]

The six months for withdrawal.

The withdrawal of United States and allied forces before the elections.

President Thieu's offer to step down one month before the new presidential elections.

The United States' being willing to have limitations on military and economic aid to South Vietnam if North Vietnam would accept limitations on aid it would receive from its allies.

The United States was prepared to undertake a $7\frac{1}{2}$ billion dollar five year reconstruction program in which North Vietnam could share up to $2\frac{1}{2}$ billion dollars.

The following dates reveal the persistence of the United States.[55] On January 26, 1972 President Nixon sent a message to Hanoi indicating readiness to resume private negotiations. On February 14, 1972 Hanoi replied that she was willing to meet any time from March 15 on. On February 17, 1972 the United States suggested March 20 and said she was ready to discuss Hanoi's points. She said that proposals of both sides should be considered. On February 29, 1972 Hanoi accepted the date of

---

54. *WCPD*, Vol. 8, No. 7, p. 333.
55. *WCPD*, Vol. 8, No. 843.

March 20 but on March 6 she postponed the date until April 15, 1972. The United States accepted the date of April 15, 1972 on March 13 but proposed instead the date of April 24. The United States did not hear from Hanoi so Ambassador Porter interrupted the plenaries. On March 23, 1972 President Nixon said the United States would not return to the table unless North Vietnam showed some willingness to negotiate seriously. On March 27, 1972 Hanoi accepted the date of April 24, 1972 provided the United States recalled Ambassador Porter to the table. The United States called Ambassador Porter back and sent a message that was delivered on March 31, 1972 in which she agreed to resume the plenary sessions on April 13 and April 24. There were two plenary sessions and a private one.

The United States did not know, when the arrangements were made, that a major offensive had started at the demilitarized zone. On March 30, 1972 the North Vietnamese launched their first conventional attack of war against the South, and on May 8, 1972 Hanoi threw her whole army into battle. At that time the United States had 60,000 troops in Vietnam. On May 15, 1972,[56] in full accord with the Republic of South Vietnam, by an Executive Agreement of Class I, the United States announced that all entrances to North Vietnam ports would be mined; that rail and all other communications would be cut off to the maximum extent possible; and that air and naval strikes against military targets in North Vietnam would be continued. Ships of other nations were notified that ships would have three daylight periods to leave in safety. The United States refused to return to public forums in Paris until North Vietnam withdrew its forces and the North Vietnamese refused to return to talks until the United States bombing stopped. On July 13, 1972, after a ten week lapse, the Paris peace talks resumed and there was another session on July 20, 1972.[57]

Another flurry of peace talks hit the headlines in mid-August, 1972 and hope was raised for a break in the deadlocked talks at last. By the end of August, 1972, however, Hanoi wanted unconditional surrender and replacement of the current leadership in South Vietnam. So only one issue was left—the United States would not collude with her enemies to overturn her friends. The United States would not impose a future on South Vietnam that

56. *WCPD*, Vol. 8, No. 20, p. 839.
57. *Current History*, September, 1972, p. 139.

North Vietnam had not been able to gain militarily or politically. So long as North Vietnam held United States men as prisoners, calculated at the time to be 1500 of the armed forces and 40 civilians, the United States said that there would be United States forces in South Vietnam.[58]

On September 11, 1972 the North Vietnamese hinted that they would accept a cease-fire in South Vietnam without the removal of President Nguyen Van Thieu and a general compromise seemed possible. On October 12, 1972 Henry A. Kissinger and North Vietnam's Le Duc Tho arrived at a draft of a Nine-Point Agreement, leaving some vital details to be filled in. It seemed to constitute a major breakthrough. The plan separated the purely military issues from the political ones. It provided for an in-place cease-fire immediately, for a United States withdrawal and the return of the American prisoners of war within 60 days, and for the establishment of a purposely vague political process whereby the Vietnamese would work out their future later on. The North Vietnamese wanted an October 31 signing but Mr. Kissinger pointed out on six occasions that the draft would have to be accepted by all parties. From October 13 to 16, 1972, President Nixon and Secretary of State Rogers studied the draft. They saw that some provisions needed tightening up and the understandings for the cease-fire machinery made more definite; but on the whole they registered pleasure at the progress. Mr. Kissinger was sent to Saigon to sell the plan to President Thieu. The latter complained that he was not ready for a cease-fire and repeatedly asked for clarifications and comparisons between the Vietnamese and the English texts but he gave the impression that he would accede. On October 21 President Nixon, acting on this assurance from Mr. Kissinger sent a message to Hanoi, stating that though a few matters needed clarification, "the text of the agreement could be considered complete" and an October 31 signing seemed feasible. The plan was for a bombing halt on October 23 and Mr. Kissinger would go to Hanoi on October 24 to tie up loose-ends in a two-day negotiating session and initial an Agreement. Formal signing would take place in Paris on October 31, 1972.[59]

On October 23, 1972 at the fifth and last meeting of Mr. Kissinger in Saigon, attended only by United States Ambassador Bunker, President Thieu, his Chief Assistant Hoang Duc Nha,

58. *Congressional Quarterly, Weekly Review*, Vol. XXX, p. 219.
59. *Time*, January 1, 1973, p. 21.

and Mr. Kissinger, President Thieu violently denounced the nine-point plan. He insisted on a total withdrawal of North Vietnamese forces and the establishment of the DMZ as a political frontier. He scorned the interim National Council of Reconciliation and Concord as a coalition government in disguise. President Nixon then sent a second message to Hanoi, saying that the October 31 signing was impossible because of difficulties in Saigon and asked for a new round of talks. On October 24 President Thieu took his case to the Vietnamese people emphasizing the sovereignty issue and saying that for the time being two Vietnams would have to be accepted. The next day, October 25, Hanoi broke the secrecy of the Agreement and broadcast a summary of its provisions. This was aimed at forcing the United States to adhere to the original deal despite President Thieu's protests. Mr. Kissinger did not go to Hanoi but back home he still believed that a cease-fire would exist in a few weeks. On October 26, Mr. Kissinger and President Nixon met to consider the position of Hanoi and to discuss the United States' response. It was decided that Mr. Kissinger should go on TV to give the Administration's version in order to maintain the momentum of peace, but Mr. Kissinger was really to be addressing Saigon and Hanoi. President Nixon approved of Mr. Kissinger's saying "We believe that peace is at hand." Six hours later North Vietnam cabled agreement to another round of talks in Paris. Since the Presidential election in the United States was imminent, President Nixon did not want to be accused of playing politics with peace, so decided not to resume negotiations until after the election on November 7, 1972. He was reelected for a second term. Meanwhile not all opinions of the Agreement were favorable in the Pentagon and the State Department. The President ruled that Mr. Kissinger would try to get a concession on the DMZ aspect but that not all of President Thieu's doubts on the sovereignty issue would be dealt with. If the concession on the DMZ was achieved, they would then try to force President Thieu to sign. If he still refused, the United States would make a separate peace with Hanoi.

From November 20 to 25, 1972 Mr. Kissinger, back in Paris, got the North Vietnamese to agree on language affirming the DMZ as a provisional political division line but then the talks stalled, and the two sides broke for an eight-day recess.

On November 29, 1972 President Thieu's special emissary, Nguyen Phu Duc, flew to Washington to tell President Nixon that Hanoi's concessions were insufficient. President Nixon rejected almost all of Nguyen Phu Duc's demands but told Mr. Kissinger to bring up the DMZ issue again at Paris. On December 3, apparently anticipating a breakdown in the talks and a resumption of bombing by the United States, Hanoi began evacuating the capital's school children to the country-side. From December 4 to 13 Mr. Kissinger was again in Paris and for a time the talks went well enough for his deputy, General Alexander Haig, to return to Washington to prepare to take a completed Agreement to Saigon. But when Mr. Kissinger raised the DMZ issue once more, Le Duc Tho became angry, retracted concessions made in earlier sessions and flung down new demands. The long delayed protocol of Hanoi concerning the Interational Control Commission, calling for a force of 250 men to handle what the United States thought would require a force of 5000 men; and a reversal of the fundamental issue of the return of prisoners in South Vietnam, a matter earlier left to later negotiations among the Vietnamese, caused President Nixon to call Mr. Kissinger back and to interrupt the Paris talks. On December 14 President Nixon sent an ultimatum, giving Hanoi 72 hours to resume serious negotiations, and when no answer was received, on December 18 sent bombers to the north again and remined the harbors.[60]

On December 30, 1972 President Nixon announced that he was suspending the air raids on Hanoi and that North Vietnam had agreed to return to "serious" talks in Paris with Mr. Kissinger. On January 8, 1973 Mr. Kissinger had his first talk with Hanoi's Le Duc Tho and on January 11, 1973 Tho indicated that he would make some concessions. The negotiations ended on January 13, 1973 and Mr. Kissinger went to Florida to present the draft of a proposed settlement to President Nixon, picking up his aide, General Alexander M. Haig, Jr., en route in Washington. On January 13, 1973 Mr. Kissinger and Tho had initialed the Agreement but technical teams from both sides remained in Paris to work on the "protocols." On January 15, 1973 President Nixon issued an order that bombing of North Vietnam, already halted, should cease. This was the signal to Hanoi that President Nixon was satisfied and President Thieu got the message. President Nixon then sent General Haig to talk with President Thieu concerning the draft of the Agreement. General Haig warned President Thieu against making any diversionary peace demands of

60. *Time*, January 1, 1973, pp. 21–22.

his own and made clear that if he demurred about signing, Congress would probably end assistance, for the House had a new attitude since the election, and President Nixon would not press Capitol Hill to do otherwise. President Thieu's advisers admitted that the delay in the negotiations and the bombing by the United States had given President Thieu time to consolidate his political position at home and had all but eliminated any chance that North Vietnam would launch a Tet-style offensive in the near future. President Thieu then sent his own technical team to Paris to work on uncompleted details. Announcement was made in Hanoi and Washington on January 18, 1973 that Mr. Kissinger and Tho would meet again in Paris "for the purpose of completing the text of the Agreement."

On January 23, 1973 President Nixon went before the American people on television to say that "Peace with Honor" had been achieved in Vietnam and Southeast Asia. The texts of the Agreement and four Protocols were released by common agreement with North Vietnam, having been initialed in Paris on January 23, 1973 by Mr. Kissinger and Le Duc Tho. On Wednesday, January 24, 1973 Mr. Kissinger made a television appearance in the United States to explain the details of the texts and gave a brilliant account. The Accord and three of the Protocols were drafted in two versions. The "four party" versions were signed in Paris on the morning of January 27, 1973. Because South Vietnam was unwilling to imply recognition of the Vietcong's Provisional Revolutionary Government, "two party" versions mentioning that Government were signed in the afternoon of January 27, 1973 only by the United States and North Vietnam. The Protocol on Clearing Sea Mines related to North Vietnam so it was signed only by the United States and North Vietnam. In all there were 72 signatures necessary.

The parties participating in the Paris Conference were immediately to designate representatives to form a Four-Party Joint Military Commission with the task of insuring joint action by the parties. This Commission was to end in 60 days. After the signing of the Agreement, The International Commission of Control and Supervision was to be established. The headquarters would be at Saigon and it was to be organized in teams. Its reports were to be made on the principle of unanimity.[61]

After five years of negotiation the cease-fire throughout North

61. *New York Times,* January 24–25, 1973.

and South Vietnam was to be effective at 7:00 p.m. Eastern Standard Time of the United States, January 27, 1973. All Americans, military and civilian, engaged in combat were to be withdrawn from Vietnam in 60 days. North Vietnam troops might remain in the South but no replacements were to take place. Foreign troops were to be withdrawn from Laos and Cambodia, although no dateline was set; bases were to be prohibited in these countries and the movement of troops and supplies through them was prohibited. The prisoners of war were to be handed over to American authorities within 60 days. (The first group of the P.O.W.'s arrived in the Philippines on February 12, 1973.) An International Commission of Control and Supervision with a force of 1160 was to supervise the release of prisoners, troop withdrawals, elections and other aspects of the Agreement; the force was to consist of troops from Canada, Hungary, Indonesia and Poland and would be based throughout South Vietnam, including border crossing points. An International Conference, including the Soviet Union, China, the Secretary-General of the United Nations, and the interested states would be convened within 30 days. The United States and North Vietnam agreed to respect "the South Vietnamese people's right to self-determination" and the present government would remain in office pending an election, for which no date was set. The election would be supervised by a National Council of National Reconciliation and Concord, made up of members from the South Vietnamese Government, Communists and neutrals. All sides agreed to respect the Demilitarized Zone, and there would be no military movement across the zone. The use of force to bring about the reunification of North Vietnam and South Vietnam would be prohibited.

President Nixon in his television address emphasized that he had had the closest support of President Thieu and other allies, and appealed to the world to see that the peace would last and be a peace that would heal. He made clear that the peace had to be kept; and he expected other interested countries to assist in respect for the Agreement and in exercising self-restraint. The people of South Vietnam were given the "precious right" to defend their own future. It was to be a peace of reconciliation and its terms had to be scrupulously adhered to. He said that the United States could be proud that she had not betrayed her allies. He mentioned that President Johnson, who had died the previous day, would have welcomed this peace. In the few days before the peace went into effect there was military activity to grab land but it was hoped that it was a peace that would last. President Thieu announced the completion of the Agreement to his people at the same time. A cease-fire in Laos and a unilateral withdrawal of troops in Cambodia were soon to be expected.[62]

Here then was the most heralded Executive Agreement of Class I of the New Era. There was no question of making it a Treaty. It seemed to be accepted gratefully as an Executive Agreement, even by Congress!

Section C—New Congressional Opposition

Increased United States activities in Southeast Asia had given rise to new efforts in Congress to curb the Executive power and to legislate an end to the Vietnam War. How the United States got involved in, and its strategy for disengaging from, this war provided the framework for the war-powers debate of 1971 and 1972. The debate recalled the Bricker Controversy, emphasizing the power of Congress to declare war and requiring Congressional consent for Executive Agreements.

There was a series of bills by which the Foreign Relations Committee challenged the assumption of larger foreign powers by the President since World War II. In 1971 the Senate on three different occasions passed amendments to bills setting specific dates for withdrawal of troops from Vietnam. Sponsored by Senator Mike Mansfield the amendments were opposed by the White House and on all three occasions were either killed or watered down by the House of Representatives. On January 19, 1971 the Foreign Relations Committee also reported a bill requiring that Congress receive promptly the text of any International Agreement made by the Executive branch (S 596). The Subcommittee on United States Security and Commitments Abroad, chaired by Stuart Symington, criticized the secrecy surrounding United States commitments and military bases abroad in hearings and reports produced by a 1969–1970 investigation on military activities overseas. Senator Clifford P. Case, a member of the subcommittee, had introduced S596 on February 4, 1971.[63] In its report the committee said it might in the future ". . . explore the question whether the executive is exceeding its constitutional authority in making some of these agreements." S596, however,

62. *New York Times,* January 24–25, 1973.
63. *Congressional Quarterly, Weekly Review,* Vol. XXX, p. 219.

was addressed to ". . . . the prior, more elemental obligation of the executive to keep the Congress informed of all of its foreign transactions, including those of a sensitive nature. . . . As the committee has discovered, there have been numerous agreements contracted with foreign governments in recent years, particularly agreements of a military nature, which remain wholly unknown to Congress and the people. A number of agreements have been uncovered by the Symington subcommittee . . . including, for example, an agreement with Ethiopia in 1960, agreements with Laos in 1963, with Thailand in 1964 and again in 1967, with Korea in 1966 and certain secret annexes to the Spanish bases agreement." The Nixon Administration opposed the bill during hearings held on October 21, 1971, proposing instead that Congressional knowledge of such agreements should be assured by "practical arrangements." The committee suggested, however, that the "practical arrangements" would still fail to establish the obligation of the Executive to report all agreements with foreign powers to the Congress.

The House on August 2, 1971 passed a resolution requiring the President to submit a written explanation to Congress if he acted without Congressional consent to commit United States troops to combat, sent combat-equipped forces to foreign countries or significantly enlarged military forces stationed abroad. The resolution urged the President to consult Congress before sending Americans into conflict but recognized his authority to defend the nation and its citizens in emergencies without specific legislative approval.[64]

On February 9, 1972 the Senate Foreign Relations Committee by unanimous vote reported a bill (S2956-S Rept 92-606) setting limits to the President's use of armed forces without specific Congressional authorization. The chief sponsors were Senators Jacob K. Javits and John C. Stennis. The bill although not made effective, defined emergency conditions in which the President could commit forces "in the absence of a declaration of war by the Congress." It also prescribed procedures by which Congress could terminate the emergency use of American forces if it disapproved of the President's action. The Committee exempted United States participation in the Indochina fighting from its provisions.[65]

The Bill S2956 provided that the situations where imminent

64. *Congressional Quarterly, Weekly Review,* Vol. XXX, No. 8, p. 219.
65. *Congressional Quarterly, Weekly Review,* Vol. XXX, No. 5, p. 219.

involvement was clearly indicated were to repel an armed attack on the United States, or to forestall the "direct and imminent threat of such an attack"; to repel an armed attack on the United States armed forces outside the United States or to forestall the threat of such an attack; and to protect and evacuate United States citizens and nationals in another country if their lives were threatened. The Bill required the President to report promptly to Congress the commitment of forces for such purposes; limited to thirty days the length of involvement of the United States forces unless Congress by specific legislation authorized their continued use; provided that Congress by act or joint resolution could terminate the use of United States forces by the President before the end of the thirty-day period; set procedures to require prompt consideration in both houses of any bill or joint resolution authorizing or terminating use of United States forces committed by the President; made the bill's provisions effective on the date of enactment; but exempted hostilities in which the United States forces were involved on the effective date.

The Senate on July 24, 1972 by a roll call rejected the fiscal 1973 foreign military aid authorization bill. It was the second rejection of a foreign aid bill in less than a year but the importance was that a Senate amendment that was attached was the first provision approved by either chamber that would have imposed a cutoff of funds for continuing United States participation in the Vietnam War.[66] Little headway had been made for such a cutoff.

By April, 1972 the controversy concerning the President's powers had spilled over to the court system. Representative Mitchell and twelve other Democratic House members filed a suit in the United States District Court for the District of Columbia seeking an injunction against the Administration's continuing the war without Congressional authorization; and on May 11, 1972 a suit was filed by two Senators and 20 Representatives and the District of Columbia Delegate. The cases were pending in 1973.[67]

Section D—The Pacific

The United States in 1972 was remaining a Pacific power. She had withdrawn some of her troops—20,000 from South Korea; 12,000 from Japan; 5,000 from Okinawa; 16,000 from Thailand;

66. *Congressional Quarterly, Weekly Review*, Vol. XXX, No. 27, p. 1573.
67. *WCPD*, Vol. 8, No. 7, p. 325.

and 9,000 from the Philippines—but she made it known that she would respect all of her commitments, both Treaties and Executive Agreements, with Asiatic countries, including Taiwan, although she was unable to prevent the United Nations from admitting the Democratic Republic of China to the Assembly and giving the Council seat to her. All insignia of the Republic of China were removed from the headquarters of the United Nations but Secretary Rogers said that the United States' support of Taiwan would be "unaffected." [68]

Japan by 1972 had become the United States' most important ally and her second most important trading partner. The wellbeing of both countries required cooperation and a shared commitment to the same fundamental goals. Japan in 1972 was playing a major and steadily increasing role in assisting other Asian nations with their developing needs. She had pledged 1% of her gross national product to assisting less developed countries; she was playing a greater role in the Asian Development Bank; and she was prominent in the international groupings providing assistance to Indonesia and the Philippines.[69]

Okinawa had been under American administration for over twenty-five years. In November, 1969, as has been stated, Prime Minister Sato and President Nixon met and accepted through an Executive Agreement of Class I broad principles which should govern the reversion of Okinawa to Japanese administration. On June 21, 1971 negotiations resulted in a new Treaty which terminated the last vestige of World War II on May 15, 1972. The United States retains her military installations in Okinawa but on the same basis as those in the Japanese home islands.[70]

In the fall of 1971 President Nixon traveled to Alaska to welcome to American soil the Emperor and Empress of Japan on the first visit abroad of a Japanese reigning monarch. In September, 1971 in Washington seven Japanese Cabinet officers and their American counterparts had a joint meeting for a wide-ranging and authoritative examination of the trade relationships of the two countries. Prime Minister Sato and President Nixon also met at San Clemente in California in January, 1972 to discuss the relationship of the two industrial powers. Then came President and Mrs. Nixon's trip to Communist China from February 21 to 28,

---

68. *Current History*, December, 1971, p. 379.
69. *WCPD*, Vol. 8, No. 7, p. 282.
70. *WCPD*, Vol. 8, No. 7, p. 929.

1972 and Japan's trying to respond by building her own trade with Communist China and by establishing diplomatic recognition of her.

President Nixon and Japan's new Prime Minister, Kakuei Tanaka, met for two days of summit talks the end of August, 1972 in Hawaii. At this time the United States seemed to make clear the necessity of Japan's liberalizing her import practices.[71] The difficulty was recognized as being Japan's archaic distribution system with its large trading companies, which funnel the consumer goods through wholesalers to the small shops, each step requiring fees to be added.

By keeping a Pacific naval presence, as well as having United States' possession in that area, the United States was able to command respect for her promise to keep her commitments.

Section E—European Commitments

The United States after World War II had, as a member of NATO, been one of the strong adversaries of Communism and considered NATO the insurance against Communism in the Western world. One of the objectives of President and Mrs. Nixon in taking their trip to the U.S.S.R. in May, 1972 was to follow the breakthrough in the SALT talks, which had occurred in May, 1971. The talks had been engaged in at Helsinki and Vienna alternately since 1969 to limit the nuclear competition between the United States and the U.S.S.R. and resulted in a summit meeting because of President Nixon's direct contact with Soviet leaders. In addition to the economic Executive Agreements of Class IV that had been framed before and during the visit and that had created a cordial atmosphere in 1972, the security agreements that were accomplished were a couple of Executive Agreements of Class IV, a Treaty, and an Interim Strategic Arms Limitation Agreement, an Executive Agreement of Class III.

The first Executive Agreement of Class IV included a pledge to take steps each considered necessary to guard against accidental or unauthorized use of nuclear weapons; arrangements for rapid commuication, should a nuclear war arise from such nuclear incidents or from detection of unidentified objects on early warning systems; advance notification of certain planned missile launches.

The second Executive Agreement of Class IV, which served in

---

71. *New York Times,* September 1, 1972.

part to implement the first one, provided for the improvement and modernization of the Washington-Moscow Direct Communications Link or "Hot Line," which was established in 1963.[72]

The Anti-Ballistic-Missile Treaty was a defensive one. It had the following provisions: [73]

"Each nation is limited to a maximum of 200 ABM's—half to be deployed in defense of land-based intercontinental missiles, the others around Moscow and Washington.

"ABM sites must be at least 806 miles apart and may occupy a circular area with a diameter not exceeding 186 miles. . . .

"ABM's must be emplaced in fixed land positions. Each side agrees not to 'develop, test or deploy ABM systems or components which are sea-based, air-based, space-based or mobile land-based.'

"Each nation is limited to two large and 18 smaller radars, for tracking and guidance, in six complexes around each site. . . .

"Each side agrees to provide any other nation with an ABM defense. . . .

"Neither nation will test ABM's with more than one warhead. . . .

"ABM systems will be limited to interceptor missiles, launchers and radars. . . .

"Neither side is permitted to give antimissile capabilities to existing antiaircraft systems.

" 'National means'—that is, spy satellites—will be used by each side to determine whether the other is cheating. . . .

"Although the treaty is of unlimited duration, it can be abrogated on six months' notice by either side."

The Interim Agreement on Offensive Arms is an Executive Agreement of Class III. It had the following provisions: [74]

"The U.S. and the Soviet Union pledge a limitation on the deployment of offensive missiles for the next five years. . . .

"Essentially, the Soviets can possess 2,359 offensive missile launchers; the U.S., 1,710. (Note: While this gave the Russians a lead in launchers, . . . the U.S. reportedly led in warheads by a margin of 2 to 1.)

"Each nation is permitted to retire old land and sea-based missiles and replace them on a 1-for-1 basis with newer submarine-launched rockets. The Soviets could have 950 missiles in 62 sub-

---

72. Weekly Compilation of Presidential Documents, September 27, 1971.
73. *U.S. News and World Report,* July 3, 1972, p. 59.
74. *Ibid.*

marines under this arrangement, while the U.S. would be limited to 710 in 44 submarines.

"Neither side may construct new fixed-position, land-based launchers for missiles.

"In modernizing and replacing land-based missiles, neither side may substitute a launcher 'significantly increased' in size. The growth limit is 10 to 15 per cent of the present size of rockets.

"Spy satellites also will be used to verify compliance, as in the ABM Treaty.

"The five-year agreement may be abrogated by either nation on six months' notice."

The Agreements do not cover the following items:

"No numerical limit is placed on bombers. The U.S. has 457 long-range bombers, compared with the Soviets' 140.

"No prohibition is extended to MIRV's—multiple, independently targeted re-entry vehicles. (Note: The U.S. planned to equip 550 of its 1,000 Minutemen missiles and 31 of its 41 missile-firing submarines with such multiple warheads. The Soviets had tested somewhat similar re-entry vehicles.)

"No restriction is placed on research, development and testing in the field of new weapons, although actual deployment is restricted in some instances."

The Treaty was held for ratification, after the Senate had acted, so that the Interim Agreement could have Congressional approval at the same time. This sanction was given the third week of September, 1972, although the Interim Agreement carried an amendment, proposed by Senator Jackson, to assure equality when a Treaty on Offensive Arms was finally arrived at. Further discussions would continue in Geneva.

At the end of President Nixon's Moscow visit there was issued a Joint Communiqué, an Executive Agreement of Class IV, which included "measures to prevent incidents at sea and in air-space over it between vessels and aircraft of the U.S. and Soviet navies." By indirection, in one sea, the Soviet Union complied for the TU-Badger reconnaissance planes that had overflown the U.S. Sixth Fleet in the Mediterranean from Egyptian bases had gone home. The Soviets hoped to retain the use of Egyptian naval bases at Alexandria and Mersa Matruh as well as Port Said and were said in September, 1972 to have been granted the right to build up naval facilities in Latakia and Tartus in Syria. The Russians were reported to have had orders to withdraw their naval personnel from repair facilities and spare parts warehouses in Egyptian ports.[75]

Cultural relations between the U.S.S.R. and the United States were revived and in the summer of 1973 the State University of New York at Binghamton sent an art exhibit to the U.S.S.R., reciprocal to the exhibit of the U.S.S.R. on its campus in 1968, and the Director of the Art Gallery was invited to be a guest of the Government of the U.S.S.R.

The United States, although it operated a "naval train" from Norfolk, Virginia to the Mediterranean to replenish the Sixth Fleet, also maintained naval facilities in Spain, Italy and Greece.[76] On December 8, 1971 Portugal negotiated a five-year extension of an Executive Agreement of Class IV granting an extension of the use of air and naval bases in the Azores.[77] The pact provided for economic aid to Portugal in the form of up to $435 millions in economic and social development credits.

The United States had other contacts with the continent of Europe. As a member of the United Nations she in recent years felt the weakness of that body but she had been a member of the Committee on Disarmament at Geneva out of the deliberations of which had come a number of multilateral Treaties that she had ratified. On September 3, 1971 she was a party also to the Four Power Treaty on Berlin, in which the Soviet Union guaranteed unimpeded and preferential civilian traffic between the Western Sectors of Berlin and the Federal Republic of Germany.[78] As a result of negotiation between the United States and Turkey it was announced on June 30, 1971 that the cultivation of the opium poppy in Turkey would cease within one year and that an Executive Agreement of Class IV had been signed.[79]

The United States stated that she was not withdrawing any troops from NATO in the early seventies and seemed to welcome the enlargement of the European Economic Community even though, with half of the world trade, the Common Market would be a competitor.

75. *New York Times,* September 14, 1972.
76. *Time,* August 14, 1972.
77. *Current History,* February, 1972.
78. *WCPD,* Vol. 8, No. 7, p. 267.
79. *WCPD,* Vol. 7, No. 27.

Section F—The Third World

The Third World was an emerging world made up of Southern Asia, Africa, and Latin America. In Southern Asia the United States kept a naval presence and had bases, the last of which was acquired by an Executive Agreement of Class IV at Bahrain in December, 1971. The United States had had no previous agreement with Bahrain, an independent sheikdom on the Persian Gulf under British protection until 1971. Since 1949, however, several United States Navy vessels, designated as the Middle East Force, had been deployed in the area, sharing British base facilities at Bahrain. Great Britain in August, 1971 decided to withdraw from the area and the Nixon Administration subsequently decided to keep the Middle East Force in the gulf and to negotiate a direct agreement with Bahrain. There was to be an annual leasing of facilities occupying about 10% of the area of the former British base but there was to be no political or military security commitment involved.[80]

The United States had a non-interference policy in African political affairs. There was a growing trade with Africa, however, and in 1971 there was the opening of the United States sugar market to Malawi and Uganda and an increase in the quotas for Madagascar, Mauritius and Swaziland. From August to December, 1971 the United States exempted many African raw material exports from the temporary import surcharge. President Nixon wished to submit to Congress legislation to implement a system of generalized preferences for the exports of developing areas including Africa. In 1972 the United States opened in Nigeria her first Regional Trade Center in Africa.[81]

South Africa had rejected the holding of the International Court of Justice in 1971 that she was obliged to quit Nambia but the United States has accepted the Court's holding and has discouraged private investment there.

In South Rhodesia after six years of economic sanctions designed to end the rebellion of that country against Great Britain, the two countries reached an agreement in November, 1971 on terms of a proposed settlement. These terms were to be put before the people of Rhodesia. On March 9, 1970 the United States announced that she would close her consulate in Rhodesia on March 17, 1971 but

80. *Congressional Quarterly, Weekly Review,* Vol. XXX, No. 10, p. 497.
81. *WCPD,* Vol. 8, No. 7, p. 322.

on November 17, 1971 President Nixon ended the ban on the importation of Rhodesian chrome as of January 1, 1972. He said, however, that he would take no action under this Executive Agreement of Class II during the course of negotiations between Great Britain and Rhodesia.[82]

In 1969, as far as Latin America was concerned, there was still the easy assumption of a hemisphere community because of geography, history and a common heritage of self-government. This feeling was enhanced by a shared experience in World War II and the new inter-America system. In the 70's, however, all of this was challenged by the new intensity of nationalism, pluralism, and pressures for change.

The United States was not responsible for all of Latin America's problems but she needed a new approach to hemisphere policy in order to respond to new conditions constructively. She concluded that geography and history did give the relationship with Latin America a special importance, for political ties in the unique hemisphere were unique, but a growing sense of national and regional identity in Latin America brought differentiation from the United States. The problems were at their roots political. Solutions would be found in reconciliations of basic interests and not merely in economic programs. In the long run the United States hoped that after development the achievement of progress would boost national self-assurance. However, the frustration of the developing process and the mobility of national energies brought some anti-United States sentiment. President Nixon then attempted a new approach which reflected the Nixon Doctrine.[83]

The United States changed the manner of participation in both bilateral and collective efforts and encouraged the initiatives of partners. She assumed a new role of leadership and support doing justice to the national dignity of her partners. The policies of the United States reflected a wider sharing of ideas and responsibilities in hemisphere collaboration; a mature response to political diversity and nationalism; a practical and concrete contribution to economic and social development; and a humanitarian concern for the quality of life in the hemisphere. Since consultation fosters shared objectives there were face to face talks of President Nixon with the Presidents of Brazil, Colombia, Venezuela, Nicaragua and Mexico. The Latin American nations frequently consulted among

82. *Current History,* January, 1972, p. 62.
83. *WCPD,* Vol. 8, No. 7, p. 311.

themselves before consulting the United States. The Special Coordinating Commission for Latin America, for example, produced the Consensus of Vina del Mar, which contributed to the Nixon program announced in October, 1969. The task of the United States was to respond constructively to change.

There was a welcome reform in October, 1969—the relaxation of restrictions which "tied" United States loans to Latin America to the purchase of United States exports. The United States gave financial and technical support to enhance the effectiveness of multilateral institutions as vehicles for Latin American leadership in planning development assistance and setting development priorities. In 1970 she created the Inter-American Social Development Institute to assist the growth of non-governmental institutions. She sent assistance to victims of disaster and aid to Peru after the earthquake of 1970.[84]

The United States exempted the hemisphere from the 10% reduction of bilateral foreign aid which was a part of the August 15, 1971 emergency New Economic Policy of the United States. She supported efforts to develop capital markets, tourism, and export promotion and to facilitate the transfer of technological information for development needs. She gave assistance to the Central American Bank for Economic Integration and the Caribbean Development Bank.

Executive Agreements of Class I were signed with Panama and Colombia on the financing of the last unfinished link of the Pan American Highway—the Darien Gap. Construction could begin in 1972. The United States and Nicaragua in 1971 abrogated the Bryan-Chamorro Treaty, relinquishing canal construction rights in Nicaragua which the United States no longer required. Presidential Counsellor Finch, visiting six Latin American countries on behalf of the President in November, 1971, signed an Executive Agreement of Class IV, recognizing Honduran sovereignty over the Swan Islands. The two governments agreed to establish a cooperative meterological program on the islands. The United States entered upon new negotiations with Panama to achieve a mutually acceptable basis for the continuing efficient operation and defense of the Panama Canal.[85]

Fisheries disputes and the problem of expropriation flared up in 1971. A fisheries dispute came in 1971 with Ecuador when a

84. *WCPD*, Vol. 8, No. 7, p. 318.
85. *WCPD* Vol. 8, No. 7, p. 314.

number of United States owned tuna boats fishing within the claimed 200-mile territorial sea were seized and fined. There were similar disputes with Peru and Brazil. Since the technical issue was a dispute over the legal definition of the territorial sea, the United States believed it was salutary to negotiate an interim solution: to halt the seizures and sanctions while continuing the juridical positions of both sides until the 1973 United Nations Conference on the Law of the Sea.

As to the problem of expropriation International Law permits nondiscriminatory nationalization of property for public purposes but it also requires reasonable provision for prompt, adequate and effective compensation. Some Executive Agreements of Class IV were negotiated but in some cases legitimate interests of private investors were treated arbitrarily and inequitably. In January, 1972 President Nixon announced principles that were to govern the United States policy on this matter worldwide. The United States would deal realistically with governments right and left. Chile was an example concerning copper companies. There were ideological differences between Chile and the United States but relations were to hinge not on ideology but on conduct toward the outside world, for International Law is a world interest.

Cuba engaged in subversive violence and increased her military ties with the U.S.S.R. The United States declared that she would consider change in the OAS sanctions against Cuba only when the evidence demonstrated a real change in Cuba's policies.[86]

There was an especially close relationship between Mexico and the United States. Presidential talks were held in 1969 and 1970. These resulted in Executive Agreements of Class IV on such matters as narcotics control, boundaries, civil air routes, agricultural imports, Colorado River salinity, joint flood control projects and the return of archaeological treasures. On May 16, 1972 the twelfth Mexico-United States Interparliamentary Conference was held in Washington.[87] On June 15, 1972 there was an exchange of diplomatic notes between Secretary Rogers and the Mexican Secretary of Foreign Relations bringing into effect an Executive Agreement of Class IV in the scientific, technical and cultural fields.[88]

The regions of the Third World thus seemed to have many different Executive Agreements for many were in need of AID, de-

---

86. *WCPD*, Vol. 8, No. 7, p. 316.
87. *WCPD*, Vol. 8, No. 7, p. 881.
88. *WCPD*, Vol. 8, No. 25, p. 1054.

sired the Peace Corps, wanted financial credits and loans for their trade, expected preferential tariffs, and welcomed private investment.

Section G—The New Challenge

The Nixon Doctrine was applicable on a global basis and pointed the way for a new kind of leadership. There was a transition in policy, for the United States was at the end of one era and the beginning of another. The configuration of power that emerged from World War II was gone and a new kind of strength on the part of the United States was displayed.

Increasingly there had been new issues that transcended geographic and ideological borders and confronted the world community of nations. Many flowed from the nature of modern technology. Travel had become commonplace, on the part not only of government leaders but on the part of the general public. Contacts reflected a shrinking globe and expanding interdependence. The global issues showed a new dimension of international cooperation that called for commitments in the form of Executive Agreements and Treaties.

By January 20, 1973, the date of the Vietnam cease-fire, the number of International Agreements in the TIAS had reached 7470 and there had been a huge increase in Executive Agreements. More care was going into the framework of Executive Agreements and they had more specific provisions for renewal and for termination.

The controversy between the Executive and the Congress, precipitated by the great use of Executive Agreements and the great complexity of modern living, needed to be faced squarely. The controversy was no longer a game of criticism of the President for being desirous of power but it was a challenge to Congress itself to be informed concerning the details of international relations and to give time to the exercise of high office.

Appendix A

PRINCIPAL VERSIONS OF THE BRICKER AMENDMENT—1952–1957

See U.S. Senate, 84th Congress, 2d Sess., Report No. 1716 by Mr. Dirksen on S. J. Res. 1, p. 24; and U.S. Senate, 85th Congress, 1st Sess., Hearing before a Subcommittee of the Committee on the Judiciary on S. J. Res. 3, pp. 10, 22, and 415 (Washington: Government Printing Office).

(1)

Introduced by Sen. Bricker
S. J. Res. 130 (82d Cong.)
Feb. 7, 1952

"SECTION 1. No treaty or executive agreement shall be made respecting the rights of citizens of the United States protected by this Constitution, or abridging or prohibiting the free exercise thereof.

"SEC. 2. No treaty or executive agreement shall vest in any international organization or in any foreign power any of the legislative, executive, or judicial powers vested by this Constitution in the Congress, the President, and the courts of the United States, respectively.

"SEC. 3. No treaty or executive agreement shall alter or abridge the laws of the United States or the Constitution or laws of the several States unless, and then only to the extent that, Congress shall so provide by Act or joint resolution.

"SEC. 4. Executive agreements shall not be made in lieu of treaties.

"Executive agreements shall, if not sooner terminated, expire automatically one year after the end of the term of office for which the President making the agreement shall have been elected, but the Congress may, at the request of any President, extend for the duration of the term of such President the life of any such agreement made or extended during the next preceding Presidential term.

"The President shall publish all executive agreements except those which in his judgment require secrecy shall be submitted to appropriate committees of the Congress in lieu of publication.

"SEC. 5. Congress shall have power to enforce this article by appropriate legislation."

(2)

Introduced by Sen. Bricker
S. J. Res. 1 (83d Cong.)
Jan. 7, 1953

"SECTION 1. A provision of a treaty which denies or abridges any right enumerated in this Constitution shall not be of any force or effect.

"SEC. 2. No treaty shall authorize or permit any foreign power or any international organization to supervise, control, or adjudicate rights of citizens of the United States within the United States enumerated in this Constitution or any other matter essentially within the domestic jurisdiction of the United States.

"SEC. 3. A treaty shall become effective as internal law in the United States only through the enactment of appropriate legislation by the Congress.

"SEC. 4. All executive or other agreements between the President and any international organization, foreign power, or official thereof shall be made only in the manner and to the extent to be prescribed by law. Such agreements shall be subject to the limitations imposed on treaties, or the making of treaties, by this article.

"SEC. 5. The Congress shall have power to enforce this article by appropriate legislation."

(3)

Introduced by Sen. Watkins
S. J. Res. 43 (83d Cong.)
1953

"SECTION 1. A provision of a treaty which conflicts with any provision of this Constitution shall not be of any force or effect.

"A treaty shall become effective as internal law in the United States only through legislation which would be valid in the absence of treaty.

"Executive agreements shall be subject to regulation by the Congress and to the limitations imposed on treaties by this article.

"SEC. 2. The Congress shall have power to enforce this article by appropriate legislation."

APPENDIX   195

(4)

Revised Version of S. J. Res. 1 (83d Cong.), as Proposed by the Committee on the Judiciary
1953

"SECTION 1. A provision of a treaty which conflicts with this Constitution shall not be of any force or effect.

"SEC. 2. A treaty shall become effective as internal law in the United States only through legislation which would be valid in the absence of treaty.

"SEC. 3. Congress shall have power to regulate all executive and other agreements with any foreign power or international organization. All such agreements shall be subject to the limitations imposed on treaties by this article.

"SEC. 4. The Congress shall have power to enforce this article by appropriate legislation."

(5)

George Substitute
Jan. 27, 1954

"SECTION 1. A provision of a treaty or other international agreement which conflicts with this Constitution shall not be of any force or effect.

"SEC. 2. An international agreement other than a treaty shall become effective as internal law in the United States only by an act of the Congress."

(6)

Ferguson-Knowland Substitute
Feb. 2, 1954

"SECTION 1. A provision of a treaty or other international agreement which conflicts with this Constitution shall not be of any force or effect.

"SEC. 2. Clause 2 of article VI of the Constitution of the United States is hereby amended by adding at the end thereof the following: "Notwithstanding the foregoing provisions of this clause, no treaty made after the establishment of this Constitution shall be the supreme law of the land unless made in pursuance of this Constitution.'

"SEC. 3. On the question of advising and consenting to the ratification of a treaty the vote shall be determined by yeas and nays, and the names of the persons voting for and against shall be entered on the Journal of the Senate."

(7)

Bricker Substitute
Feb. 4, 1954

"SECTION 1. Clause 2 of article VI on the Constitution of the United States is hereby amended by adding at the end thereof: 'Notwithstanding the foregoing provisions of this clause, no treaty made after the establishment of this Constitution shall be the supreme law of the land unless made in pursuance of this Constitution.'

"SEC. 2. A provision of a treaty or other international agreement which conflicts with this Constitution shall not be of any force or effect.

"SEC. 3. A treaty or other international agreement shall become effective as internal law in the United States only through legislation by the Congress unless in advising and consenting to a treaty the Senate, by a vote of two-thirds of the Senators present and voting, shall provide that such treaty may become effective as internal law without legislation by the Congress.

"SEC. 4. On the question of consenting to the ratification of a treaty the vote shall be determined by yeas and nays, and the names of the persons voting for and against shall be entered on the Journal of the Senate."

(8)

Introduced by Sen. Bricker
S. J. Res 181 (83d Cong.)
Aug. 5, 1954
and S. J. Res. 1 (84th Cong.)
Jan. 6, 1955

"SECTION 1. A provision of a treaty or other international agreement which conflicts with this Constitution, or which is not made in pursuance thereof, shall not be the supreme law of the land nor be of any force or effect.

"SEC. 2. A treaty or other international agreement shall become effective as internal law in the United States only through legislation valid in the absence of international agreement.

"SEC. 3. On the question of advising and consenting to the ratification of a treaty, the vote shall be determined by yeas and nays, and the names of the persons voting for and against shall be entered on the Journal of the Senate."

(9)

Dirksen Substitute (84th Cong.), as Proposed by the
Committee on the Judiciary
Mar. 5, 1956

"SECTION 1. A provision of a treaty or other international agreement which conflicts with any provision of this Constitution shall not be of any force or effect.

"SEC. 2. On the question of advising and consenting to the ratification of a treaty, the vote shall be determined by yeas and nays, and the names of the persons voting for and against shall be entered on the Journal of the Senate."

(10)

Introduced by Sen. Bricker
S. J. Res. 3 (85th Cong.)
Jan. 7, 1957

"SECTION 1. A provision of a treaty or other international agreement not made in pursuance of this Constitution shall have no force or effect. This section shall not apply to treaties made prior to the effective date of this Constitution.

"SEC. 2. A treaty or other international agreement shall have legislative effect within the United States as a law thereof only through legislation, except to the extent that the Senate shall provide affirmatively, in its resolution advising and consenting to a treaty, that the treaty shall have legislative effect.

"SEC. 3. An international agreement other than a treaty shall have legislative effect within the United States as a law thereof only through legislation valid in the absence of such an international agreement.

"SEC. 4. On the question of advising and consenting to a treaty, the vote shall be determined by yeas and nays, and the names of the Senators voting for and against shall be entered on the Journal of the Senate."

Appendix B

LETTER OF PRESIDENT NGO DINH DIEM TO PRESIDENT JOHN F. KENNEDY, December 7, 1961

Dear Mr. President:

In the course of the last few months, the Communist assault on my people has achieved high ferocity. In October they caused more than 1,800 incidents of violence and more than 2,000 casualties. They have struck occasionally in battalion strength, and they are continually augmenting their forces by infiltration from the North. The level of their attacks is already such that our forces are stretched to the utmost. We are forced to defend every village, every hamlet, indeed every home against a foe whose tactic is always to strike at the defenseless.

A disastrous flood was recently added to the misfortunes of the Vietnamese people. The greater part of three provinces was inundated, with a great loss of property. We are now engaged in a nationwide effort to reconstruct and rehabilitate this area. The Communists are, of course, making this task doubly difficult, for they have seized upon the disruption of normal administration and communications as an opportunity to sow more destruction in the stricken area.

In short, the Vietnamese nation now faces what is perhaps the gravest crisis in its long history. For more than 2,000 years my people have lived and built, fought and died in this land. We have not always been free. Indeed, much of our history and many of its proudest moments have arisen from conquest by foreign powers and our struggle against great odds to regain or defend our precious independence. But it is not only our freedom which is at stake today, it is our national identity. For, if we lose this war, our people will be swallowed by the Communist Bloc, all our proud heritage will be blotted out by the "Socialist society" and Viet-Nam will leave the pages of history. We will lose our national soul.

Mr. President, my people and I are mindful of the great assistance which the United States has given us. Your help has not been lightly received, for the Vietnamese are proud people, and we are determined to do our part in the defense of the free world. It is clear to all of us that the defeat of the Viet Cong demands the total mobilization of our government and our people, and you may be sure that we will devote all of our resources of money, minds, and men to this great task.

But Viet-Nam is not a great power and the forces of International Communism now arrayed against us are more than we can meet with the resources at hand. We must have further assistance from the United States if we are to win the war now being waged against us.

We can certainly assure mankind that our action is purely defensive. Much as we regret the subjugation of more than half of our people in North Viet-Nam, we have no intention, and indeed no means, to free them by use of force.

I have said that Viet-Nam is at war. War means many things, but most of all it means the death of brave people for a cause they believe in. Viet-Nam has suffered many wars, and through the centuries we have always had patriots and heroes who were willing to shed their blood for Viet-Nam. We will keep faith with them.

When Communism has long ebbed away into the past, my people will still be here, a free united nation growing from the deep roots of our Vietnamese heritage. They will remember your help in our time of need. This struggle will then be a part of our common history. And your help, your friendship, and the strong bonds between our two peoples will be a part of Viet-Nam, then as now.

NGO DINH DIEM

THE PRESIDENT
The White House
Washington, D.C.
[Attachment to White House press release dated Dec. 14, 1961 (text as printed in the Department of State *Bulletin,* Jan. 1, 1962, pp. 13–14).]

Appendix C

LETTER OF JOHN F. KENNEDY TO PRESIDENT NGO DINH DIEM, December 14, 1961

Dear Mr. President: I have received your recent letter in which you described so cogently the dangerous condition caused by North Viet-Nam's efforts to take over your country. The situation in your embattled country is well known to me and to the American people. We have been deeply disturbed by the assault on your country. Our indignation has mounted as the deliberate savagery of the Communist program of assassination, kidnapping and wanton violence became clear.

Your letter underlines what our own information has convincingly shown—that the campaign of force and terror now being waged against your people and your Government is supported and directed from the outside by the authorities at Hanoi. They have thus violated the provisions of the Geneva Accords designed to ensure peace in Viet-Nam and to which they bound themselves in 1954.

At that time, the United States, although not a party to the Accords, declared that it "would view any renewal of the aggression in violation of the agreements with grave concern and as seriously threatening international peace and security." We continue to maintain that view.

In accordance with that declaration, and in response to your request, we are prepared to help the Republic of Viet-Nam to protect its people and to preserve its independence. We shall promptly increase our assistance to your defense effort as well as help relieve the destruction of the floods which you describe. I have already given the orders to get these programs underway.

The United States, like the Republic of Viet-Nam, remains devoted to the cause of peace and our primary purpose is to help your people maintain their independence. If the Communist authorities in North Viet-Nam will stop their campaign to destroy the Republic of Viet-Nam, the measures we are taking to assist your defense efforts will no longer be necessary. We shall seek to persuade the Communists to give up their attempts of force and subversion. In any case, we are confident that the Vietnamese people will preserve their independence and gain the peace and prosperity for which they have sought so hard and so long.

John F. Kennedy

His Excellency Ngo Dinh Diem
  President and Secretary of State for National Defense
    The Republic of Viet-Nam
      Saigon, Viet-Nam
[White House press release dated Dec. 14, 1961 (for release Dec. 15; text as printed in the Department of State *Bulletin,* Jan. 1, 1962, p. 13).]

Appendix D

CEASE-FIRE AGREEMENT AFTER THE VIET NAM WAR
(See *New York Times,* January 24 and 25, 1973.)

The Cease-Fire Agreement had nine chapters: Chapter I—The Vietnamese People's Fundamental Rights; Chapter II—Cessation of Hostilities, Withdrawal of Troops; Chapter III—The Return of Captured Military Personnel and Foreign Civilians, and Captured and Detained Vietnamese Civilian Personnel; Chapter IV—The Exercise of the South Vietnamese People's Right to Self-Determination; Chapter V—The Reunification of Vietnam and the Relations between North and South Vietnam; Chapter VI—The Joint Military Commissions, The International Commission of Control and Supervision, The International Conference; Chapter VII—Regarding Cambodia and Laos; Chapter VIII—The Relations between the United States and the Democratic Republic of Vietnam; Chapter IX—Other Provisions. The four Protocols were named as follows: Protocol on Clearing of Sea Mines; Protocol on the Cease-Fire; Protocol on Control Commission; and Protocol on the Prisoners.

Bibliography

Indexes

Bulletin of Public Affairs. New York: Kraus Reprint Corporation.
International Index—A Guide to Periodical Literature in the Social Sciences And Humanities. New York: H. W. Wilson Co.
Reader's Guide to Periodical Literature. New York: H. W. Wilson Co., 1900— .
The New York Times Index. New York: New York Times Co., 1913— .
U.S. Congressional Hearings—Cumulative Index, 1935–1959. Washington: Government Printing Office, 1959.

Published Public Documents

A Decade of American Foreign Policy: Basic Documents, 1941–1949. Washington: Government Printing Office, 1950.
American Foreign Policy, 1950–1955: Basic Documents. 2 vols.; Washington: Government Printing Office, 1957.
American Foreign Policy: Current Documents, 1956— . Annual volumes; Washington: Government Printing Office.
Documents of American Foreign Relations, 1939–1951. Boston: World Peace Foundation.
Documents of American Foreign Relations, 1952–1966. New York: Harper and Brothers for Council on Foreign Relations.
Foreign Relations of the United States, through 1945. Washington: Government Printing Office.
Statutes at Large. Washington: Government Printing Office.
U.S. Code, 1964 Edition Containing the General and Permanent Laws of the U.S. in Force on January 3, 1965. Washington: Government Printing Office.
U.S. Treaties and Other International Agreements (UST). Compiled, edited, indexed and published by authority of law (1 U.S.C. #112a) under the direction of the Secretary of State. Washington: Government Printing Office.
League of Nations Treaty Series, through 1946. Geneva: League of Nations.
Whiteman, Marjorie M., *Digest of International Law.* 11 vols. to date (1968); Washington: Government Printing Office.
The U.S. Supreme Court Records, October Term, 1956. Cases Contained in U.S. Reports, Vol. 352, 353, 354. Lawyer's Edition, Second Series, Vol. I. Rochester: The Lawyers Co-operative Publishing Co., 1957.
The Constitution of the U.S. of America. Analysis and interpretation; annotations of cases decided by the Supreme Court of the U.S. to June 30,

1952. Prepared by the Legislative Reference Service, Library of Congress, Edw. S. Corwin, editor. Washington: 1953.

The Constitution of the U.S. of America. Analysis and interpretation; annotations of cases decided by the Supreme Court of the U.S. to June 22, 1964. Prepared by the Legislative Reference Service, Library of Congress, Norman J. Small, ed. Washington: 1965.

U.S. Senate, 85th Congress, 1st Sess., Hearing before a Subcommittee of the Committee on the Judiciary on S. J. Res. 3, proposing an amendment to the Constitution of the U.S. relating to the legal effect of certain treaties and other international agreements, on June 26, 1957. Washington: Government Printing Office.

U.S. Senate, 82nd Congress, 1st Sess., Hearings before the Committee on Foreign Relations and the Committee on Armed Services on the Mutual Security Act of 1951. Washington: Government Printing Office.

U.S. Senate, 82nd Congress, 2nd Sess., Hearings before the Committee on Foreign Relations on the Mutual Security Act of 1952. Washington: Government Printing Office.

U.S. Senate, 85th Congress, 1st Sess., Hearings before the Committee on Foreign Relations on the Mutual Security Act of 1957. Washington: Government Printing Office.

Weekly Compilation of Presidential Documents. Contains statements, messages and other Presidential materials released by the White House during the preceding week. Vol. I (1965)–(1972). Published by the Office of the Federal Register, National Archives and Records Service, General Services Administration. Washington: Government Printing Office.

U.S. Senate, 84th Congress, 2d Sess., Constitutional Amendment Relative to Treaties and Executive Agreements, March 27 (legislative day, March 26), 1956; Senate Report 1716; Mr. Dirksen, from the Committee on the Judiciary, submitted the Report together with Individual Views, to accompany S. J. Res. 1. Washington: Government Printing Office.

U.S. Senate, 84th Congress, 2d Sess., Constitutional Amendment Relative to Treaties and Executive Agreements, April 11 (legislative day, April 9), 1956; Report 1716, Part 2. Washington: Government Printing Office.

U.S. Senate, 88th Congress, 2d Sess., The Republican Report of U.S. Senator Everett McKinley Dirksen, Minority Leader for the Second Session, 88th Congress; Document No. 108. Washington: Government Printing Office.

U.S. Senate, 85th Congress, 1st Sess., Technical Assistance, Final Report of the Committee on Foreign Relations, March 12 (legislative day, March 2), 1957; Report No. 139. Washington: Government Printing Office.

The Battle Act Report, 1964; Seventeenth Report to Congress on Mutual Defense Assistance Control Act of 1951. Released Jan., 1965; Department of State Publication 7736. Washington: Government Printing Office.

The Battle Act Report, 1965; Eighteenth Report to Congress on Mutual Defense Assistance Control Act of 1951. Released Feb., 1966; Department of State Publication 8019. Washington: Government Printing Office.

Pamphlet Documents

Treaty Series, 1908–1946 (TS). Washington: Government Printing Office.

Executive Agreement Series, 1929–1946 (EAS). Washington: Government Printing Office.

Treaties and Other International Acts Series, 1946– (TIAS). Washington: Government Printing Office.

Miscellaneous Publications of the Department of State and Various Agencies. Washington: Government Printing Office

Foreign Aid by the U.S. Government, 1940–1951.
U.S. Foreign Aid in Review, 1945–1960.
Principles of Foreign Economic Assistance; Agency for International Development; first printing, September, 1963, revised September, 1965.
The Aid Story. Agency for International Development, August, 1966.
A Supplement to the Survey of Current Business, Foreign Aid by the U.S. Government, 1940–1951. U.S. Department of Commerce.
Foreign Aid; Report 1957.
U.S. Treaty Development, July, 1948 through 1952. A loose-leaf service.
Challenges and Choices in U.S. Trade Policy.
Treaties in Force. Annual publication.
The Legality of U.S. Participation in Vietnam.
Foreign Affairs Outline.
Foreign Policy Briefs.
News Letter.
A B C's of Foreign Trade.
Patterns for Peace in Southeast Asia, April 7, 1965.
Questions and Answers—Vietnam. The Struggle for Freedom.
How Foreign Policy Is Made.
The U.S. Department of State. What It Is. What It Does.
The U.S. Policy toward Cuba.
The Pledge of Honolulu, 1966.
The Anatomy of Foreign Policy Decisions by Dean Rusk.
Department of State. The Work of the Department.
East–West Trade Relations Act of 1965; and of 1966.
The American Republics in Partnership; 75 Years of International Cooperation.

Periodicals and Newspapers

Press Releases. Weekly Issue, No. 1-508, October 5, 1929–June 24, 1939.
Department of State Bulletin, superseding *Press Releases.*
American Journal of International Law.
The American Political Science Review.
Congressional Digest.
Congressional Quarterly Service—Weekly Report.
Congressional Record.
Current History, A Monthly Magazine of World Affairs.
Foreign Affairs.
Harvard Law Review.
International Conciliation.
Minnesota Law Review.
Reader's Digest.
Saturday Review.
Time.
U.S. News and World Report.
The Yale Law Journal.
The New York Times, Daily and Sunday editions.

Books and Addresses

Congressional Quarterly Almanac, Congressional Quarterly Service. Washington: 1945— .

World Almanac and Book of Facts. New York: N.Y. World-Telegram and Sun, annual through 1966.

American Bar Association, Committee on Constitutional Aspects of International Argreements, *Report to Section of International and Comparative Law on Senate Joint Resolution 1 and the Knowland Substitute Amendment.* Chicago: 1953.

Bloomfield, Lincoln P., *The U. N. and Vietnam.* New York: Carnegie Endowment for International Peace, 1968.

Davids, Jules, *America and the World of Our Times: U.S. Diplomacy in the Twentieth Century.* New York: Random House, 1960.

McBride, Roger Lea, *Treaties versus the Constitution.* Caldwell, Idaho: Caxton Printers, 1955.

McClure, Wallace Mitchell, *International Executive Agreements, Democratic Procedure under the Constitution of the United States.* New York: Columbia University Press, 1941.

Phleger, Herman, *U.S. Treaties; Recent Developments* (Address made before the New York State Bar Association at Saranac, New York, on June 23, 1956). Washington: Department of State, 1956.

U.S. in World Affairs, Annual Volumes 1945–1966, published by the New York Council on Foreign Relations. New York: Harper and Bros., 1945–1947 through 1961; Harper and Row, 1962— .

Robinson, James Arthur, *Congress and Foreign Policy-Making, A Study in Legislative Influence and Initiative.* Homewood, Illinois: Dorsey Press, 1962.

Wightman, David R., *Food Aid and Economic Development.* New York: International Conciliation, No. 567, Published by the Carnegie Endowment for International Peace, March, 1968.

Wilcox, Francis O. and Thorsten V. Kalijarvi, *Recent American Foreign Policy; Basic Documents 1941–1951.* New York: Appleton-Century-Crofts, 1952.

Index

ABM system of U.S., 107; of U.S. and U.S.S.R., 185
Action for Progress, 147
Africa, 143, 188
African Development Bank, 166
Agency for International Development (AID), 78
Agricultural Trade Development and Assistance Act, 43, 45, 96
Aid, 20-21, 24; Mutual Defense Assistance Agreement, 25, 29, 35; to Indochina, 37; to Cambodia, Laos and Vietnam, 37; Mutual Defense Assistance Agreement with France and the Associated States of Indochina, 38; to Indochina, 39; to South Vietnam, 41-42; as instrument of foreign policy, 42; Mutual Security Act of 1951, 42; of 1954, 42; 43; Mutual Security Act of 1958, 44; in 1960 number of countries receiving, 44; 46, 48, 50, 55; to Vietnam, 82, Appendix B and Appendix C; Foreign Assistance Act of 1961, 78; Agency for International Development (AID), 78; 86; Agricultural Aid, 96-97; Food Aid, 98; 99-100, 105; Asian aid, 118; Laos aid, 121, 124; Bill of 1970, 130-131; 144, 146-147, 150-151, 163-164, 168, 191
Algeria, 47, 98
Alliance for Progress, 78, 143-146
Ambassadors of U.S. at Paris, 170
American Selling Price System, 149
American Treaty of Specific Settlement, 19

Andean Group, 147
Anti-war demonstrations, 124
Apollo 11, 119
Appropriations of Congress, 143
Aqaba, 47-48
Arab states: boycott against Israel, 47
Asian Development Bank, 165, 183
Asian Doctrine of President Nixon, 118
Assembly of the Western European Union, 139
Associated States of Indochina, 38
Aswan Dam, 47-48
Atlantic Charter, 15
Australia: communiqué, 92
Austria, 16; treaty with, 54

Baghdad Pact, 46
Balance of Payments, 99; run on dollar, 99
Barall, Milton, 143
Bases, 12-13, 18, 50, 52; of Great Britain east of Suez, 111; of U.S. in Japan, 133; naval, 134; in Philippines, 136; in Spain, 142, 187; in Italy and Greece, 187; in Azores, 187; in Bahrain, 188
Battle Act of 1951, 43
Bay of Pigs, 80
Berlin, 24; Foreign Ministers Conference, 34; 54, 187
Bermuda Meeting (with Heath and Nixon), 158
Bonin Islands, 133
Bricker Movement, 57-77; change in status and role of U.S., 57-58; Constitutional issues, 58-61, 67-69; as-

Bricker Movement (continued) sessment of Executive Agreements, 59, 63; tests in the courts, 61-63, 68-74, 76-77; treaty making power, 64; hearings, 65; list of persons and organizations in favor of, 65-67, 72; list of persons and organizations against, 67, 72, 74-75; assessment, 65-70, 76, 77; 104; Appendix A
Buddhist: troubles, 84
Bunker, Ambassador, 175

Cairo, 15-16
Cambodia, Kingdom of: recognition by U.S., 37; aid to, 37; under SEATO, 40, 81; 86, 88, 125-130
Canada, 12-13, 25, 40
Caribbean, 143; Caribbean Free Trade Association, 147
Cease-Fire Agreement in Vietnam, Appendix D
CENTO, 44, 49-50
Central American Common Market, 147
Central Intelligence Agency (CIA), 80-81
Charter: of American States, 19; of Punta del Este, Uruguay, 78, 143-144; of United Nations, 19
Chiang Kai-shek, 26, 32, 51
Children's Emergency Fund, 20
Chile: Foreign Minister, 145
China, 26; Nationalists to Formosa, 26; Red China, 108, 160-162; Nixon trip to, 183-184
Chou En-lai, 32
Churchill, Winston, 23
Colombia, 145
Commercial Commission with U.S.S.R., 167-168
Commission on International Trade and Investment Policy, 148
Common Market, 112, 114, 187
Communism: in Indochina, 39; U.S. Understanding under SEATO against Communism, 41; in Middle East, Latin America and Pacific, 46; anti-Communism, 80; 81, 85; in Santo Domingo, 87; 97, 104, 111; anti-Communism, 111-112; 115, 125-127; in Latin America, 147; 151; in Hanoi, 169

Communist China, 47, 126, 134
Concerned citizenry, 154
Concurrent Resolution in Senate, 129, 131
Congress: powers, 1, 5, 6, 153; criticism, 123-124, 129-132; controversy with Executive, 153; responsibility of, 154; new Congressional opposition, 180-182, 192
Cooper-Church Amendment, 129-131
Corn: to U.S.S.R., 162
Counterpart fund, 22
Cuba, 50, 80, 98, 191
Cultural Agreements, 56, 107; cultural changes, 112; with U.S.S.R., 187
Curtiss-Wright: embargo against, 62
Cyprus, 46
Czechoslovakia, 24, 107, 137, 150

Defense Appropriations Bill (HR 15090): amendment to, 124, 131
Defense Department, 42, 44, 52
De Gaulle, President, 140
Democratic Republic of Vietnam, 36, 93, 113
Development Assistance Group, 45
Development Loan Fund, 43, 78
Diem, Ngo Dinh, 41, 83, 84; assassinated, 84; letters, Appendix B and Appendix C
Dienbienphu, 39
Disarmament: Conference of United Nations, 138; Committee on, at Geneva, 187
Dollar, 99-100, 157, 158
Dominican Republic, 87
Dulles: Sec'y John Foster, 53-34, 64; Allen, 80

Eastern Europe, 140-141
Eastern Germany, 50
ECA, 21, 24, 29
Ecuador, 145, 150
Egypt, 47; deal with U.S.S.R. concerning cotton from Czechoslovakia, 47-48; 186
Eisenhower, Pres.: aid to Pres. Ngo Dinh Diem, 41, 43, 48; Eisenhower Doctrine, 48-49; 51, 53-55; increase of Executive Agreements under Eisenhower Administration, 55, 80
Era, New, 155-192

European Adjustments, 137-143
European Economic Community (EEC), 79, 95, 111, 159, 163, 165, 187
European nuclear force, 140
European Security Pact, 137
Executive Agreements, 1, 3-4, 14, 17, 42-43, 46, 56, 59, 63-64, 66-72, 74-75, 77; number in 1960, 106; 112, 132, 150-152; procedures of termination, 152-153; Class I, 73, 81, 85, 87, 99, 133-136, 140, 158, 162, 169, 171-172, 174, 178, 180, 183, 190; Class II, 14, 19-22, 25-26, 30, 38-39, 43-46, 50, 52, 54, 78-79, 83, 85-86, 91, 95-96, 99, 142, 144, 160, 162-164, 168; Class III, 15-16, 20, 25, 27-28, 48-49, 87, 102, 109, 116, 119-121, 123, 169, 171, 184; Class IV, 15, 18, 20, 22, 34, 41, 47, 51-52, 54-56, 81-82, 87, 99, 106, 109-110, 119, 126, 132, 140-143, 146, 150, 158, 161, 167-168, 181, 183-188, 190-192
Export-Import Bank, 19, 78, 141-142, 160-161
Expropriation in Latin America, 191

FAO Consultative Sub-Committee on Surplus Disposal (CSD), 97-98
Far Eastern Economic Assistance Act, 30
Federal Republic of Germany, 25
Fifth Japan-United States Conference on Cultural and Educational Exchange, 135
Fisheries: disputes in Latin America, 190-191
Food Aid Convention, 166
Food and Agriculture Organization (FAO), 97-98
Food: Food for Freedom Program, 78; 97; surpluses, 97; food aid, 98; World Food Program (1963), 98-99
Foreign Aid Bill of 1970, 130
Foreign Assistance Act (of 1961), 78; Foreign Assistance Act (of 1965), 86; 153
Formosa, 26, 30-31, 33
Four-Nation Declaration in 1943, 17
France: in Saigon, 36; Vietnam in French Union, 36-37; military equipment to, as member of NATO, 38, 47-48, 52-53, 108, 111, 120; French Union, 120; removal of NATO headquarters, 140, 152
Fulbright, Senator, 128, 142

GATT, 22, 80, 95-96, 141, 149
Geneva Conferences: on Korea in 1954, 34; on Indochina in 1954, 34; 39-40; elections in Indochina not held, 41; International Conference on the Peaceful Uses of the Atom, 53; on Laos in 1962, 82, 91, 120, 127
Geneva Protocol of 1925, 148-149
Germany, 16, 112, 140, 187
German Democratic Republic in Eastern Germany, 25
Germany: East, 137; West, 137, 150
Girard, William S., 76-77
Gold, 99, 100; paper gold, 100; Special Drawing Rights, 100-101; 101, 157-158
Great Britain: chairman of 1954 Conference, 39; 48-49, 53, 108, 111, 118, 140, 166
Greece, 23-25, 46
Group of Ten: at London, 157; at Rome, 157; at Smithsonian Institution, 158
Guam, 118
Gut Dam in Canada, 150

Hanoi: Communists of, 41-42; 91, 93
Helsinki, 137
Hiss, Alger, 57
Ho Chi Minh, 36, 38, 41, 119; Trail in Laos, 123
Honolulu Declaration, 102
Hoover Moratorium, 11
Hot line with U.S.S.R., 81, 185
House: support of President Nixon, 124
Hungary, 50, 140
Hydrogen test and bomb, 52

Iceland, 25
India, 40, 118
Indo-China, 26; policy of U.S. toward, 29; Military Assistance Advisory Group to, 38; French responsibility, 39
Indonesia, 118, 134
Inflation, 100

Inter-Allied Declaration, 14-15
Inter-American Development Bank, 79, 165
Inter-American Treaty of Reciprocal Assistance, 19
Inter-American Development Bank Act in 1959, 44, 147
International Agreements, 1, 2; categories, 2, 3; number. 7-8; publication of, 7-8; competent evidence in courts of law, 8; heritage of World War II, 10; 18, 58, 60-61
International American Economic and Social Council at Caracas, Venezuela, 146
International Atomic Energy Agency, 53
International Bank for Reconstruction and Development (World Bank), 17, 19, 45
International Coffee Agreement: Act of 1970, 162; Treaty of 1962, 162; Treaty of 1968, 162
International Committee of the Federal Council for Science and Technology (Latin American Subcommittee), 147
International Conference on the Peaceful Uses of the Atom, 53
International Control Commission of 1954: complaint of Cambodia, 126
International Cooperation Administration (ICA), 42, 44-45, 78
International Development and Humanitarian Assistance Act, 164-165
International Development Association (IDA), 45, 166
International Finance Corporation, 45
International Monetary Fund, 17, 19, 45, 100-101; Special Drawing Rights, 156
International Security Assistance Act, 164-165
International Supervisory Commission for Vietnam (1954), 40
Interposition: in Dominican Republic, 87
Investments, 100, 145, 165, 192
Iran, 25-26
Iraq, 49

Israel, 46-48
Iwo Jima, 133

Japan, 16, 26; Japanese troops, 27; Japanese in Saigon, 36; Treaty with, 132; Constitution of, 132; bases of U.S. in, 133; demonstrations against U.S., 133-136; 159, 163, 165, 182; Treaty with and Emperor's trip to Alaska, 183; Summit talks with U.S. at Hawaii, 184
Johns Hopkins Speech, 86
Johnson Administration, 85-111; Johns Hopkins Speech, 86; 87-88, 91-92; announcement, 93-94; 98-100, 106, 109, 112-113, 143-144
Joint Resolution, 87
Jordan, 48-49
Judiciary, 1, 6

Kennedy: Administration, 78-84; letter to President Kennedy from President Diem, 83 and Appendix B; letter to President Diem from President Kennedy, 84 and Appendix C; assassinated, 84; 100
Kennedy Round, 80, 95, 163
Khrushchev, 53-55
Kissinger, Henry A., 168, 170, 175-178
Korea, 26; Korean War, 27; 27-28; Korean Democratic People's Republic, 28; Republic of Korea, 28-29; Mutual Defense Assistance Agreement, 29; 30; Korean War, 30-32; talks for Truce, 33; Geneva Conference of 1954, 34; U.S. responsibility, 39; aid, 42; casualties, 112; Mutual Defense Treaty with U.S., 135; Korean troops in Vietnam, 135; reduction of troops in, 136; 182
Ky, Nguyen Cao, 87

Laos: recognition by U.S., 37; aid to, 37; under SEATO, 40, 81; Geneva Conference (1962), 82; 86, 120-122, 124-129, 132
Latin America, 12-14; Act of Chapultepec, 16; Inter-American Treaty of Reciprocal Assistance, 19; Charter of the American States, 19;

INDEX

American Treaty of Specific Settlement, 19, 50; Eisenhower visits, 54; Charter of Punta del Este, 78; 143-147, 165, 188
Latin-American Common Market, 144, 189-191
League of Nations, 11, 19
Lebanon, 49
Lend-Lease Act, 13-14, 16, 20-21; debt of U.S.S.R., 168
Litvinov Assignment, 62
Lon Nol, 126

MacArthur, General, 31-33
Marcos, President of Philippines, 136
Marcus Island, 133
Marshall Plan, 21
Matsu, 51, 55
Malacca Straits, 101
McCarthy, Joseph R., 57
Meat: import quota, 168
Micronesian Islands, 18-19, 26
Middle East: U.S.S.R.'s interest in, 46; Joint Resolution, 153
Middle East Treaty Organization, 46
Midway Islands, 115
Military Assistance Advisory Group to Indochina, 38
Military Bases Agreement with Philippines, 136
Military Sales Bill, Amendment to (in 1970), 129, 131
Moscow, 15, 92
Moscow Agreement, 27
Mutual Defense Assistance Agreement with France and the Associated States of Indochina, 38
Mutual Defense Treaties, 151
Mutual Defense Treaty with Japan, 132
Mutual Security Act of 1951, 42, 134

Nasser, 47, 50
National Commitments Resolution of the Senate, 132
National interest, of U.S., 4-5, 112, 151
National Liberation Movement, 42, 91-92, 113; N.L. Front, 113
National security, of U.S., 4-5, 112, 151

NATO, 25; French rearmament program within, 38; 39, 44, 46, 111, 137, 139-140; removal of headquarters from France, 140, 152; American forces not to be reduced, 140; removal, 153; 184, 187
Negotiations at Paris: Lodge, 114; Bruce, 117
Neutrality Acts, 11-12
Nixon, Richard M., 111-112; 113; 115; 117-118; travels in Asia, Rumania and Great Britain, 118; 120; Nixon Policy, 120; new rationalization, 128; peace proposals of 1970, 130; Policy, 132; 135, 137, 140; Nixon Administration, 143-148, 150, 164-166, 169
Nixon Doctrine, 134, 155, 164, 166, 169; in Latin America, 189-190, 192
Non-Proliferation Treaty, 88, 137, 151
North Vietnam, 87-88, 93, 98, 113, 125
Nuclear: warheads, 52; arsenal, 152

O.E.E.C., 21
Office of Strategic Services (OSS), 80-81
Oil Pollution, 148
Okinawa, 133-135, 182-183
Operation Pan-America, 78
Organization of American States, 50, 78-79, 87
Organization of Economic Development and Cooperation, 159, 165

Pacific: Charter, 41; 50, 132, 182-184
Pakistan, 118
Panama, 50
Pan-Americanism, 19
Paris Summit: (1960), 55; talks of 1968 concerning Vietnam War, 93, 113; shape of table, 114; 115; ten-point program, 115; eight point peace plan, 115; peace talks, 169-175
Park, President Chung Hee, 135
Pathet Lao, 120-121
Peace Corps: Act, 78; 150, 192
Pentagon Papers, 94
Peru, 145, 150

Philippines, 19, 26, 118, 134, 136, 150, 183
Philosophy for Seventies, 155
Pipeline, 137
Point-4 Program, 22, 46
Poland, 40, 50, 137, 141
Policy: definition of, 4; change, 111
Potsdam, 15, 16; Potsdam Declaration, 27
Presidency, 1, 5
Prisoners of War, 179
Provisional International Civil Aviation Organization, 17
Provisional Revolutionary Government, 116
Public Law 480, 43, 45, 96-97; New (1966), 98-99; 147

Quemoy and Matsu, 51, 55
Quotas, 168

Republic of Vietnam, 37; diplomatic recognition by U.S., 37
Rhodesia: chrome, 166, 188-189
Rice, Mrs., 61
Rockefeller, Governor, 146-147
Rogers, Secretary, 142
Roosevelt, Pres. F. D., 12; bases, 13; meetings, 15; Good Neighbor Policy, 19
Rumania, 91, 118, 141; accession to GATT, 160; most favored nation treatment, extended to, 160
Ryukyu Islands, 133-134

Saigon: French coup d'etat, 36; economic mission of U.S. in, 38; Saigon Harbor incident, 85; 92, 113
Santo Domingo, 87
San Antonio Formula, 93
Seabed: uses of, 148
SEATO, 40, 44, 85, 104, 128
Sei Fujii, 61
Senate: Foreign Relations Committee, 143-144
Senate Resolution, 123, 151; 85; 123-124, 187
Shoes, 150, 162-163
Sihanouk, Prince, 125-127; Sihanoukville, 127
Singapore, 111

Southeast Asia: Southeast Asia Joint Resolution, 85, 87, 94, 104; 134
Southern Asia, 188
South Vietnam: as non-signator of Geneva Agreements, 40; 118, 120, 128-129
Souvanna Pouma, 120
Spain, 25, 142-143
Sputnik I, 43, 52
State Department, 42-43, 50
Steel, 160, 163
Strategic Arms Limitation Talks (SALT), 137, 139
Suez, 47-48, 50, 143
Supreme Court: cases against participation in Vietnam War, 105

Tachens, 51
Taiwan, 137
Tariffs, 158, 159, 165-166, 168, 192
Teheran, 15
Textiles, 150, 160, 162
Thailand: under SEATO, 81; 86, 118, 120, 122, 123-124; troops, 127; 132, 182
Thieu, President Nguyen Van, 92, 109, 113-116, 169-176, 178
Technical Assistance to Latin America, 147
Third World, 188-192
TIAS: number of Treaties and Executive Agreements in, in 1960, 109; 150, 152, 192
Tonkin Bay: Resolution, 85, 87, 103-104, 128-129; repeal of Resolution, 131; 142, 144, 153
Trade: Trade Agreements Act of 1934, 11, 22, 50; Trade Expansion Act (1962), 79-80, 95; Trade Act of 1969, 149; 158-159; barriers, 159; with Communist countries, 160; new bill, 162-163, 192
Trade Information Committee, 95
Treaties, 1, 3, 17, 25; Mutual Defense Treaty with Republic of Korea, 34; SEATO, 40, 58-64; 65-70, 72, 74-75, 77; Multilateral Treaty banishing nuclear weapon tests, 81, 85, 87; ban on nuclear weapons in outer space, 106; Nuclear Non-Proliferation Treaty, 106-107; number in 1960, 109; 132, 138-139, 142, 148, 158, 162, 166,

INDEX

168; Treaty with Japan, 183; Treaty with U.S.S.R., 184-186, 187, 190, 192
Tripartite Declaration of 1950, 47
Truman: Truman Plan, 24; 26, 29; policy for Asia, 29; 31-33, 35, 39, 46
Turkey, 23-25, 46, 147

United Arab Republic, 98
United Kingdom, 152, 163
United Nations, 19, 25-26; U.N. Temporary Commission on Korea, 28; 28-33, 47-49; U.N. Atomic Energy Committee, 53; U.N. Commission on Conventional Armaments, 53; Geneva Summit Conference (1955), 53; United Nations Economic commission for Latin America, 79; Cuba, 81; Vietnam, 87-92; Food and Agriculture Organization, 97-98, 108; 120, 137-138, 148, 151, 183, 187
U.N. Food and Agriculture Organization, 17
UNRRA, 16, 20; Post UNRRA Relief Act, 20
United States, 33; declaration after Geneva Agreements of 1954, 40; 48, 50, 87, 125, 127, 138-139, 143-144, 147, 151-152, 159, 163, 169, 182-183; beginning of New Era, 192
U.S.-Japan Mutual Security Treaty of 1951, 132, 134
U.S. Seventh Fleet, 134
U.S. Tariff Commission, 95
U.S. Troops, 18-19, 27; number in South Vietnam, 93; withdrawal of troops, 128; 132; 134-135; reduction in Japan, 136; in Germany, 140; 169, 174; from Pacific, withdrawals, 182-183, 187
United States–U.S.S.R. Commission, 27
U.S.S.R., 16, 21, 23, 26; policy of U.S. toward, 24; 27-30, 33; chairman of 1954 Conference, 39; 46-48, 50, 53; cultural exchanges, 54; forces in Cuba, 81; detente between U.S.S.R. and U.S., 106; Consular Convention with U.S., 106; Commercial Agreement, 107; Cultural Agreement, 107; detente jeopardized in 1968, 107; circling of moon, 107; 108, 137-138; submarines off northern coast of S. America, 143, 152; truck factory, 166; Nixon visit, 167; Commercial Commission, 167-168; World War II debt, 168; Soviet-American Trade Agreement, 168; Jewish emigrants, 168; Agreements and Treaties with, 184-185

Vienna: headquarters of International Atomic Energy Agency, 53, 137
Vietcong, 42, 85, 91, 119, 127
Vietnamization, 128, 147, 151, 169
Vietnam War, 36; aid to, 37; free territory of Vietnam under SEATO, 40, 81; 82; Control Commission in, 83-84; President Diem, 83; 86-87; elections, 89; terms for halt of bombing, 92-93; negotiations, 93-94; 101; criticism of, 101-106; Senate debate, 106; 112; as symbol, 112, 119; conference steps, 112-114, 116; withdrawal of troops, 117, 119-120, 169; negotiations for peace, 169-175; attack on South, 174; mining of harbors of North, 174, 177; Cease-Fire Agreement, 178-180 and Appendix D
Vina del Mar, Chile, 144
Volcano Islands, 133

Warsaw Pact, 46, 92
Wheat: Agreement, 95-96; large sowings, 98; bought by Communist China, 161-162; to U.S.S.R., 162; Wheat Trade Convention, 166
Withdrawal of troops from Vietnam, 117, 119-120, 169
World Changes: by 1968, 108

Yalta, 15-16, 30
Yugoslavia, 25, 98, 141